TREKKING IN GREECE

THE PELOPONNESE AND PÍNDOS WAY

About the Authors

Tim Salmon first visited Greece in 1958. He has lived and worked in the country, visited countless times, written and translated books and articles, and made a film about shepherd life for Greek TV.

Michael Cullen was brought up in Greece and, after university, set up a trekking business there. He spent the 1990s leading hikes throughout the country, before moving to the UK, where he now runs a travel website.

Updates to this Guide

While every effort is made by our authors to ensure the accuracy of guidebooks as they go to print, changes can occur during the lifetime of an edition. Any updates that we know of for this guide will be on the Cicerone website (www.cicerone.co.uk/968/updates), so please check before planning your trip. We also advise that you check information about such things as transport, accommodation and shops locally. Even rights of way can be altered over time.

The route maps in this guide are derived from publicly available data, databases and crowd-sourced data. As such they have not been through the detailed checking procedures that would generally be applied to a published map from an official mapping agency, although naturally we have reviewed them closely in the light of local knowledge as part of the preparation of this guide.

We are always grateful for information about any discrepancies between a guidebook and the facts on the ground, sent by email to updates@cicerone.co.uk or by post to Cicerone, Juniper House, Murley Moss, Oxenholme Road, Kendal, LA9 7RL.

Register your book: To sign up to receive free updates, special offers and GPX files where available, register your book at www.cicerone.co.uk.

TREKKING IN GREECE

THE PELOPONNESE AND PÍNDOS WAY

by Tim Salmon and Michael Cullen

JUNIPER HOUSE, MURLEY MOSS,
OXENHOLME ROAD, KENDAL, CUMBRIA LA9 7RL
www.cicerone.co.uk

© Tim Salmon and Michael Cullen 2018
Third edition 2018
ISBN: 978 1 85284 968 9
Second edition 2006 The Mountains of Greece
First edition 1986

Printed by KHL Printing, Singapore
A catalogue record for this book is available from the British Library.
All photographs are by the authors unless otherwise stated.

Route mapping by Lovell Johns www.lovelljohns.com
Contains OpenStreetMap.org data © OpenStreetMap contributors,
CC-BY-SA. NASA relief data courtesy of ESRI

Warning

Mountain walking can be a dangerous activity carrying a risk of personal injury or death. It should be undertaken only by those with a full understanding of the risks and with the training and experience to evaluate them. While every care and effort has been taken in the preparation of this guide, the user should be aware that conditions can be highly variable and can change quickly, materially affecting the seriousness of a mountain walk. Therefore, except for any liability that cannot be excluded by law, neither Cicerone nor the author accept liability for damage of any nature (including damage to property, personal injury or death) arising directly or indirectly from the information in this book.

Front cover: Asprórema gorge (Píndos Way, Stage 12)

CONTENTS

Acknowledgements

I would particularly like to thank Penelope Matsoúka and Ivy Adamakópoulos for all their help with maps and GPS problems, Florica Kyriakópoulos for helping to sponsor the book, Nicolas and Marie Chochoy for their stalwart work with saw and clippers, Bob Simpson for driving me around and doing his share of sawing, Ian Payne for teaching me how to use a GPS in the first place, Jane and Alan Laurie for lots of useful information gleaned from their epic walk across Greece, Vasílis Nasiákos for checking the Zagóri routes, Kóstas and Yióta Gantzoúdis for their kindness and advice in the Ágrafa, and countless other people who, for more than 40 years now, have directed me around these mountains, offered me hospitality, let me into their lives, dried my clothes and told me fascinating stories about exile in Tashkent, hand-to-hand fighting in the Korean war, encounters with bears and all sorts of other adventures that do not often come a Londoner's way. And, far from least, I would like to thank my co-author Michael for joining this great project to promote the wonderful mountains of Greece and promising to go on with it when I am finally put out to pasture in the Elysian Fields!

Tim Salmon

Thanks to Rolf Roost and Yiórgos Kanelópoulos for nobly maintaining the Peloponnese stretch of the E4 trail, and the accompanying website; to my brother Matthew for accompanying me, with unstinting patience and good humour, every step of the way from Dhiakoftó to Pantazí beach (not to mention all the variants, the backtracking and the dead ends); and to my family for taking up the slack while I was away, or beavering over maps and keyboards until the small hours.

Michael Cullen

Symbols used on route maps

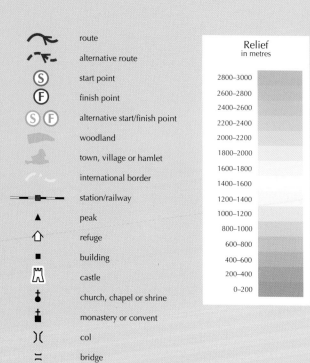

	route
	alternative route
(S)	start point
(F)	finish point
(S) (F)	alternative start/finish point
	woodland
	town, village or hamlet
	international border
	station/railway
▲	peak
⌂	refuge
■	building
	castle
	church, chapel or shrine
	monastery or convent
)(	col
⸗	bridge
©	cave
(W) •	spring/water feature

Relief
in metres

2800–3000	
2600–2800	
2400–2600	
2200–2400	
2000–2200	
1800–2000	
1600–1800	
1400–1600	
1200–1400	
1000–1200	
800–1000	
600–800	
400–600	
200–400	
0–200	

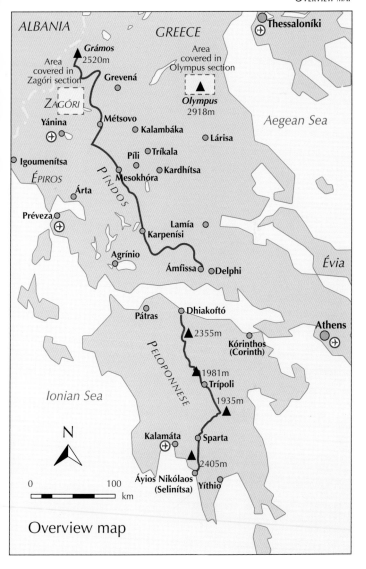

Overview map

9

Going up towards Skolió (Mount Olympus, Stage 2)

FOREWORD TO 2018 EDITION

In the 1970s I was teaching in Athens and came across the account by Lord Hunt, of Everest fame, of his 1963 traverse of the Píndos mountains with a mixed party of Greek and English youngsters. I decided that I would try to retrace his itinerary and my route became the backbone of the first edition of this guide in 1986. Since then I have added descriptions of most of the interesting mainland massifs so that the book became a general guide to mountain trekking in Greece.

At the time of the last revision I acquired a colleague, Michael Cullen, who was born and grew up in Greece and founded its first ever trekking company. This time we decided to change the format of the guide quite radically, ditching almost everything in favour of a single route that runs pretty much the length of the country from the northern frontier with Albania to the southernmost reaches of the Peloponnese. We have accordingly also changed the title to *The Peloponnese and Píndos Way*, in the hope that this will give the book a clearer focus and identity and help to attract walkers to come and sample the real charms and beauties of Greece's mountains.

If you are in any doubt, there is no better taster than the blog of Jane and Alan Laurie (http://greekhiking.com) describing their epic 2014 walk from the Préspa Lakes on the Albanian–Greek border to their home in the southern Peloponnese, most of it following a route identical with or very close to ours. And keep an eye on our websites, www.thepindosway.com and www.thepeloponneseway.com, for additional photographs and various extra snippets and bits of information which we will add as time goes by.

Tim Salmon

Ascent from Ayía Paraskeví to the Tsoúma col. Smólikas in the background

INTRODUCTION

Looking north-west from Áï-Liás chapel (Peloponnese Way, Stage 9)

Mountains cover most of Greece; many are over 2000m (6500ft) in altitude. Most are limestone, the massifs cut by a complex geometry of deep ravines. To people who know only the summertime seaside, the mountains are surprisingly green, forested and well watered. In their more southerly reaches, the Greek fir, *Abies cephalonica*, is the characteristic tree cover from 800m to 1800m. Further north, the black pine, *Pinus nigra*, takes over, with extensive beech woods on the colder faces. Springs abound, and rivers run all year round. Snow lasts from November to April. But the mountains' special beauty lies in the fact that they have remained not untouched, but largely bypassed by modernity.

They are hillwalkers' rather than climbers' mountains, but you do need to be in good physical shape to explore them. Routes – although not technical – are physically demanding because of the variations in altitude, the distances involved and the absence both of organised facilities for the walker and of restorative creature comforts. Meals and supplies – when available – are basic. There are a number of fairly active local branches of EOS, the Greek mountaineering club (known in English as the Hellenic Alpine Club or HAC), but they are not really of any use to the visiting walker and their huts are, with only two or three exceptions, unstaffed and locked.

Since the early editions of this guide, modern life has impinged on the mountains, mainly in the form of roads and bulldozed tracks. This has made navigation more difficult, because road construction has both destroyed paths and – more importantly – made them redundant. People travel by vehicle and the paths are no longer maintained.

On the plus side, there is a growing awareness among Greeks that their own back country is worth exploring and that walking, climbing, canyoning and mountain biking are worthwhile ways of doing it. There are also signs that even the local authorities have woken up to the fact that there may be some commercial advantage in encouraging such pursuits. It is not always consistent, but there are several areas where there have been attempts to clear and waymark paths. Guesthouses have sprung up in the remotest villages. Most importantly, from the walker's point of view, the mapmaking publisher Anávasi (www.anavasi.gr) has appeared on the scene with an extensive series of detailed, accurate and GPS-friendly maps.

Armed with map, compass and guide, and possibly also with GPS, you should not encounter too many problems. Indeed, our hope is that you will come to see the relatively uncommercial and primitive nature of these mountains as an essential part of their charm.

TRADITIONAL MOUNTAIN LIFE

You can still get a sense of how traditional mountain life must once have been, although much has changed over the 40 years since this book was first researched. The biggest change has been the end of all economic – essentially agricultural – activity in the mountains. Already in the 1970s the population had been drastically reduced by emigration, but those who remained were still able to maintain a bit of farming activity. Now they are too old and too few. There is no longer any cultivation. There are no young children, no schools anywhere. The only economic activity is the arrival of the shepherds in May, bringing their flocks to the mountain pastures for the summer, and the seasonal return from the cities of now retired émigrés,

Sheep grazing above Anavriti (Peloponnese Way, Stage 12)

sometimes with their children and grandchildren in the school holidays. Many villages are almost completely deserted in the winter.

There is a certain melancholy in the overgrown fields and crumbling houses. Yet, paradoxically, there is more life and investment than there has been for years. The children of those who emigrated have become prosperous enough to rebuild family homes for holiday times. Village squares are freshly paved. Churches are restored. There is at last a sense that there was something valuable about the life that has been lost, and people have begun to take a pride in saving what they can.

A LITTLE HISTORY

In the north and west of Greece you still find descendants of the shepherd clans, the Sarakatsani and the Vlachs, who have preserved a separate and distinctive identity to this day. The Vlachs in particular are interesting because their language, in contrast to all the other Balkan tongues south of Romania, is Latin-based. No one quite knows who they are or how they come to speak Latin. Traditionally semi-nomadic, with no written language, they have left no records. They call themselves *arumani* – Romans. While they are obviously not Romans, the language they speak is probably not much different from that heard round shepherds' campfires 2000 years ago.

There are villages throughout the mountains, and you wonder why places so rugged and inaccessible should ever have been populated. But it is this very inaccessibility which provides the answer. People sought refuge in these natural fastnesses, especially from the Turks, who overran and controlled the lowlands from their capture of Constantinople in 1453 until, in the case of northern Greece,

Mt Veloúkhi and the site of old Víniani (Píndos Way, Stage 9)

World War I. The outlawed sheep-rustlers and brigands – the *klephts* – made their hideouts in the mountains and formed what we would now call the liberation army that finally drove the Turks out and instituted the beginnings of the modern Greek state in the 1820s.

During World War II, many Greeks took to their mountains again to form one of Europe's biggest Resistance movements. With the outbreak of Civil War in 1946 – for which many Greeks blame the British – a new generation of outlaws made the mountains their base. This time they were Communist guerrillas, mostly veterans of the Resistance, who felt that Anglo-American domination, restoration of the monarchy and the return of the old politicians from their safe wartime haven in Egypt was not what they had fought for. It was this war which occasioned the promulgation of the Truman Doctrine and America's first attempt to halt the feared domino

Clockwise from left: Autumn crocus; Marsh orchid; Lilium albanicum; Astragalus angustifolium; Lilium heldreichii

effect: the conviction that if one state fell under Communist influence, then others would follow.

The mountain communities endured 10 years of war in the 1940s, more than their fragile economy could stand. Populations were evacuated to the lowlands to prevent them supporting the guerrillas. Children went to school, adults found jobs. By the time peace came in the 1950s, village fields had reverted to nature and there was no other work. Many families never returned to their mountain homes.

FLOWERS AND WILDLIFE

You see surprisingly little wildlife for such wild and remote terrain. The

Kernítsa convent (Peloponnese Way, Stage 5)

occasional fox or hare, perhaps a deer, an adder, salamander, or tortoise, the odd eagle or griffon vulture, and smaller species like chough, partridge, wheat-ear, accentor, perhaps a wallcreeper. If you are lucky you might see mountain goats or a wild boar in the north-west. Bear and wolf exist – both, reportedly, in increasing numbers – but you would be extremely lucky to meet either.

Flowers, on the other hand, abound. The best season for seeing them depends on altitude and latitude. In the first half of May in the Peloponnese and southern central Greece, for instance, you will find fritillaries, orchids, ophrys, violets, aubretia, iris, anemones and *Daphne oloeides* up to 1200m or so. As you approach the melting snow patches, around 1600–1800m, there are crocuses, squills, *Corydalis solida*, saxifrages and many others. Further south, spring comes earlier; further north, later. Tulips, gentians, narcissus, campanulas, geraniums, aquilegias, lilies – all sorts of glorious species are to be found, over 600 of them endemic.

NAVIGATION AND MAPS

The problem of finding reliable maps has been largely resolved by the appearance on the scene of Anávasi, specialist mapmakers and publishers. They are essentially a mother-and-daughter team, themselves experienced mountaineers. Their maps, varying in scale from 1:25,000 to 1:50,000 and 1:100,000, cover the majority of the most interesting walking areas of the country. No other maps are remotely as good. Penelope Matsoúka also produces beautiful books of aerial photographs which cover islands as well as mountain massifs and make a wonderful souvenir of Greece's spectacular landscapes.

The maps are all GPS compatible. The digital versions in various formats can be downloaded from the Anávasi website (www.anavasi.gr). Until we are able to get the routes properly and consistently waymarked, they are an absolutely crucial tool. Where their traced paths and our routes coincide – which is not everywhere – and the path on the ground is not easy to follow, you can absolutely rely on them, which is why we strongly recommend using a GPS. If your GPS shows you have wandered off the route, you can trust it.

GPS SET-UP

Add the metric grid Greek Geodetic Reference System (GGRS87) to your GPS as follows:
User grid
Longitude of origin E024°00.000
Latitude of origin N00°00.000
Scale factor +0.9996000
False easting +500000
False northing 0.0
User map datum
Dx –00201
Dy +00076
Dz +00246

In the UK, maps are available from Stanfords (www.stanfords.co.uk) and The Map Shop (www.themapshop.co.uk). In Athens, the Anávasi Bookshop is five minutes' walk from the central Síntagma Square. For addresses and contact details, see Appendix D.

A PRACTICAL TIP ABOUT PATH-FINDING

Right up until World War II in many parts of Greece and up to the 1970s in the furthest mountains, there were few roads. The paths were the roads. The traffic was four-legged and two-legged and had been for many centuries. As a consequence, the paths, even in rugged mountain terrain, were well worn into the ground, a bit like sunken cart tracks in England. The line of them, even when they have not been regularly used for a long time, is often still quite clear to a practised eye. They were made principally by the mules, who have a much better feel for a gradient than a human. They unerringly find the line of least resistance, winding up spurs and along contours, avoiding over-long or over-steep steps.

So, whenever a path is not clear and you find yourself striking straight uphill or straight downhill, pause and ask yourself: would a laden pack animal be doing this? And the answer is almost certainly: no. Goats go straight up and straight down, mules never, and their human drivers, never.

If you have been on a fairly clear path and suddenly it ceases to be clear, don't panic. One of you should stay put and the other cast around systematically and patiently, thinking of those laden mules with a load of 100kg on their backs. Sections of path get destroyed by landslips; but entire paths seldom disappear completely. You will find the continuation.

There is no uniform system of waymarking in Greece. You will find Bonne Maman jam-jar lids, fading red discs, splashes of parti-coloured paint, more sophisticated plastic squares and diamonds with variously coloured symbols, E4 and E6 signs left over from 40-year-old attempts to hook Greece into a trans-Europe network of paths, plus ribbons, streamers and paint spray added by us – and long stretches with no waymarks at all. It is all part of what the Greeks call 'the Greek reality'.

SLEEPING AND EATING

Country towns almost always have at least one reasonable hotel, and increasing numbers of mountain villages offer informal rooms or guesthouses – the latter at around €20–40 per room. On the Píndos Way there is no point really in trying to book ahead, except perhaps in towns like Ámfissa, Karpenísi and Métsovo. The villages you go through are not places that have outside visitors. But if you do find the inn full, someone will certainly find you an alternative place to sleep. Besides, you will have your tent or your bivvy bag: vital equipment on the Píndos Way.

The Peloponnese Way, however, is a different story. There, you will need to book ahead, if you plan to hike without camping gear, which should be possible as there is currently accommodation available at every stage. Remember that if calling a Greek number from outside Greece, you must prefix the number with the +30 international code for Greece.

Local produce for sale in Vitína (Peloponnese Way, Stages 5–6)

Most villages do not have shops any more. What they do have is a coffee-shop-cum-general-store, the *magazeé*. This is the place to make for on arrival, for information about a place to sleep or eat or where to get supplies. They will always go out of their way to help. If there is a menu it will be basic – costing (with a beer) around €15–20.

Food for the road can be a problem. Special backpacking products do not exist. In general you have to make do with local fare: bread, cheese and olives, supplemented by endless tins of sardines or spam, which is all that is available in remote places.

The rule has to be: whenever you hit a place with a restaurant and shops, have a blow out and stock up. Avoid things that leak and squash in rucksacks or are dry and salty – they are horrible when you are hot and thirsty. Be careful with cheeses, especially the ubiquitous feta. The dry variety is often salty, and the more edible wet one leaks. Better to go for the hard Gruyère type of cheese – *graviéra* or *kefalotíri* – if you can get it. Taste cheeses before committing yourself. Whole salamis are good, and although they sweat they keep. Halva (*khalvá*) is a good sugary energy-giver. Nuts, sultanas and dried fruit are readily available in the towns. Muesli is light, unmessy and quite palatable when mixed only with spring water, but unobtainable outside Athens supermarkets. Greeks eat no breakfast, so you need to bring something with you if you do not like the idea of cheese and olives first thing.

The refuge huts are really of little use to the visitor. With the exception of those on Olympus, Gamíla, Smólikas and possibly Taïgetos, they are unstaffed and locked. The palaver involved in

Camping is possible anywhere in the mountains

getting and returning the keys far outweighs any benefits.

Monasteries are a better bet, if you are a man. You can always ask for food and shelter, but you have to be modestly dressed, which means no shorts. Women are not always allowed in.

Camping, on the other hand, is possible anywhere in the mountains and no one will object. As the land belongs to no one, there is no question of trespassing. You do not need a tent in summer; a bivvy bag is quite sufficient. Just be careful of sheepdogs.

DOGS

This is a serious warning. The sheepdogs – guard dogs, not collies – are the greatest danger you are likely to encounter in the mountains. It is not the little mongrels that guard some flocks that you

have to worry about, but the Molóssi. They are wolf-sized, half-starved, unused to strangers and very fierce and, like the arrows of outrageous fortune, rarely come one at a time but in gangs. If at all possible, give them a very wide berth. Do not approach the flock they are minding and certainly do not walk through it. If possible attract the attention of the shepherd; he will call them off. Always carry poles or a stout stick and be aggressive. Keep them at pole's length and throw rocks at them – with the intention of hurting them. Don't panic. You will survive.

GETTING ON WITH PEOPLE

Mountain people are extremely friendly and hospitable. It is, however, up to you, the stranger, to break the social ice by saying hello first. The simplest greetings

21

are *kaleeméra*, good day, or *yásoo*, good health to you (*yásas*, if there is more than one person). That immediately dispels what can appear to be hostility, but is in reality merely polite reserve.

Do not forget that mountain people are still rather old-fashioned in their attitudes. Women, in particular, should be careful how they dress and act.

WEATHER AND WHEN TO GO

There is snow on the mountains from November to April. Quite extensive patches sometimes persist until mid June, and later on the higher and more northerly ones. The weather begins to settle in April or May, and to break again some time in October. June–September is the most settled period. It is also the hottest, but once you get into a big range like the Píndos, and high up, the heat is not too bothersome. Above 2000m the temperature rarely rises above 25° even in July and August, and at night drops to 10° or 12°. I have found my water frozen in the morning at 2000m near the Albanian border in September.

The table shows average monthly temperatures (°C) throughout the year 2016–17 in Thessaloníki (north), Yánina (mid-north in the mountains), Athens,

*Vália Kálda in June
(Píndos Way, Stage 23)*

and Sparta (close to the southernmost point of the Peloponnese Way).

Certainly, the weather can be beautiful, but you should not be lulled into a false sense of security. Greek mountains behave like other mountains. Even in midsummer violent storms can blow

Average monthly temperatures (°C) (Aug 2016–Jul 2017)												
Aug	Sep	Oct	Nov	Dec	Jan	Feb	Mar	Apr	May	Jun	Jul	Aug
Thessaloníki	31	26	19	13	6	3	11	15	15	20	26	32
Yánina	29	22	17	10	4	1	7	12	13	18	24	30
Athens	32	27	22	17	10	9	13	16	17	22	27	33
Sparta	28	23	19	12	5	4	9	12	11	16	22	30

Source: www.worldweatheronline.com

up with little warning. Nights are cool, especially in contrast to daytime temperatures; you definitely need a fleece.

WHAT TO TAKE

In summer conditions, you need a combination of light and warm clothing. We would recommend a hat, and shirts with collar and sleeves, if you are at all susceptible to sunburn. Take sunscreen if you have a vulnerable Anglo-Saxon nose and, especially, do not forget the backs of the knees, and the thumb and index area of the hand, one of the most exposed if you are using poles. Warm clothing (including your sleeping bag) does not need to be heavy, just enough to protect you in bad weather and against the chill of tiredness and night. Take a windproof and waterproof cagoule. A good pair of lightweight Vibram-soled boots is sufficient in the way of footwear, although consider taking hiking sandals or water shoes if you are likely to do any of the riverbed sections. Take a tent or survival/bivvy bag and basic first-aid kit, including some mosquito repellent for use in the lowlands.

If you are packing a stove, petrol is the most widely available fuel; but remember that, if you are travelling by air, empty fuel bottles need to be scrubbed clean enough to pass for water bottles. There must not be any whiff of petrol, otherwise you risk having them confiscated at the airport. Self-sealing camping gas cartridges are available in specialist shops in Athens and big towns, but not elsewhere. A safe bet is Polo Center at 52 Patisíon Avenue, in Athens, close to the National Archaeological Museum.

EMERGENCY SERVICES

There are no emergency services or mountain rescue, so you would be wise to have an insurance policy that will get you home if you need serious treatment.

ACCESS TO THE MOUNTAINS

For most destinations in this book, buses are the best means of transport. All major country towns have daily connections with Athens. Buses for the Peloponnese and parts of central Greece west of the Píndos mountains (Yánina, for instance) leave from the terminus at 100 Kifisoú Street (referred to as 'KTEL Kifisoú'); to get there, take bus 051 from the corner of Vilará and Menándrou Streets near Omónia Square. Buses for Delphi, Ámfissa and parts east of the Píndos leave from 260 Liosíon Street ('KTEL Liosíon'), near Áyios Nikólaos metro stop. The only way to be absolutely certain about departure times is to go to the appropriate terminus.

Onward journeys from provincial centres into the mountains are more problematic. Bus services are much less frequent than formerly and the only way to find out times is generally on the spot. There is always the chance of a lift – easiest to arrange from village to town, when you can ask in the *magazeé* (village shop, café) if anyone is going. Alternatively, just step into the road and flag someone down. That is what the locals do. Vehicles are rare birds in out-of-the-way places, and you cannot afford not to make your intentions absolutely plain.

Dhrakólimni tarn (Zagóri, Stage 4)

Of the four sections of the Píndos Way, only Mesokhóra, the end point of Section 2/start of Section 3, and Mt Grámos, the very end of Section 4, are unreliably served by buses. The Peloponnese Way is better served, with daily connections to Dhiakoftó (start point), Kalávrita, Vitína, Kápsia, Trípoli (mid point), Áyios Pétros, Sparta and Áyios Nikólaos (end point); plus occasional services to Dhára, Vamvakoú and Árna.

Taxis can always be summoned with the help of the *magazeé* and are not expensive by general European standards. Ask the locals beforehand what the fare is and be sure to agree the price before you get in.

USING THIS GUIDE

The book comprises four parts. The main route, the Peloponnese and Píndos Way, which constitutes by far the greater part of the book, is split into two: Part 1 covers the Peloponnese Way, and Part 2 the Píndos Way. Parts 3 and 4 cover the Zagóri district, which can easily be incorporated into the Píndos Way, and Mt Olympus, home of the gods of the ancient Greeks.

It may at first glance strike the reader as rather illogical that the two parts of our main route should be described as running in opposite directions – north to south for the Peloponnese and south to north for the Píndos – rather than as a continuous route. We accept that this will create some difficulties for hikers wishing to do the whole route in one fell swoop. For example, it would entail having to do one of the two halves in reverse – probably the Peloponnese Way, since it is the shorter half and better signed; and in terms of transport, getting to the further end of both halves would prove relatively complicated.

There are, however, some persuasive reasons for running the two halves in opposite directions. First, sea divides the two, in the form of the Gulf of Corinth. Second, Athens, the most convenient place to arrive, the only place likely to meet any last-minute shopping requirements and by far the most useful communications hub, lies smack between the two, pretty much equidistant from the starting points of both halves.

All the routes are broken down into and described as day stages. Practical information relevant to each – how to get there, maps, places with accommodation – is contained in the section and stage introductions. Information about distances, height gain and loss, difficulty, approximate walking times and waymarks is given at the beginning of each day stage. (The route summary tables in Appendix A provide an overview of the key statistics for each walk.)

Walks are graded on a scale of 1 to 3. You will find that nearly all are graded 3, not because they require a high degree of technical expertise or involve any serious danger – with rare exceptions they do not. But they do demand a considerable degree of commitment because of their remoteness and inaccessibility, and the absence of organised facilities. Routes are often long, with nowhere to stop between start and finish. The terrain is arduous and navigation not always easy.

Estimates of walking times exclude halts, and are records of our own times. (I was accused of walking too fast in earlier editions. Youth is well behind me now, so the times should be more generous.)

Following the route directions

L(eft) and R(ight) directions are given in relation to the walker's line of march.

This applies also to the flanks of valleys and gullies. The only exception is when referring to the banks of streams or rivers, when L and R are indicated in relation to the direction of the current. We have also given compass bearings and GPS positions (using GGRS87 – see 'Navigation and maps' above) when available.

We have used the word 'path' (*monopátee* in Greek) to describe the old mule trails and footpaths. We use 'track' to describe a rough unsurfaced road, more suitable for a four-wheel drive vehicle: the kind of road used by shepherds to get to their mountain sheepfolds or into the forest. Until not long ago, many country roads intended for ordinary vehicles were unsurfaced but maintained and relatively even. Where these still exist we have called them 'dirt roads' or 'earth roads' (*khomatódhromos* in Greek). When it is not suitable for an ordinary car, Greeks will call it *anómalos* ('anomalous', or uneven).

Significant features that you pass en route and that are marked on the maps are highlighted in **bold** in the route descriptions. Altitudes are given in metres (m), for example 2637m. Throughout each stage, cumulative walking times (approximate and based on our own times) are shown in brackets, in hours (hr) and minutes (min).

Greek place names

One problem peculiar to writing guides to Greece is the alphabet and what to do about rendering Greek place names and words in English letters in a form that allows English-speakers to pronounce them in a way that Greek-speakers in

*Road sign near Vamvakoú
(Peloponnese Way, Stage 10)*

turn might have a chance of understanding. There is no consensus, no official system; chaos reigns. Some people no doubt will think the system used in this book crazy too. We have given place names in a spelling not too different from what you are most likely to encounter on bilingual road signs. See the glossary in Appendix B for pronunciation tips together with a list of Greek words and phrases that you may find useful along the route.

For the most important route, the one that gives this book its title, we have used the traditional English name for the Peloponnese and the compromise, Píndos, for what used to be known by the Latin name of Pindus. The Greek for Peloponnese, spelt kind of phonetically, is *pelopóneesos* and for Píndos it is *peéndhos*, the English 'd' being pronounced like 'th' in the word 'then.'

PART 1
THE PELOPONNESE
WAY

Mt Ménalo: the descent to Kardharás (Stage 6)

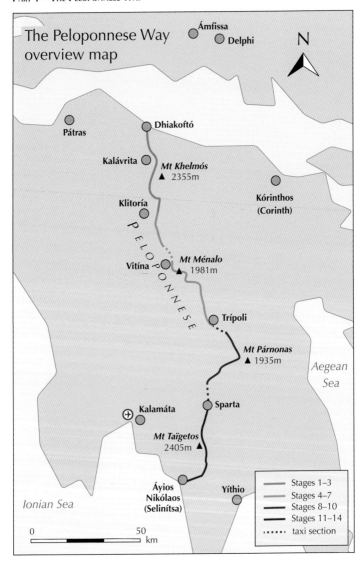

The Peloponnese Way overview map

Ascent to Méga Spílio (Stage 1)

The Peloponnese is the detached, three-fingered landmass south-west of Athens, which is neither really part of the mainland, nor considered to be one of the Greek islands. The name means the 'island of Pelops', after a mythical king venerated at Olympia; the Byzantines called it the Morea ('mulberry leaf'), and modern administrative boundaries often group it with Attica or the western mainland. It can be thought of as a region unto itself: a dense, varied, self-contained landscape of long sandy beaches and ancient cities, of rolling vineyards, hilltop hamlets and olive groves, market towns and unexpectedly wild mountain ranges – seven of them reaching around 2000m (6500ft) or more – all packed into an area the proverbial (and actual) size of Wales, or of New Jersey, if that means more to you.

It is this variety which makes the two-week hike across it – from north to south, in our book, starting and ending at the sea – such a memorable trip. On Mt Khelmós there are alpine meadows carpeted with flowers in May, high crags pocked with snowpack until June, and a river gorge threaded by a tiny, gravity-defying rack-and-pinion railway line. In rural Arkadhía (yes, that's ancient Arcadia, home of wilderness-loving Pan and bear-hunting Arcas), you'll still find isolated shepherds' hamlets and maquis-covered hills where time ticks at a slower pace. After a brush with modern life at Trípoli, you'll escape again to the fir forests and historic monasteries of Mt Párnonas (or Párnon), then the citrus groves and ancient ruins of Sparta and Mistrás, before a final hurrah across the steep flanks of lunar Mt Taïgetos and down to the coast in sunset-facing Messinía. If time permits, linger on in one of the lovely, low-key resort villages of Áyios Nikólaos, Stoúpa or Kardhamíli:

fresh fish, olive groves, clear seas. Or you can, if you prefer, end the trail at the handsome harbour town of Yíthio (Gythion), which has ferry links to Crete.

The length of it – two full weeks, a bit more if you want to bag the summits, a bit less if you're prepared to cab or bus the flatter stretches – is very manageable, with the town of Trípoli handily placed midway in case you want to break it into two week-long chunks (express buses whisk you to Kalamáta or Athens along the E65 motorway). If you have more time, three or four additional days are outlined below, which can be slotted in after Stage 5 (to visit Dhimitsána, Stemnítsa and the monasteries of the Loúsios gorge), during Stage 6 (to summit Ostrakína, 1981m, the highest point on Mt Ménalo), and after Stage 12 (to summit Taïgetos, 2405m).

Finally, the logistics are not – touch wood – too complex. Staying in village guesthouses or hotels every night, plus one night in a mountain refuge, means you can hike light – no camping gear necessary – but you will need to check and book these ahead of time, as some have a habit of closing midweek, or randomly, or altogether. Our route, which follows the E4 trail for large parts, is generally well waymarked; and the excellent website www.e4-peloponnes.

info (in German only, at the time of press) gives free GPS/route information on those sections, as well as handy tips for accommodation and taxi transfers. Our own www.thepeloponneseway. com is also useful for additional photos, updates and help with accommodation bookings. In terms of altitude, the trail rises to 1600m four times – once for each of the major ranges crossed – but no higher, unless you choose to bag a summit. This helps you avoid spring snowpack and extends the season: April and November are feasible if you don't mind the cooler weather and shorter days, May–early June and mid September–October are ideal.

Two planning tips. Check accommodation in Vamvakoú (Stage 9) first – the hostel may well be restricted to weekend openings, or closed completely (some alternatives are suggested in Stage 9). Contact the mountain refuge (Stage 12) second – the warden charges a hefty fixed fee (€120 in 2017) to come and open it, so flexibility on dates may help you coincide with other hikers and share this cost. The refuge provides food, bunks and blankets; just bring a sheet sleeping bag and torch. The alternative to the refuge is a crude stone shelter at Pendavlí (1hr further), for which you would need sleeping mat, sleeping bag and food, but no tent.

SECTION 1
DHIAKOFTÓ TO TRÍPOLI

Méga Spíleo monastery: the fortress (Stage 2)

The first half of the Peloponnese Way crosses two massifs: rugged Khelmós, which we skirt beneath its ski station, and Ménalo, whose uplands are cloaked in evergreen forests. Between these is a lower stretch among maquis-covered hills and sleepy shepherds' hamlets: this has its own Arcadian charm, despite some stony paths and one section of road (but you could hitch the road section or take a cab).

- Anávasi Topo 30 (1:30,000) 8.2 *Mt Chelmos*
- Anávasi Topo 50 (1:50,000) 8.5 *Mt Mainalo – Arcadia*
- Lyhnia (1:25,000) *Ménalon Trail* (http://menalontrail.eu/maps)
- For the side trip after Stage 5: Anávasi Topo 25 (1:22,000) 8.51 *Lousios*

LOCATION

Dhiakoftó is on the north coast of the Peloponnese, facing the Gulf of Corinth. It is 160km (2hr by road or train) west of Athens and 55km (45min by road or train) east of the city of Pátras.

BASES

Kalávrita has banks, shops (including outdoor gear), restaurants and hotels. In **Klitoría** you will find Mont Helmos Hotel (tel 26920-31221, http://monthelmos.gr), rooms, restaurants and a few shops. **Vitína** has a bank, shops,

Zakhloroú hamlet (Stage 1)

restaurants and hotels, including the Hotel Sinói (tel 27950-22354, mob 694-5632241, www.sinoi.gr).

ACCESS

Regular daily buses run from Athens (Kifisoú Street terminus) to Dhiakoftó – not all buses to Pátras will drop you in Dhiakoftó, so ask first; buses to Aigio will drop you in Dhiakoftó (www.ktelachaias.gr in Greek only).

There are four trains a day from Athens (airport or Akharnés SKA station) to Dhiakoftó, using the *proastiakó* (suburban) train as far as Kiáto and the rail replacement bus from Kiáto to Dhiakoftó (www.trainose.gr/en).

Regular daily buses go from Trípoli to Athens (Kifisoú Street terminus) (www.ktelarkadias.gr in Greek only).

STAGE 1
Dhiakoftó (0m) to
Méga Spílio monastery (1000m)

Start point	Dhiakoftó
Distance	15km
Difficulty	1
Walking time	4hr 30min
Height gain	1000m
Height loss	0m
Waymarks	E4 (yellow + black) to Zakhloroú

The first day of the trans-Peloponnese hike could hardly be easier, at least in terms of route-finding: you simply follow the narrow-gauge railway line from Dhiakoftó on the coast, up through the impressive cleft of the Vouraïkós gorge, to the tiny hamlet of Zakhloroú, halfway to Kalávrita (12km/600m climb). Passing some spectacular tunnels and galleries, you walk between or alongside the tracks. There are only a few trains each day and they chug along at a gentle jog, hooting as they go.

At Zakhloroú, you could stay in one of the small hotels, including the Romántzo (tel 26920-22758), Káto Zakhloroú (tel 26920-22789, mob 698-3125616) or the swankier Olympios Zeus (tel 26920-22595, www.olympioszeus.gr). Alternatively, to get a useful head start on the next day's long hike, follow the path up to Méga Spílio monastery and sleep in its guesthouse or the nearby Grand Chalet roadside motel. The former is more atmospheric, but you'll need to nip down to the Grand Chalet for dinner and back by sunset; the latter is easy but soulless; both are bookable (tel 26920-23357, info@grandchalet-ms.gr).

A few tips: be aware of train times in both directions and keep a torch handy for the tunnels. If a train does come when you're in a tunnel, don't panic: stand hard against one side of the tunnel and shine your torch towards it. Cross bridges on the side with the iron boardwalk and handrail, and don't worry about the 'no pedestrian' signs!

Take a stick: underfoot is chunky gravel, with the occasional girder to trip you; and carry plenty of water: the stream is not drinkable, and there are only one or two springs en route. Avoid the second Sunday in May, when thousands of Greek hikers descend the gorge.

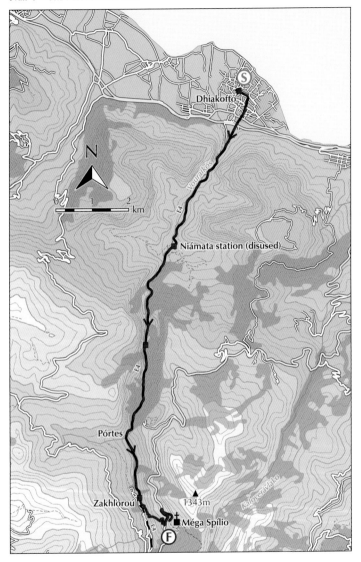

Entering the Vouraikós gorge

From Dhiakoftó railway station, follow the tracks heading S. After about 3km, a dirt road appears alongside, which makes for easier walking; it crosses the tracks again about 2km further. Here, resume along the railway tracks S past the abandoned **Niámata station (1hr 15min)** and into the wild section of the gorge. Clumps of purple cistus, yellow Jerusalem sage and pink valerian spring from orange-grey cliffs; crag martins and falcons flit overhead; the roaring stream is hidden by oleanders, Judas and plane trees below. The gradient steepens; rack-and-pinion cogs appear between the rails, and the tunnels start.

At the 8km mark, the gradient levels out and, 2km later, you pass the small guards' hut of Trikliá (unlocked in 2016) and a weak spring in the trunk of a plane tree. At 10.6km, the track splits to cross a narrow defile (the disused L fork is easier) before passing through the tunnel gates known as **Pórtes**, designed to keep livestock out. Look out for wagtails, dippers, freshwater crabs and even otters in this stretch of the river. Soon, walnut meadows appear on L and R – possible campsites – before you reach **Méga Spílio station** and **Zakhloroú (3hr 30min)**.

In the hamlet of **Zakhloroú**, shaded tavernas and rented rooms await, if you have not managed to book the Méga Spílio monastery guesthouse or the Grand Chalet motel.

For Méga Spílio monastery, from the station, walk through the second café terrace and find a path signed 'Great Cave Monastery/Méga Spílio' with a green circle and

35

blue triangle (and suggesting a generous walking time of 1hr 30min). You are leaving the E4 trail. A broad gravelly path climbs steadily between huge composite boulders, spiny broom and juniper saplings. After 15min the path bears L and levels out briefly; up ahead, a crag towers above the monastery guesthouse. Some 10min later, you join a dirt road at a hairpin and keep L (up). After a further 5min, you meet the main road by a yellow-and-black signpost ('Zakhloroú 20mins') and turn L along the road.

You pass a covered spring bedecked with icons (R) to reach a large stone-clad building (L), the Grand Chalet motel, whose owners currently run the monastery guesthouse. **Méga Spílio monastery** itself is a 5min walk up the paved road R (**4hr 30min**). It is open daily until sunset, with an hour's closure at lunch. The guesthouse is at the R (S) end of the complex, on a prominent outcrop.

To visit **Méga Spílio monastery**, ensure your shoulders and legs are covered, then enter through the huge door guarded by sculpted lions and head upstairs.

The frescoed hall tells the story behind the monastery, starting with the discovery in AD361 of a miraculous icon by local shepherdess Efrosíni; the finding of an exact replica in the hollow of a plane tree at Plataniótissa village; and the holy fathers' escape from the Ottoman sword in the 1820s. You pass the smoke-darkened Byzantine chapel (on the right) and the gold-glinting treasury (left) – both worth a visit (note: no photos); then descend to the cave where the shepherdess, pictured with founding monks Simeon and Theodore, was saved from a dragon by the divine icon.

Méga Spílio monastery

STAGE 2

Méga Spílio monastery (1000m) to Áno Lousí (1050m)
via Kserókambos/Mt Khelmós (1687m)

Start point	Méga Spílio monastery
Distance	17km
Difficulty	2
Walking time	6hr
Height gain	750m
Height loss	700m
Waymarks	Blue (and some yellow) to Livádhi Louká, some orange across Kserókambos, green to Valvoúsi

This is a long but truly beautiful hike climbing through dense fir forest, then across a 1600m plateau beneath the high peaks and ski slopes of Mt Khelmós, before descending through Alp-like meadows to the shepherds' village of Áno Lousí. This is remote terrain. You probably won't see a soul for most of the day. There's no reliable water after Psilós Stavrós and low cloud can roll into the plateau, so be prepared.

If it sounds too strenuous (and especially if you have overnighted in Zakhloroú), you could instead take the train to Kalávrita and then follow the E4 road route – or the red-waymarked mountain bike trail – up to the col of Áyios Nikólaos and down to Áno Lousí (about 3hr). Both are well marked on the Anávasi map.

Either way you should pre-book the Hotel O Spérhos – simple but friendly, and the only option in the village (Andréas and Toúla Pavlópoulos, tel 26920-83348, mob 694-4542413, little or no English spoken).

In front of the monastery guesthouse, turn sharp L (blue arrow) up a stepped path, then R passing a cemetery and through a gate in the lee of an overhanging boulder – note the blue-on-white (BW) and yellow-on-white (YW) waymarks which guide us for much of the morning.

Follow the broad path for a minute or so. Our preferred route then turns sharp L up a path which climbs to the restored stone fortress atop the monastery cliffs. The balustrade is still largely intact, but for those who might find the exposure disturbing, an alternative route is suggested below. Continue N behind the fort – there may be fallen trees – to a dam of round stones in wire blocks; then up to a second dam, in front

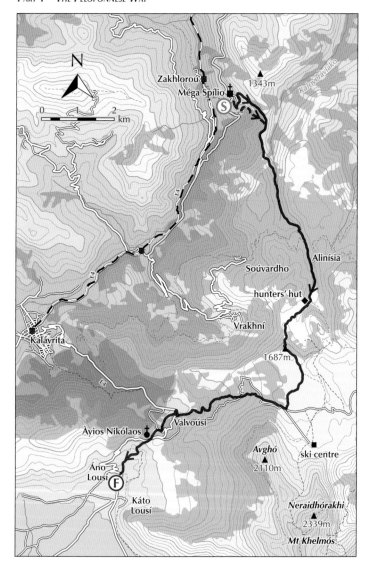

of which you turn R and scramble up to a clear track (**20min**). Follow this R (SE), with expansive views to the south past Kalávrita to distant Mt Olonós. The going is easy, apart from three washed-out gullies (take care). After about half an hour, you reach the 1150m ridge of Psilós Stavrós, with five interlinked wooden water troughs filled by a big black hosepipe (**50min**).

Alternative route to the ridge
An alternative route, avoiding the exposure, follows the broad path to a cross, then descends L on loose stones, past the base of a crag (BW and YW waymarks), before climbing steeply through fir forest, across a wooden footbridge, and up to the ridge just S of the troughs.

From the troughs, continue briefly S along the ridge, then follow a good path (and the hosepipe) R, contouring round a gentle summit. Resume along the ridge line, climbing steadily through fir forest (BW and a few YW waymarks). Look out for harebells, leopard's bane, nodding cyclamen, squeaking chaffinches and the occasional squawking woodpecker. About 20min from the troughs, with large lumps of conglomerate rock ahead, bear L along a small clear path descending gently, then round a corner and more steeply, over loose stones.

You enter the fir-cloaked Kaloyerávlako valley – mossy rocks, forget-me-nots, green marten droppings – and almost meet the stream (normally flowing until late May/early June). Continue along the R (true L) bank, joining an old cement conduit. Where the conduit crosses on a flimsy bridge (**1hr 30min**), walk down to the stream, jump

On the ridge near Psilós Stavrós

Livádhi Louká

across and up the far bank for 30 metres to rejoin the path alongside the conduit. About 20min later, you reach the broader, meadowy area of **Alinísia** (1300m); great camping.

Keep following the L (true R) bank near the pipe and stream. The path ascends briefly, then drops to cross the stream (faded BW waymark on a low rock) and resumes its climb more steeply; red paint splodges help through some messy switchbacks. It levels out around 1400m and follows the daisy-specked banks of the now-dry stream, before joining a dirt road (**2hr 15min**) at a yellow-and-black signpost pointing back to 'Méga Spílio 1h45'. Follow this L/straight, towards 'Xerokampos Helmos Ski Center 1h10'. After a minute or so, ignore a second signpost ('Peristéra 4h45', etc) and stay on the dirt road, ignoring smaller jeep tracks L. After 15min along the valley floor you reach the lovely open meadows of Livádhi Louká, carpeted with millions of daisies in May. Stay on the dirt road to a fork (**2hr 45min**) near a **hunters' hut** with two benches.

As the Anávasi map shows, there are several routes up to the Kserókambos plateau. In low cloud, you could follow the main dirt road (L, then keep R). Otherwise, our preferred route is to fork R past the hut. After 5min, at a multiple fork, keep R and immediately L to skirt the base of a grassy hump. Behind this, ignore a jeep track climbing steeply ahead and bear R (W) up a gentler jeep track, which then climbs in earnest – with a few unnecessary curves – to reach the grassy watershed (**3hr 10min**). This is a good lunch spot, with far-reaching views west over endless layers of jagged, blue-grey mountains.

Follow the ridge L (S) – largely trailless, with occasional orange splodges – becoming steeper, stonier and treeless: rock partridge terrain. After a steep step between two outcrops of conglomerate boulder, bear R and resume L to reach the concrete **1687m trig point** (**3hr 40min**). The rocky pyramid of Neraidhórakhi (2339m) is visible ahead (south), with the Khelmós ski slopes and buildings below.

Here, turn L (ESE) following the ridge and orange splodges (note: these also continue R/WSW). After 8min, descend a lip into a grassy gully and follow a faint jeep track down this (SSE) to rejoin the main dirt road (**3hr 55min**).

Follow this R (SSE), passing a crude shepherds' hut after 15min, to reach an asphalt road (**4hr 15min**). Turn R and immediately join the main road from Kalávrita to the ski centre; continue along this (NW). After 2min, at a L bend, take the path R, signed 'Kalávrita 2h30'. The clear path, waymarked with green triangles, descends steadily W through fir forest, crossing the main road twice. Be prepared for passing mountain bikers, and even motocrossers at weekends. After 45min, you see the new chalets of **Valvoúsi** ahead/R, tucked among alpine meadows, and soon join the dirt road that serves them, next to an old yellow-black post. Continue straight (W) along the dirt road for 5min to join the main Kalávrita–Lousí road by a small blue sign ('Valvoúsi alt. 1140m') above some new stone chalets (**5hr 15min**). Here, the route may become messy, especially if more chalets are built; if so, follow the main road L (SW) to the ridge and Áyios Nikólaos chapel (1.2km).

From the small blue sign, turn R along the main road for 150 metres and, by two telephone poles and a wooden sign 'Aroania Village II', turn sharp L into a field. Follow the L edge of the field to a wooden telephone pole, passing right next to it, climbing very slightly and bearing L (200°) onto a short section of old path, then up a small streambed to a new but uninhabited chalet. Behind this, follow the concrete track uphill. At a dirt road, turn R down to a walled spring (dry); you rejoin the E4 trail here. Turn L up a jeep track (230°) to a telephone pole on the skyline, next to the **chapel of Áyios Nikólaos** (**5hr 35min**).

Turn R along the road and after 50 metres fork L (E4 signpost) down a steep and stony dirt road. After 7min, ignore a R turn. The road (now concrete) enters the village of **Áno Lousí**. Turn R, passing the village church, spring and plane trees. Shortly before the road bears R, turn L down a steep concrete lane signposted 'ΟΔΟΣ ΚΟΣΜΑ ΠΑΥΛΟΠΟΥΛΟΥ' (ODOS KOSMA PAYLOPOYLOY) to reach Hotel O Spérhos (**6hr**).

STAGE 3
Áno Lousí (1050m) to Tourládha (750m) via Planitéro (590m)

Start point	Áno Lousí
Distance	17km (+ 1km for Cave of the Lakes detour)
Difficulty	2
Walking time	6hr (+ 1hr–1hr 30min for Cave of the Lakes guided tour)
Height gain	450m
Height loss	750m
Waymarks	E4 (yellow + black) all the way

This is another longish day but, apart from a short steep climb in the afternoon, it is largely downhill. You're following the E4 trail, but out of step with its daily stages. Long views stretch over fertile valleys and half-forgotten villages to serrated skylines. The terrain is a mix of meadows (flower-speckled in spring, dry thereafter) and Greek maquis (prickly kermes oak), stony underfoot, with little forest. This is the classic pastoral landscape of ancient Arcadia (although it now belongs to the administrative region of Achaia), and you may well meet shepherds tending their flocks. It is best to set off early, to allow time for the Cave of the Lakes detour (an additional 1hr–1hr 30min). In the afternoon, you pass the pretty village of Planitéro and the plane-shaded springs of the Aroánios river (possibility of rooms c/o Panayiótis 'Belénis' Melitsópoulos, tel 26920-31831, mob 697-2058496, mob 697-6699898).

The only reliable accommodation is in Káto Klitoría (also called Mazéïka), a friendly little market town 5km off the walking route, with an excellent hotel (Mont Helmos, tel 26920-31221, http://monthelmos.gr), several tavernas and an English-speaking taxi driver (Andréas Kazánis, mob 697-3819130) who can collect you from Tourládha (or elsewhere) and bring you back the following day to resume the route; book him a day ahead and take a mobile phone in case timings change.

Opposite Hotel O Spérhos, take the rightmost of the three tracks, passing L of some stone chalet-maisonettes and bearing R uphill. At the cemetery and cypress trees, continue straight (E4). At the church, continue straight/R ('Planitéro 3h30') down the concrete track into **Káto Lousí** (**15min**). At the square with springs and plane trees (part-time café on L), turn sharp L along a concrete lane, which curves R and climbs into the S part of the village. Leave the village by a chapel and big bushy oak tree, descending a gravelly jeep track in the direction of the half-fir-clad summits of Profítis Ilías (1489m).

About 150 metres before rejoining the asphalt road (**35min**), bear L onto a small goat trail (E4 sign). Keeping your eyes peeled for E4 plaques and plastic ribbons on trees, proceed SE across flat stony meadows, maintaining height and staying parallel to the road. Convolvulus, vetch and butterflies brighten your way in spring. After 5min, bear a few degrees L (up) across a very rocky stretch, then a few degrees R again to hit a gravel track by an E4 signpost. Cross straight over, passing a yellow-and-black (YB) waymark on a low rock. The path squeezes between kermes oak trees.

At **1hr 5min**, ignore the more trodden path bearing L up towards the peaks of Khelmós, and continue SSE across trailless ground to crest a slight rise. At an E4 post, turn R down a stony jeep track. Near a tiny corrugated iron hut (**1hr 15min**), turn L along a clearer jeep track. Where it starts to rise, bear L (E4 plaque) on a path to cut a corner. Cross another jeep track (**1hr 25min**); a deep gully opens up on your R. Where the track swings L, turn R (not signed) down a stony track, with views ahead over the gravelly Langádha riverbed. The track lurches L, then R down stony ground, past a house (dogs), to join a dirt road at a stone shrine (**1hr 40min**).

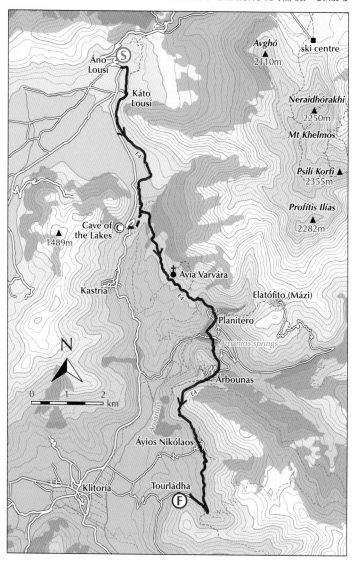

Descending into the Langádha valley

Detour to the Cave of the Lakes

The Cave of the Lakes lies 15min to your R – a worthwhile detour, although you'll need 1hr–1hr 30min in total (not included in timings below). To reach it, follow the dirt road R for 400 metres to a fork, then make your way R across the streambed and up to the road.

You get a 30min guided tour through a sequence of well-lit passages and subterranean lakes, festooned with stalactites. Take a jumper and some cash. It's open daily from 9am–4.30pm (5.30pm at weekends). Return the same way.

From the stone shrine, head straight down the slope (E), past a walled spring, to cross the wide gravelly riverbed (**1hr 50min**). Continue SE along a path (E4 sign), traversing up the L bank to reach a meadow. The path levels and broadens into a jeep track. Pass a weak spring L (**2hr 5min**). The **chapel of Ayía Varvára** is visible on a wooded spur ahead. You reach this after 20min and join a larger dirt track.

Continue straight/R and after 50 metres fork L up a smaller track (E4 post), and keep L again. After 12min, ignore a track L and continue (SE). Some 8min later (**2hr 50min**), at a R bend where the ground falls away steeply in front of you, the E4 trail strikes L (YB waymark on rock) down a very stony hillside, to join a concrete track just above a walled spring (**3hr**). You can also reach this point by staying on the track and then forking sharp L down a smaller track. Ahead, the village of Planitéro nestles spectacularly against a backdrop of darkly forested mountains (Dourdouvána).

Follow the concrete track into **Planitéro**, ignoring an asphalt road R, to reach a wide square with the health centre L, spring, kids' slide and a second asphalt road forking R. From here, the E4 takes you L up through the highest part of the village; but it is quicker to turn R down the (second) asphalt road and, at the junction by a forest of plane trees, L to the restaurants and trout farms of the **Aroánios springs (3hr 30min)**.

Planitéro village

From here, there is apparently a gentle **cycle route** (*podhilatódhromos*) along the banks of the Aroánios river to Klitoría, about 7km away.

However, our preferred route (and the E4 trail) climbs steeply to the hamlet of Árbounas before traversing, with lovely views south-west, to the village of Áyios Nikólaos and then Tourládha, from where you can cab, hitch or walk the 5km into Klitoría.

From the Aroánios springs, start by locating an arched bridge just before the restaurant Sólas (Rigoyiánnis). Cross this and bear L past some shelters (market stalls), heading 100° through plane forest. E4 markers are sparse. Bear R up a dirt track until, 5min above the chapel of Áyios Konstantínos, at a yellow-on-white waymark painted on the rock, you scramble up the bank R to find a tiny path threading through kermes woods. After 6min (**3hr 45min**), cross straight over the track (YB waymark on rock). The path, now clearer, climbs at 100° and after 10min eases off. You pass beneath a makeshift sheepfold, bear R up to a jeep track and steeply up this to the asphalt Árbounas road (**4hr 10min**).

Cross over (ascend the steep bank from the R) and make for the cypress tree below the L cluster of houses. Just below the cypress, bear R towards a big building with a painted cross (Áyios Athanásios church; **4hr 20min**). To the R of this, climb up the steep concrete track to the top of **Árbounas** village and keep R to reach a breeze-block chapel (**4hr 30min**) next to an abandoned playground. To the north-east and east, the rocky peaks of Khelmós encircle you: the dominant pyramid of Profítis Ilías (2282m), Gardhíki (2182m) and Dourdouvána (2107m).

Turn L and slightly uphill (YB waymark) along a jeep track which very soon becomes a clear goat path, contouring at 1150m, with views over the lush fields of Klitoría to the serrated peaks behind. After 25min (**4hr 55min**), you pass L of a rocky outcrop, lose height and veer unexpectedly R before switchbacking L towards the

45

houses of **Áyios Nikólaos**. At **5hr 20min** you pass just below the cemetery and climb up to join a concrete track. Follow this through the village to just above the main church (**5hr 30min**). You could get the taxi from Klitoría to collect you here.

To continue to Tourládha, turn L (E4 sign) and at a four-way junction go straight over, up a lane with tall cypresses and pines on your L. Pass a signpost ('Tourládha 0.30, Likoúria 4.30') and a gushing spring, then fork L (E4 sign) along a flat concrete lane which leaves the village heading S. After 2km, and just beyond a spring shaded by plane trees (possible campsite), ignore a L turn, follow the track sharp R, past an E4 plaque on a tree L, and enter the village of **Tourládha** (**6hr**). The E4 plaque on a tree marks the onward E4 route to Krinófita, which we don't advise – see beginning of Stage 4.

The taxi from Klitoría can collect you from Tourládha. At 1.5km along the road to Klitoría, look out for tomorrow's 'pleasant dirt road' forking L at a R bend.

STAGE 4

Near Tourládha (700m) to Dhára (660m)
via the Ládhonas river (480m)

Start point	Road bend 1.5km below Tourládha
Distance	18km
Difficulty	2
Walking time	6hr
Height gain	560m
Height loss	600m
Waymarks	E4 from below Pangráti to Dhára

This morning's route follows a lower, gentler and more direct route than the E4 (with which it overlaps briefly in the village of Krinófita) to the head springs of the Ládhonas (or Ládhon) river. Be prepared for some route-finding challenges around the river valley – including finding the one tiny, rickety bridge. After this you rejoin the E4 path to climb up to the near-deserted village of Pangráti, and contour round to Dhára (often written 'Daras'), a bigger village with the luxury of an indulgent guesthouse, Arkhontikó Kordhopáti (www.arhontiko-kordopati.gr/en). The going is mostly stony, over kermes-oak-covered hillsides with the occasional grassy meadow.

The E4 trail from Tourládha climbs steeply over a 1000m saddle before descending messily to Krinófita in about 1hr 45min. Given today's time constraints, we advise instead following the pleasant dirt road which starts about 1.5km below Tourládha, at a bend with a house, heading S past a concrete trough/spring (L).

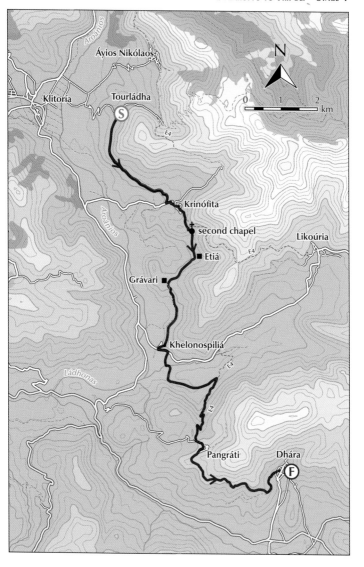

You contour S, then SE for 3.5km (**50min**) to join the asphalt road just below **Krinófita**, and head up into the village (**1hr**). Follow the E4 signs past two simple cafés to the highest houses and pick up a track (initially concreted) heading S. It climbs steadily past the chapel and vaulted spring of Panayía (L), after which you ignore a switchback L and continue straight along a smaller track (no sign) to a second **chapel** at a L bend (**1hr 15min**).

> The **E4 trail** continues to the end of the track and along a stony path, climbing broadly east to cross a 1000m saddle and descend to Likoúria, then southwest to the Ládhonas springs (about 3hr 30min from the second chapel). Our more direct route rejoins the E4 just south of the Ládhonas springs in about 1hr 45min, but depends on a rickety bridge and some fiddly route-finding.

Turn R at the second chapel down a stony but clear path through Jerusalem sage bushes. After a few zigzags, it bears L (E) and then R (S) to pass below the ruined houses and porticoed chapel of **Etiá** (**1hr 35min**), where one shepherd still lives part-time with his 150 sheep and 6 dogs. Follow the fence down to the cypress trees (unreliable spring) and skirt the top of the walnut grove, following the most trodden of the many sheep trails climbing gently SW. At **2hr** you crest the grassy saddle of **Grávari** (640m). This is idyllic in spring, with bright pink pyramid orchids, purple vetch, diligent stag beetles and shiny green rose chafers.

Behind the southernmost of three stone ruins, pick up a jeep track wiggling gently and then more steeply down to the S. After 15min you pass beneath a stone hut and then, where the track turns 90° R (W), continue straight on (S) on a tiny jeep track, past an oak tree and then a seasonal pond (R). There is no clear trail, but stay on the same bearing (210°), climbing very gently and ignoring any red dots to your R.

The path, becoming clearer, threads between kermes oak trees, descends slightly, levels out, then climbs again to cross a rocky spur (**2hr 40min**) above a very ruined stone hut. Here, turn R down the spur and make your way past an old threshing floor to what looks from here like a large white balcony – the **monument of Khelonospiliá** (**2hr 45min**).

Khelonospiliá monument

> When you reach the **Khelonospiliá monument**, you'll see the arresting statue of a woman with broken chains and a sword pointing defiantly skywards, in commemoration of the first anti-Ottoman liberation battles in 1821.

48

A few paces down the road, fork L down a stepped, white-edged path to the asphalt Likoúria road. Follow this L (E) for about 250 metres to a stone sheepfold on the L. Opposite this, turn R on a small path heading 190°, which after a few minutes bears L, to find a rickety wooden and metal bridge across the fledgling, gin-clear Ládhonas river (E00338367 / N04188568; **3hr**). Electric-blue and green dragonflies abound here in spring; you may also spot turtles if you're lucky.

This is where the route briefly becomes tricky; it may be worth scouting ahead. Turn L along the bank for 2–3min, then bear R (120°) towards the end pair of a row of poplars, on a faint path which continues past a twin-trunked poplar and, curving R, through a muddy cow path into a field. Here, continue 150° towards the lowest part of the cliff, across a trailless field (you may want long trousers), before bearing R to hit a good jeep track (**3hr 15min**).

Follow this L (E), ignoring a small fork L, and climbing gently through meadows with sparse oak and hawthorn trees. The track swings L until, bearing almost N, you reach a level meadow and join the E4 (post on L; **3hr 40min**). Here, turn 90° R (SE) for a few minutes, crossing terraced fields and passing E4 plaques on spiny trees; then step up L into the oak woods. Keeping your eyes peeled for faded red ribbons hanging from branches, follow the increasingly clear and part-shaded path steadily uphill (210°). At a gully (**4hr 20min**), pick up a jeep track climbing R (NW). After 5min, turn L along a more level track (E4). At the top (**4hr 35min**), turn L into the village of **Pangráti**.

Follow the main road up past the playground (water tap by seesaw) and the now-closed hostel. After a couple of minutes, fork R (E4); the lane levels out. At a hairpin bend, keep straight, taking the uppermost of two tracks and climbing steadily SW on a good path to the 870m saddle (**4hr 50min**). You can see the forested bulk of Mt Ménalo spread out to the south.

Dhára village

49

Here, the path turns SE, descending steadily over stony ground. After 7min, you descend to cross a streambed and clamber up a few paces before resuming SE on a gentle ascent. About 20min later, you round a barren spur – keep looking for the old path's border stones (don't descend). After a further 20min, you descend to join a farm track (**5hr 40min**).

Turn L into the village of **Dhára**; for Arkhontikó Kordhopáti guesthouse, 100 metres before the big church, turn R down a small lane and it is on your L (**6hr**).

STAGE 5

Nimfasía (920m) to Vitína (1030m) via
Kernítsa convent (850m)

Start point	Nimfasía
Distance	7km
Difficulty	1
Walking time	2hr 50min
Height gain	350m
Height loss	240m
Waymarks	Green squares (Nimfasía–Kernítsa and Tzavárena–Vitína)

The E4 route from Dhára to Nimfasía follows a road (much of it paved), which is flat, rather featureless and hot in summer. We therefore suggest taking a taxi for the 20km to Nimfasía – book it in advance, as there is only one in Dhára (Spílios, mob 694-4276544, no English spoken).

From Nimfasía, we've found a short but lovely and varied route, looping anticlockwise, to Vitína. It takes in the wild gorge and hilltop convent of Kernítsa (Kernítsis), an old stone bridge over a verdant valley (swimmable river pools until the end of May), and a dramatic limestone cleft. The first and last sections follow the green-waymarked Ménalon Trail (http://menalontrail.eu); try to get a copy of the 1:25,000 map produced by Lyhnia (www.lyhnia.com), although it – like the route itself – may be hard to locate as time goes on.

Vitína is a surprisingly large mountain village, bustling in summer and cool all year round, with shops, tavernas, guesthouses and even a boutique hotel. Athenians love coming here for snowy winter weekends. You could take the taxi all the way to Vitína, find a hotel and drop your bags, then walk the E4 trail back (north) to Nimfasía (3km/40min) to pick up our route.

Beehives near Nimfasía

From the central square of Nimfasía, head NW along the road between the 'ΧΑΣΑΠΟΤΑΒΕΡΝΑ (963m)' (HASAPOTABERNA) taverna (L) and the Ménalo map-board (R). At the bell tower, turn L and then bear R, following green square (GS) way-marks and signs to Ierá Moní Kernítsis.

Where the road bears L at a cemetery (**5min**), continue straight ahead (W) on a dirt road towards the flat-topped summit of Aryirókastro. Ignore side tracks to L and R. After 10min, you pass a shrine and a Ménalon Trail (MT) sign; shortly after this, just beyond a L bend in the track, fork R and immediately R again (GS) down a small path (W). This enters a ditch, bears R (first views of the convent) and zigzags down, part-shaded by oaks, to just above the road bridge over the Miláontas stream (**40min**). Don't drop down to the road, but keep R, climbing and then dropping steeply to cross the river on an old stone bridge (**45min**). This is a lovely shady spot, but tantalisingly there is no way down to the blue-green pools (dry after June).

Shortly before the road, the path turns sharp R and then splits: both ways lead to the convent but L (GS) is gentler. Reunited, the old mule path zigzags up, through a gate, to emerge at the top of the car park for **Kernítsa convent** (**55min**).

To visit **Kernítsa convent** (open daily from 9am–2pm and from 4pm until sunset), follow the stepped lane to the right, up through a rose garden and a wooden gate to the chapel, perched on a limestone crag above the gorge.

The site is 900 years old, the buildings much newer; they now house 14 nuns – and, on the 15 August feast day, many visiting pilgrims. A door to the left of the chapel takes you down to the tiny vaulted crypt, with a copy of the miraculous icon, and dozens of censers hanging from the ceiling.

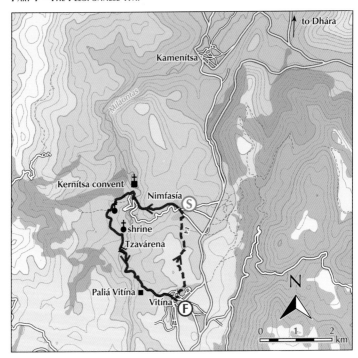

From the convent car park, follow a stepped path (W) up to a stone-faced chapel (good spring), through the gate, across the yard, out of the far gate and R up a steep path (GS). Climb a shaly spur, covered in purple cistus in May, with views back to the convent. After 10min (**1hr 5min**), you pass an overgrown circular threshing floor and pick up a jeep track continuing SW. Look left (south) to see the tiny red-roofed shrine of Áyios Ioánnis on a rocky outcrop at the end of a sandy spur: you'll pass this later.

At the end of a fence (L), leave the GS waymarks and follow a track L down to the dirt road, where you turn R. After 3–4min, fork R (uphill), watching out for vicious dogs (be prepared to throw some stones). After another 5–6min (**1hr 20min**), and 20 metres after a stone **chapel** (L), fork L down the uppermost of two tiny jeep tracks between a fence (L) and a hut (R). This bends L across a small streambed (plane trees), then winds over shrubby hillsides and down a shaly spur to the **shrine of Áyios Ioánnis** which, close up, looks like a cross between a dog kennel and a family grave (**1hr 40min**). Before the shrine, take a small path descending sharp R (W), contouring S across shale

The crypt of Kernítsa

to a small saddle, and then stonily down to a lovely meadow ringed by plane trees (**1hr 50min**): lovely camping.

From the left-hand corner of the meadow, it is worth making a **short detour** north to a point where the gorge narrows dramatically. You can either take a small path that threads its way along the left bank 20–30 metres above the stream, or follow the streambed (dry after June). After visiting, retrace your steps to the meadow.

To continue, from the upper end of the meadow, find a small path running SW parallel to the stream and about 30 metres above it, to reach the old stone **bridge of Tzavárena** (**2hr**). In pre-automobile days, this bridge used to be the main artery between Vitína and the villages of western Gortynia. Cross the bridge (signpost to 'Vitína 45 mins') and head straight (SE) up the opposite slope (GS). After 7–8min, bear R (S), still climbing steadily, across slopes speckled with yellow *Onosma* and red spurge. You cross a dry gully (880m); the path may be washed out. At a spur with views towards Vitína, turn unexpectedly R (GS) following the spur down to a wooden picnic shelter (**2hr 20min**) with plunging views over a narrow cleft of river gorge, known as Mávra Lithária (black boulders).

Tzavárena bridge

For a closer look at the **river gorge** (optional), a stepped path zigzags down to the plane-shaded riverbed, which you follow carefully to the right into the jaws of the gorge.

If, in the riverbed, you keep left and cross two wooden bridges, there is a narrow rollercoaster trail all the way to the stone bridge of Zárzi in about 45min, from where tracks lead to Vitína – but from the state of the trail in 2016 there's no guarantee it will be passable. It is better to return to the picnic shelter.

From the shelter, follow the jeep track E. After 5min, at a L bend, turn R down a path (GS) which crosses a smelly stream, swings R (W) and climbs steadily and shadily SE. It briefly rejoins the track at a hairpin (GS) before forking R (uphill) and veering R to crest the ridge. Here, turn L along a paved path, passing the ruins of **Paliá Vitína** (L).

At a gravel track, continue straight/L; after a couple of minutes, a bigger track joins from the L and you pass Áyi Apóstoli chapel and Arhontaríki guesthouse on your R (**2hr 40min**). Follow the now paved lane E into **Vitína** (**2hr 50min**). The E4-sponsored Hotel Sinói (tel 27950-22354, mob 694-5632241, www.sinoi.gr) is on the far (E) side of town.

Side trip to Dhimitsána, Stemnítsa and the Loúsios gorge (1–2 days)

There are two buses a day from Vitína to the beautiful towns of Dhimitsána and Stemnítsa on Ménalo's western flanks, overlooking the deep river valley and spectacularly sited monasteries of the Loúsios. If you have time to spare, this is a worthwhile two-day detour, using the Anávasi map or the Ménalon Trail waymarks (red squares on white) to hike from Dhimitsána to Stemnítsa via the water museum, Filosófou monastery, Prodhrómou monastery, and (optionally) a detour to the ancient riverside ruins and Asklepeion of Gortys (or Górtina) (5–6hr in total). There are several hotels and tavernas in Dhimitsána (we like the Theonimfi guesthouse www.theonimfi.gr and the Kazakou www.xenonaskazakou.gr), and a few in Stemnítsa.

The Anávasi and Ménalon Trail maps also show waymarked forest trails linking Dhimitsána or Stemnítsa with Vitína (red/yellow squares), but with 8–9hr hiking time and uncertain route-finding, you may struggle to make it in a day. We'd be happy to hear from anyone who does try it.

STAGE 6
Vitína (1030m) to Kardharás (1020m) or Kápsia
(700m) via Mt Ménalo ski area (1600m)

Start point	Vitína
Distance	17km to Kardharás (22km to Kápsia) excluding Sfendámi
Difficulty	2–3
Walking time	5hr 45min to Kardharás (6hr 45min to Kápsia) excluding Sfendámi
Height gain	930m
Height loss	940m
Waymarks	Yellow then orange squares

Today's hike climbs through pine- and fir-clad mountains more reminiscent of the Swiss Jura than of southern Greece. Most of it is shady, with a few open meadows offering glimpses of the rounded summits of Mt Ménalo (or Mainalon). Our high point is the tiny and very seasonal ski resort at 1600m, or (optionally) the 1880m summit of Sfendámi (add 35min). Keen peak-baggers could go further and book a night at the EOS refuge, allowing them to summit 1981m Ostrakína, Ménalo's highest point, and other minor summits.

The descent, again through shady forests, criss-crosses the mountain road before reaching the tiny hamlet of Kardharás – almost dead outside winter weekends, although the luxurious Neféles Mountain Resort (tel 27960-22771, tel 27960-22871, www.nefelesmainalon.gr) can normally open for you by prior arrangement. Otherwise you'll have to continue 5km along the road – you may get a lift if you're lucky – to the larger village of Kápsia, which has a conference-oriented but welcoming hotel, Arkhontikó Kalteziótis (tel 2710-235822/3, www.kalteziotis.gr).

From Vitína's central square (1030m), follow the main road E, with the church on your L. After 300 metres, at a L bend (Hotel Aígli ahead, Hotel Sinói 100 metres to your L), continue straight and immediately L, following the road R. Yellow-on-white squares (YS) guide you throughout the morning's route. After 400 metres, with a pine wood L, follow the lane L. After 300 metres, fork R up a farm track (YS) to the main road (**20min**). Go straight over (E4, YS) up a surfaced lane, soon passing a stone spring and cistern R. Where the concrete lane ends in front of a stone chapel (**30min**), turn R up a jeep track (E4). This becomes a path, still heading NE and well marked with YS.

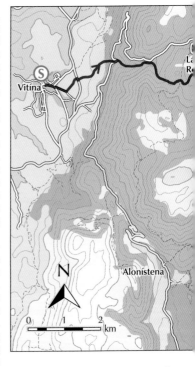

Enter the fir forest and climb steadily up a rocky defile. At weekends, be prepared for down-rushing mountain bikes from here onwards. At **50min**, you climb steeply to a surfaced road: turn L and immediately R up a jeep track in a gully heading broadly SE. The signed route forks L twice, passing a mountain bike ramp before rejoining the gully floor. At **1hr 10min**, turn sharp L up a path, then resume SE along a broader, rockier path. At a clearing, the gradient lessens; fork R along a gravelly path (E4, YS). At **1hr 25min** cross straight over the forest road, heading SSE (YS). Emerge on a small forest track and keep R/straight. This soon levels off and dwindles into a path bearing L (E); climb past several ramps to reach the junction of a forest road and smaller track (1520m – this morning's high point; **1hr 45min**).

Go straight across the dirt road and down a lovely path (E4, YS) initially heading E; the path bears R then L down to a grassy jeep track in the valley floor. Turn L, gently downhill. The next half-hour needs careful route-finding. At **1hr 55min**, bear R (two YS on tree trunk) onto a vague trail skirting the R edge of semi-open grassland (**Láki Roúkhi**). Pick up another grassy track, keep L/straight for 100 metres, then bear nearly 90° R (SE) across meadows looking for YS on trees. If you miss the YS waymarks on trees, turn sharp R at the water tank. Where the now wider track veers R, fork L (two YS and one red square on a tree) heading SSE and climbing gently up an open meadow strip. After 300 metres, turn 90° L/NE (two YS on R, pointing L), climbing up a steeper

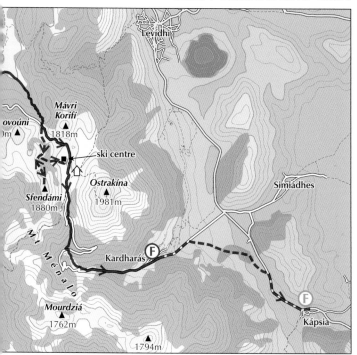

path between fir trees. Reach the top and descend for 5min or so. With the main trans-Ménalo road just visible 80 metres ahead, turn 90° R (two YS) and weave between fir trees to reach this asphalt road at its junction with a good dirt road descending NE (**2hr 30min**).

Cross straight over and pick up a small path R of the dirt road (some fallen trees), descending initially parallel to the dirt road, then bearing R. At **2hr 40min**, you cross a grassy track and remain on a small trail (YS). Some 5min later, turn R along a good dirt track (no obvious waymark); from here you are following orange squares (OS), not yellow squares (**2hr 45min**).

A couple of minutes later, continue L/straight along a smaller track aiming SE between the summits of **Mávri Korifí** (1818m) and **Mesovoúni** (1860m). The valley is now open and grassy. Where the track bears R away from the valley floor, continue straight up the gully on a smaller track (OS) which dwindles to a path. This climbs steeply – better for descending bikers than ascending hikers – but is shady and soft underfoot.

Mt Ménalo: the ski area in May with Sfendámi summit behind

At **3hr 30min** you reach the main asphalt road (1600m, the day's high point) and turn L. From this point, you can either follow the asphalt road for about 2km (25min) to just beyond the buildings and car park of the **ski centre** or take the following optional detour to Sfendámi.

Detour to Sfendámi
After 50 metres along the asphalt road, turn R across a grassy bowl and climb steeply up to a ski hut (1680m). From here, a jeep track continues R (SW then S; keep R) up to the base of **Sfendámi**; continue cross-country up to the pyramidal 1880m peak (30–40min from the ski hut). Return the same way past the ski hut and then turn R (E) down to the **ski centre** and car park (1hr total).

From the ski centre (**3hr 55min**, excluding Sfendámi detour), follow the main asphalt road S, passing the access track to the **EOS refuge** (L), and a small red square plaque (R) indicating the start of the trail to Alonístena and Mourdziá. Here (**4hr**), by an E4 and EOS info sign, hop L onto a small path running parallel to the road, which becomes a lovely corridor through the forest. At the asphalt road (**4hr 15min**), turn R along it for 50 metres, then L (OS, E4) down a gently descending path. Cross to the L side of the gully, then (**4hr 30min**) pick up a jeep track with views ahead up to Mourdziá ridge (1762m). At **4hr 35min**, the trail lurches down a stony bank to the asphalt road; or, easier, follow the track R and turn L up the road. Either way, opposite the winding-road sign 'ΣΥΝΕΧΕΙΣ' (SYNEXEIS), continue SE down a path which descends across semi-open ground, down some steep terraces, bears L and skirts just above the asphalt road before giving up and joining it by a telephone pole (E4, green EOS sign; **5hr**).

From here, it is not worth persevering with the overgrown and gravelly trail, so resign yourself to 2km (25min) of road trudge E, with little chance of a lift. At **5hr 25min**, a lane forks L to the scattered houses of **Kardharás**, including the E4-backed Neféles Hotel and the oft-closed Ostra (tel 27960-22743, www.ostra.gr, expensive) – about **5hr 45min** hiking from Vitína, excluding Sfendámi detour.

If these hotels are closed or full, stay on the main road and continue to **Kápsia** and the Hotel Kalteziótis (**6hr 45min** from Vitína, excluding Sfendámi detour): see Stage 7 for the route from Kardharás to Kápsia.

Alternative route via Ostrakína and Mourdziá

If you're coming with a group, you could, by arrangement, overnight at the EOS refuge near the ski area. This would allow you to summit Ostrakína (1981m) in the afternoon and next day follow the high-level path over Mourdziá (1762m) and E down to Kápsia; I have not done this but have heard it is wild and beautiful.

To book the EOS refuge: see www.eostripolis.gr or tel 27210-232243 midweek evenings, or try the warden Tássos on mob 694-5858862 (little English spoken; approx €120 per night for up to eight people, with an additional €15 per extra person; bring sheet sleeping bags and food to cook).

STAGE 7

Kardharás (1020m) or Kápsia (700m) to
Trípoli (670m)

Start point	Kardharás (or Kápsia)
Distance	19.5km from Kardháras (14.5km from Kápsia)
Difficulty	2
Walking time	5hr 30min from Kardharás (4hr 20min from Kápsia)
Height gain	350m
Height loss	700m from Kardháras (380m from Kápsia)
Waymarks	E4

The E4 route from Kardharás to Trípoli is one of the less interesting stages in the trail: if you're going to skip one day, skip this – especially since there is a morning bus along the main road 2km below Kardharás (it normally passes the junction between 8.30am and 9am; times vary, so check locally), continuing through Kápsia and into Trípoli. You can stock up in this bustling provincial capital, then take a taxi to Psilí Vrísi and complete the next stage all in one (longish) day.

From Kardharás, rejoin the main road and follow it downhill (ENE). About 1km below the village (or 0.5km below Neféles), turn R (E4) along a small lane passing a couple of blocky houses. Fork R (E) and after 1.5km bear R and then bend L to rejoin the main road. Turn R along the main road. After just over 2km you enter **Kápsia** (700m; **1hr 10min**).

If you have arrived in **Kápsia** at the end of Stage 6: for the Hotel Kalteziótis, continue into the village and turn left at the big church, crossing its front yard, and bearing left (tel 2710-235822/3, www.kalteziotis.gr).

For Trípoli, as you enter Kápsia, turn R (E4) up a dirt track climbing gently SW. This becomes a goat path, crossing open hillsides to another dirt track which you follow L (S), past a goat stable (**1hr 30min** or **20min**). Beyond Kápsia, walking times show the time from Kardharás first, followed by the time from Kápsia. After about 2km (**2hr** or **50min**), fork L off this track onto goat paths (E4), still heading S across stony, scrubby meadows near the valley floor. You reach the **chapel of Áyios Yiórgos** (**3hr** or **1hr 50min**) and pick up a track, part concrete part gravel, heading S. After the first side road, the path slips L (E4) and runs parallel with the track before rejoining it and then descending through a valley to the village of **Perthóri** (**4hr** or **2hr 50min**).

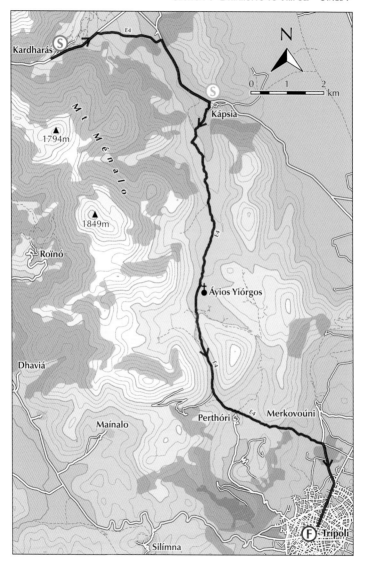

Tortoises can be seen along the Píndos Way

At the entrance to the village, keep L/straight (E4), past the old school, then L and immediately R along a small lane which dwindles to a track, descending ESE. After 2km, near an army shooting range, you pick up an asphalt road (E4) and bear R (SSE) through the ugly periphery of **Trípoli** (**5hr** or **3hr 50min**). After just over 1km, you join the main road from Kápsia (and Olympía/Pírgos), and follow it R (SSW) into the centre of this bustling provincial capital (**5hr 30min** or **4hr 20min**).

SECTION 2 TRÍPOLI TO PANTAZÍ BEACH

Track from Metamórfosi to Faneroménis monastery (Stage 11)

The second half of the Peloponnese Way crosses the massifs of Párnonas and Taïgetos, the former rounded and forested, the latter jagged and rocky, although firs and venerable black pines do shade your way in parts. In between these is Sparta, a modern town with ancient roots, sitting in the olive- and citrus-cultivated Evrótas valley; here our continuous walking route is interrupted with a taxi or bus ride.

Note that the last part of our route diverges from the E4, which descends the south-eastern flanks of Taïgetos to the harbour town of Yíthio (Gythion) in Lakonía. We, instead, descend the more direct south-western side to reach the Messinian coast near a village called Áyios Nikólaos. Note that there is another village of the same name on the eastern side, which – to add to the confusion – is an overnight stop on the E4.

Trípoli is in the centre of the Peloponnese, capital of the modern administrative region of Arkadhía. It is 160km (1hr 45min by motorway) south-west of Athens, and 85km (1hr by motorway) north-east of the city of Kalamáta.

- Anávasi Topo 50 (1:50,000) 8.7 *Mt Parnon*
- Anávasi Topo 50 (1:50,000) 8.1 *North Taygetos*
- For the last day: Anávasi Topo (1:20,000) 8.10 *Exo Mani*

Looking north past Kastrí village (Stage 8)

BASES

Mistrás has restaurants, a few shops, hotels and guesthouses, including the Hotel Byzantion (www.byzantion hotel.gr) and the Mystras Inn (www. mystrasinn.gr). **Anavrití** has one guesthouse, the Arhontikó (tel 27310-82671 or 27310-22938, mob 698-7101555, 698-7128554 or 697-9118855, https:// kaneltrekking.gr), run by Yiórgos Kanelópoulos, a trekking aficionado who also maintains the E4 Peloponnese route. **Áyios Nikólaos**, **Stoúpa** and **Kardhamíli** are three lovely villages near the trail's endpoint, offering hotels, restaurants and further gentle hikes.

ACCESS

Regular daily buses run from Athens (Kifisoú Street terminus) to Trípoli (www. ktelarkadias.gr in Greek only) and from Kalamáta to Athens (Kifisoú Street terminus) (www.ktelmessinias.gr).

There are two or three buses a day between Kalamáta and Áyios Nikólaos, passing Stoúpa and Kardhamíli (www. ktelmessinias.gr see Kalamáta–Ítilo route).

STAGE 8
Psilí Vrísi (720m) to Áyios Pétros (930m)

Start point	Psilí Vrísi
Distance	20km
Difficulty	2
Walking time	6hr 15min
Height gain	840m
Height loss	630m
Waymarks	E4 all the way

Today's scenery is not dramatic, but the afternoon's long views and easy striding give a great sense of satisfaction. From Trípoli, the 13km road to Psilí Vrísi is flat, hot and dull, so it really is worth taking a taxi, especially since the onward walk is still long (6hr 15min). The first part of the trail follows an undulating farm track over scrublands and fields; then there's a shady but pathless streambed up to pretty Dholianá, where there are cafés and seasonal hotels (including Erásmion, tel 2710-234072, mob 697-2706580, www.erasmion.gr). A steep ascent brings you to an open watershed with views south over rolling hills as far as distant Mt Taïgetos; undulating farm tracks and a stretch of road complete the journey to the small but lively village of Áyios Pétros at the foot of Mt Párnonas – which is itself tomorrow's target.

Taxi drivers may not know Psilí Vrísi (it is a tiny hamlet, almost deserted now), nor the E4 trailhead, so ask to go through Áyios Sóstis and Garéa, after which the road splits. Head left through the main cluster of houses and stop 150 metres before a war memorial at a junction of three asphalt lanes. (If you fork right at the split, you will also reach this point, 150 metres after the memorial.) In winter or early spring, when the streambed will be impassable and the days shorter, you may want to take the taxi all the way to Dholianá.

Take the lane between a small breeze-block bus shelter (L) and two blocky houses (R), and immediately turn R (E4 arrow) and R again down a farm track. Descend gently SE towards a 1417m summit topped by masts (Dholianítiko) with the village of Dholianá visible halfway up the hillside. Stay on the main shadeless track, weaving between abandoned wheat fields lined with small hawthorn trees, white or purple cistus bushes and beehives in summer.

After **15min** follow the main track forking L (E4 signpost). At the top of the rise, keep L (signpost), downhill. Cross a dry streambed and keep R. Where a track joins

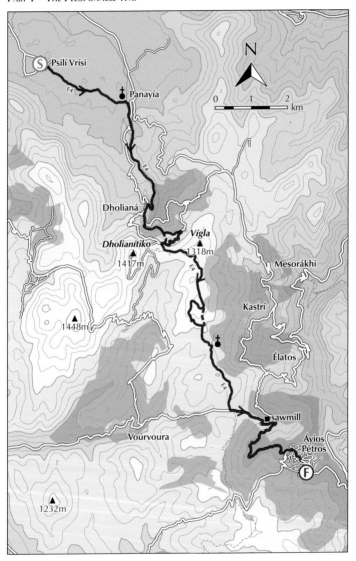

White rock roses (cistus) bordering the track from Psilí Vrísi

from the R (**35min**), keep L/straight (E4 on plane tree L) and shortly afterwards L/straight again (chestnut grove on L) and across a smaller track. At **45min** you reach the whitewashed **chapel of Panayía**, a lovely spot in the shade of plane and cherry trees (water tap in wall).

After 50 metres, turn R up a plane-shaded streambed, usually dry from May. If it is impassable, you can pick your way along the R (true L) bank for the first 300 metres. It is cool here but prone to midges; a stick is useful, as dry leaves can cover hollows. Shortly after the first rubbish spill, it is best to climb L onto the true R bank and through a small orchard to the asphalt road by a ruined mill and a church-shaped shrine (**1hr 5min**). Continue S along the road for 100 metres to a concrete ford. If the stream is flowing strongly (typically Nov–Apr), you may want to continue along the road to Dholianá (about 3km).

To follow the stream, turn L along a small streamside track (E4 on plane tree) and, where it climbs L, continue along the streambed as best you can. After 15–20min it opens out; the path follows the R, then the L side. Around **1hr 40min** you see two E4 arrows on a thin plane tree, pointing L away from the streambed along a path with walled fields on the R (E4 ribbons). After 6min, drop R to cross the streambed and up the earthy bank opposite into fields, bearing L to resume progress SE, with a side stream on your L. Watch out for silently sunbathing snakes (bang your stick), but don't worry about loud rustles in the leaves (lizards). At **1hr 55min**, drop L to the side stream and follow this R (E4), then up to the L (grassy track). At a jeep track, turn R (E4 on tree) and keep R/straight, to cross a stream. Just before a R bend, turn L along a path (E4 and red square), then up a side stream, across an old wheat field, then back alongside the stream.

Where the path heads L across the stream (**2hr 15min**), turn R (E4 arrow) and zigzag up a steep chestnut-strewn path (overgrown in places), before straightening out NW. At **2hr 25min**, you emerge on the asphalt road at the bottom of **Dholianá**, by an S-bend with a mirror, and turn L (E4). Turn L again after 50 metres up a concrete path to the lower village square (950m; tap by graveyard gate; **2hr 30min**).

Continue S up the cobbled lane and, at the T-junction, turn L and immediately R up a stepped path. At the asphalt road (**2hr 35min**), turn L to reach a parking area, with the village centre to your R. The village centre has a funky café, two restaurants and seasonal hotel(s). Stock up on water.

For the onward route, continue along the road for 150 metres, then fork R up a small asphalt lane (E4 and yellow arrow), climbing steadily. Ignore a L fork and turn

Dholianá village

sharp R (E4 only) up a small concrete lane, passing an old spring on your L. Behind the house and chestnut tree (E4 arrow and optimistic 1100m altitude sign), turn L up a steep, overgrown path. At the concrete lane (**2hr 50min**), turn L (no sign). Look back for great views over the village to the plain of Trípoli, forested Mt Ménalo behind and the stark outlines of Mts Trákhis and Kteniás further right (north). Fork R and, at the last house, fork R again up a jeep track which climbs and then wiggles more gently upwards (broadly E).

At **3hr**, you'll see a grassy track ascending R with an E4 plaque on which someone has scribbled 'Very thorny! Take the road'. By the time you read this, the thorny section should be passable, but if you prefer not to risk it, continue straight along the jeep track (another E4 sign) through still-tended chestnut groves to the asphalt road (**3hr 12min**), where you turn R (uphill) and after 5min L up a slightly prickly path (E4). Either way, you should reach the 1240m watershed and dirt road around **3hr 30min**, with your first views south over rolling hills of untrampled maquis and low woods to the distant, jagged silhouette of Mt Taïgetos. In midsummer, this unshaded, blonde earth will be baking hot.

Turn L (E), away from the antenna-topped peak of **Dholianítiko** (1417m) along the watershed dirt road. Ignore the track L up to the gentle summit of **Vígla** (1318m), with its fire-watching tower. At the T-junction (**3hr 50min**), turn L and after 150 metres, by a hut, R (E4).

There are **views** to the left (north-east) to the Gulf of Náfplio and the Argolid; and, in spring, cuckoos, tortoises and lupins. Ahead/Right (south-east), below and left of the pyramidal summit of Mt Párnonas, the big building standing out from the dark forest is Malevís convent, tomorrow's trailhead.

Optional shortcut

Where the dirt road curves R and up, it is possible (although not waymarked) to short-cut L down a rough track to some chestnut groves, descending S over rough ground with a gully on your L, to reach a cherry grove; here turn R along a small track to rejoin the original dirt road.

If you choose not to take the shortcut, remain on the dirt road, keeping L (safer, but 10min longer) to reach a five-way junction of dirt roads (**4hr 40min**). Go straight across, on a smaller dirt road (E4), and at a crossroads (**4hr 45min**) turn R (E4). The unremarkable chapel of Profítis Ilías lies 200 metres to your left (east). At **4hr 49min**, with cultivated fields on your R, turn 90° L (E4), climbing gently.

You eventually descend to reach an asphalt road (**5hr 20min**) by a yellow-and-green sign pointing back your way 'ΠΡΟΣ ΚΟΣΣΙΑΝΑΣ' (PROS KOSSIANAS). Turn L (E) along the asphalt road for 100 metres to where the E4 route turns R along a dirt road. The E4 route follows the dirt road for 3km, then, at a second asphalt road, descends L (NE) for 4km into Áyios Pétros. For a shorter route, ignore the E4 turn-off and remain on the asphalt road, descending E past a **sawmill** to the main road (1.5km) which you follow R for 3km – with chances of a lift – into **Áyios Pétros** (**6hr 15min**). The Hotel Párnon (tel 27920-31245, mob 694-7377615, www.hotelparnon.gr) is on your R, with a couple of restaurants opposite. If the hotel is closed, try Malevós Traditional Houses (tel 27920-31155, tel 27920-31375, mob 694-5377328, www.facebook.com/malevos, advance booking essential).

Áyios Pétros with the summits of Párnonas behind

69

STAGE 9

*Malevís convent (900m) to Vamvakoú (930m) via
Mt Párnonas (1670m/1935m)*

Start point	Malevís convent
Distance	17km (excluding optional peak)
Difficulty	3
Walking time	7hr (+ 1hr 45min for round trip to peak)
Height gain	1120m (+ 265m for peak)
Height loss	1090m (+ 265m for peak)
Waymarks	Red squares

Today's walk diverges from the E4, but it is one of my favourites: a classic Greek mountain ascent, with the option to climb a panoramic, rocky summit if you are feeling energetic, before the equally pretty fir- and pine-shaded descent to the forgotten village of Vamvakoú, lost in the wooded folds of Mt Párnonas. It is a long day (start early), but varied, well signed and almost entirely road-free. You start from the formidable convent of Malevís, 5km east of Áyios Pétros along the Astrós road; book a taxi a day or two ahead (Pávlos Katsís, mob 694-4858287).

Vamvakoú has a cosy village hostel, but at the time of writing, nobody to run it. Check www.xenonasvamvakou.gr for the latest, or call the village *kafeneio* (café) on 27310-81217 (Greek only). Failing that, try contacting the previous manager Kóstas Verdhékis (tel 27310-27492, tel 27310-21116, mob 694-4786798, limited English). If all that fails, you have four options:

a) Try Hotel Meterizi in the nearby village of Varvítsa (tel 27310-28332, tel 27310- 95100, mob 697-2922250, www.meterizi.com, the owner Panayiótis speaks a little English). It is most likely to be open over weekends and school holidays; at other times, he normally opens only for groups of six or more. You'll also need to arrange transport from Vamvakoú to Varvítsa (6.5km) and back.

b) Book the Arnómousga ('George Pierce') mountain refuge with EOS Spártis (tel 27310-22574 evenings, tel 27310-26343 daytime, mob 697-4454079); there's a fixed fee of about €120 for the warden (who drives up from Sparta and stays the night with you), so this option is only worth it for larger groups

c) Book Pávlos Katsís (mob 694-4858287) to collect you at the refuge or at Vamvakoú and take you back to Áyios Pétros, returning next morning to continue the route.

d) Camp in Vamvakoú: there are streamside meadows below the village and simple food is usually available at the *kafeneio* (see above).

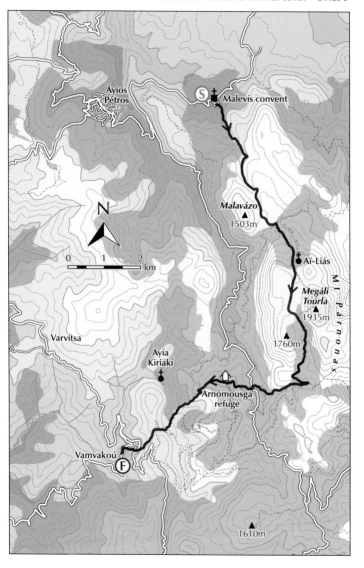

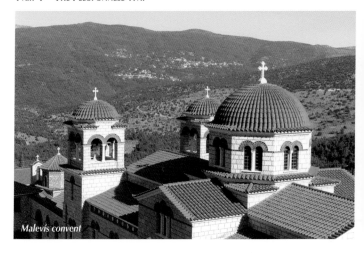
Malevís convent

Malevís convent is a large complex of 20th-century outbuildings surrounding a 17th-century *katholikón* (central church). It is home to 30 nuns and a much-venerated miraculous icon which intermittently oozes myrrh. You can normally visit from 8am (entrance on left); wear long sleeves.

Entering the convent, with the church on your L, fork R up an asphalt lane past a no-entry sign, and bear L. Behind the church, turn sharp R and immediately L (wooden sign to 'Megáli Toúrla peak 1934m, Refuge, Vamvakoú') up a path with faint steps. Join a larger path at wooden signs to 'ΔΑΣΑΡΧΕΙΟ ΚΥΝΟΥΡΙΑΣ' (DASARXEIO KYNOURIAS). From here, the route is generally well waymarked with red squares (RS).

Climb through low cedar woods (*Juniperus drupacea* sign), whose matt silvery-blue berries dot the path. After an old water station and conduit, the path drops briefly, then by two decrepit signs (**30min**) turns 90° L steeply uphill. Resume gentle progress S, past two wooden troughs (weak spring). At **1hr**, you cross a side gully and descend, curving L, to enter the main valley. At **1hr 30min** you climb steeply E (up the true R bank) before resuming S. Around **1hr 50min** you reach the grassy saddle E of **Malavázo** (1503m), with the twin summits of Párnonas clearly visible ahead.

Continue along a grassy jeep track descending gently just W of S for 4min. At a R bend, bear L (RS) along a path; if you miss this, just turn L at the junction with the next track. At a slight dip, bear R (165°) aiming towards the R peak, Megáli Toúrla. At a crude wooden shepherds' hut, keep L/up (RS), passing above a hairpin of the dirt road. Climb steadily to reach a large dirt road (**2hr 10min**).

Here turn R, downhill (RS on rock). After 200 metres, fork L (wooden sign) up a steep jeep track, ignoring any R forks. At **2hr 25min** it dwindles to a path (RS). At **2hr**

40min you emerge on a dirt road (metal sign to 'Megáli Toúrla 1:20, Katafygio Parnona 2:00') and turn R. At the first hairpin, continue straight up a broad path to rejoin the dirt road by a wooden sign. Follow this up to the unlocked **chapel of Áï-Liás** (Áyios Ilías; 1670m; **2hr 45min**), with its grassy *kámbos* (plateau) behind/S.

If you want to climb the lunar mound of **Megáli Toúrla** (1935m; 1hr 45min round trip) – only recommended if it is before noon, as you still have over four hours to go to reach Vamvakoú – a yellow signpost points the way to 'ΜΕΓ ΤΟΥΡΛΑ 1Η' (MEG TOURLA), and red splodges continue. It is usually snow-covered from December to April and often windy. The views are spectacular: east over the sea to the Argolid and the island of Spétses, south-west to the long ridge of Taïgetos, north-west to darkly forested Ménalo. Return the same way.

From Áï-Liás chapel, follow the wiggling track S across the plateau. Black-eared wheatears flit among the juniper shrubs, and rocky outcrops to your right offer views south-west. Where the track ends (**3hr 5min**), a path continues S down the gully, past a *stroónga* (stone shepherds' hut). You enter the forest – rockier underfoot, but mostly pleasant – descending steadily down the gully floor (RS). At **3hr 20min** the path climbs the R bank, then descends to the L briefly, before resuming in the gully. At **3hr 25min**, pick up a jeep track on the L bank. It climbs gently to a small saddle (**3hr 40min**), and bears L. Look out for cuckoos, chaffinches and leopard's bane on the climb. At the saddle, there's a possible picnic spot on a hilltop to the right.

The plateau below the summits of Párnonas

The mountain refuge at Arnómousga (Mt Párnonas)

At a R hairpin (**3hr 50min**) turn R off the track down a path in a nettly, occasionally wet gully (wooden sign). This soon becomes a natural corridor twisting between fir-covered slopes. At the dirt road (**4hr 15min**), turn L (uphill) for 30 metres, then continue R along a path (RS) which crosses a seasonal trickle and climbs on a soft bed of pine and fir needles. In 2016 there was a signed diversion 'ΠΑΡΑΚΑΜΨΗ' (PARAKAMWH) L around a fallen tree.

At the asphalt road (**4hr 30min**), turn L for 30 metres and R up a path (RS). Pass a weak but apparently year-round spring, then cross diagonally over a forest track, to reach another asphalt road (**4hr 42min**). Turn R (wooden sign to 'Refuge 10, Vamvakoú 1h55'), passing on your L a football pitch used by children's camps in summer.

At **Arnómousga refuge** (1415m; locked; **4hr 50min**), follow the dirt track to its L, heading W and passing to the R of a basketball pitch (RS). Descend a grassy, open spur. Where the track descends more steeply and bends R, turn L (RS) down a steep path under the pines. You join a dirt track at a hairpin and spur (**5hr 15min**). Cross and turn sharp L along a small grassy track (wooden sign). After 3–4min turn R down a steep path (wooden sign), which levels out for 5min, then descends over loose stones. Join a clearer path (two RS; **5hr 35min**) and descend steadily through kermes oak, wild plum and spiny broom bushes into a lovely valley with strips of green fields and walnut groves.

At the valley floor (1020m; **5hr 55min**), turn R along a jeep track. Where this turns L, continue straight (wooden sign) across a dry stream and up a shaly slope on a clear, steep path. This crosses the dirt road twice (RS) – if the path has eroded, just take the dirt road – to reach a four-way junction of dirt roads at the ridgetop (**6hr 30min**), near a seasonal shepherds' hut.

Cross straight over (W), down a path (wooden sign) in a slight dip, descending under chestnut trees. Cross the asphalt road, by two signs (one wooden, one metal) for a now-closed café. Ignore a small path forking L, and at the asphalt road, turn L into **Vamvakoú** village, passing a small chapel and square, and down to the 'Παραδωσιακος Ξενωνας' (Paradosiakós Xenónas) hostel – a tall stone building on your R, with a stone bust outside (**7hr**).

STAGE 10
Vamvakoú (930m) to Paleogoulás (450m)

Start point	Vamvakoú
Distance	18km (+ 7.5km for side trip to cliff hermitage)
Difficulty	1–2
Walking time	4hr 10min (+ 2hr for side trip)
Height gain	0m (150m for side trip)
Height loss	480m (+ 150m for side trip)
Waymarks	E4 from below Vrésthena to Paleogoulás

This stage is a gentle and fairly straightforward descent, initially on tracks and paths, then on dirt roads along the part-wooded valley from Vamvakoú all the way to the asphalt road by the site of Paleogoulás, near Sellasía. As it is a shortish day time-wise, start by visiting the wonderfully evocative *paliomonástiro* (cliffside hermitage) and chapel of Ayía Kiriakí, built as a hideaway from persecution in Ottoman times. It is an hour's gentle walk up the valley from Vamvakoú: two hours there and back if you return the same way.

From Paleogoulás, there are no paths to speak of and it can be hot as you descend below 500m. Call a taxi to take you the last 20–25km into Sparta/Mistrás (approx €25–30 in 2016): try pre-booking Sotíris Roïnós (mob 693-7134229), who speaks some English, asking to be collected at Paleogoulás on the road to Vrésthena, 3km from Sellasía. Alternatively, you can walk a further 3km to the Trípoli–Sparta road near Sellasía, and try hitching or hailing a bus. Some Athens–Sparta buses come this way (tel 27310-26441, www.ktel-lakonias.gr/en, limited English).

Sparta is a bustling modern town with not much to recommend it, other than the scant remains of the theatre (which is actually Roman) and the Museum of the Olive (which is out of town). We advise staying in the pretty village of Mistrás, 5km outside Sparta; this is where the onward hike resumes, and it is also the site of a stunning, half-ruined Byzantine hill town.

To visit the cliff hermitage

For Ayía Kiriakí cliff hermitage, follow the cobbled lane from Vamvakoú hostel down to the square with the big church and café (**7min**). Continue out of the village heading NE, then NW. After 1km (**20min**), another road joins from the R. Keep straight and after 250 metres, just before the bridge, fork R down a small track at a yellow-on-bronze sign 'ΑΓ ΚΥΡΙΑΚΗ' (AG KYRIAKI; **25min**). You could hide your pack here, as you will be returning to this point.

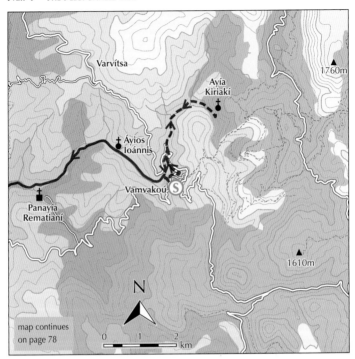

map continues
on page 78

Ayía Kiriakí cliff hermitage

The track follows the valley floor heading NNE and curving gradually clockwise to E. After 1.5km (**45min**), cross and keep R (same sign) along the track. Fir trees replace planes; you climb away from the stream and zigzag L to reach – via a short stretch of path built on a sloping rock face – the evocative hermitage or cave-chapel (**1hr**): a stack of crumbling stone facades, one of which contains a chapel, built against an orange-grey overhang.

Return the same way to the asphalt road by the bridge (**1hr 50min**). Follow the road L (the way you came) and, after 70 metres, just after a blue sign with a dozen village names, fork R onto a farm track. After 10min (**2hr**), you pass below Vamvakoú; you may see the wreck of a pick-up van and the direct track descending from Vamvakoú. Continue along the valley track.

For the direct route, without the Ayía Kiriakí detour, make your way to the bottom of Vamvakoú, cross the stream (usually dry) and at the farm track on the far side turn L along the valley (**10min**). The return route from the Ayía Kiriakí detour comes in here.

Follow the valley track curving clockwise; the stream may be flowing here. At the junction of tracks (**30min** from Vamvakoú), with the cypresses and chapels of Ayía Triádha and Áyios Yiórgos visible L, keep straight along the valley floor on a tiny farm track with fenced fields and walnut groves on your R. After 7min you pass the white **chapel of Áyios Ioánnis** on your R (**37min**), after which the track dwindles. From here you continue along the valley floor on a mix of farm tracks and meadows, staying as close to the streambed as you can.

If you find the stream is in full spate – only likely after very heavy rains – return to Ayía Triádha chapel and take the dirt road NW; it only crosses the stream once (at the 55min point below), before rejoining the route at the 1hr 45min point.

Our route was as follows: first on the L bank (**40min**), then, at **43min**, the R bank staying near the streambed, then the L again (**46min**), to pick up a jeep track near a row of tall poplars (**50min**). This joins a dirt road; keep R/straight. At **55min**, follow this across to the R bank and fork L down a small jeep track which crosses the stream (here often flowing). You may spot a red paint circle (RC) on a tree trunk. The overgrown track winds down terraced meadows to the stream and, now a path, crosses to the R bank, then L, then R again, by the stone ruins of a mill (**1hr 5min**). At the end of a meadow, nip up along an old conduit (low branches), then down and across a meadow (RC) and down to the streamside (**1hr 11min**). The next 15min may be tricky in early spring or after heavy rainfall. You pass a second ruined mill (**1hr 15min**), cross briefly to the L, then back R, then (after an ochre-coloured ruin), L again.

At **1hr 30min** you reach a tiny concrete weir feeding a concrete conduit on the R bank and, next to it, a clear path. Wild boar often congregate here. A few minutes later the valley opens up; cross to the L, then back to the R and, by a scant ruin, join a jeep

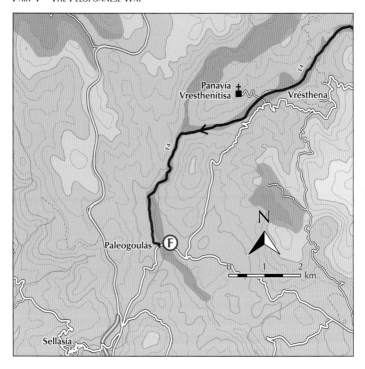

track. At **1hr 45min** you join a bigger track coming down from the R. Up a side valley to your L lie the ruins of **Panayía Rematianí monastery**.

Continue W on the track along the main valley. After 2km (**2hr 10min**), ignore a bigger track on your R (E4/Karyés) and then another to your L (E4/Vrésthena). Continue along the valley floor. After 700 metres, a first track joins from the L and, after another 700 metres, a second smaller one (**2hr 27min**). This is the E4, descending from Vrésthena; you may soon see a familiar white-yellow-black E4 waymark.

At a paved road below **Panayía Vresthenítisa monastery** (**2hr 35min**), turn R and after 100 metres fork L (no E4 sign) to stay in the valley. After 1.4km (**3hr**) you enter a plane forest. You cross the stream twice. Beware sheepdogs hereabouts – pick up a stout stick. After 1.7km (**3hr 20min**), where another valley joins from the R, turn L down a stony jeep track (E4 sign, easily missed). If you find yourself climbing the R flank, you have gone too far.

After 25min (**3hr 45min**) this jeep track passes through a lovely, densely plane-shaded section of valley floor, sometimes on one bank, sometimes the other, sometimes

Ancient Sparta with the modern town behind

in the streambed (usually dry from April–November). At the end of this, follow the main track slightly R, away from the watercourse, through olive groves (E4). A track joins from the R.

At **4hr 10min** you reach the asphalt Sellasía–Vrésthena road by a bridge (560m) near the little-known ancient site of **Paleogoulás**: you could meet the taxi here to take you to Sparta or Mistrás.

> The **E4 trail** does continue, almost opposite, along a dirt road (E4) down the valley, before climbing up to and along the paved road to Theológos – but it's not the prettiest stretch, and you'll still need a taxi from Theológos.
>
> If you want to walk further, walk to the right (from Paleogoulás) up the road for 3km to the junction with, first, the old Trípoli–Sparta road near Sellasía, and then, keeping right, the new highway (E961), where buses from Athens or Trípoli to Sparta should stop if you flag them.

STAGE 11

Mistrás (300m) to Anavrití (810m)

Start point	Mistrás
Distance	7.2km (excluding site)
Difficulty	1–2
Walking time	2hr 45min (+ 2–3hr for optional visit to site)
Height gain	610m (excluding site)
Height loss	100m (excluding site)
Waymarks	E4

This is another short day, which leaves you time to explore the ruined Byzantine hill town of Mistrás in the morning: a real highlight, even for non-history buffs. There is a Frankish castle at the peak, a restored Despot's Palace halfway down, a working convent, a dozen frescoed Byzantine chapels, various crumbling town houses and a small museum. If you've stayed in Sparta, take a taxi (or occasional local bus, www.ktel-lakonias.gr/en) to Mistrás. If you go as far as the top entrance (by the castle, or *kástro*) you can walk down through the site; allow a good two hours for this. An alternative is to walk from Mistrás village up through a mini-gorge to the top entrance, which adds nearly another hour.

The ascent to the mountain village of Anavrití (2hr 45min) is in three parts. The first threads up a spectacular gorge, past the cave-chapel of Langadhiótissa and along a narrow water conduit; if you are very prone to vertigo, you can follow the wider E4 track instead. The second follows a largely shadeless jeep track winding up the valley flank to Faneroménis monastery, with far-reaching views over the plain of Sparta. The last part follows small paths into the once populous village of Anavrití, perched on an 850m plateau in the eastern foothills of Mt Taïgetos.

Anavrití's one and only guesthouse (Arhontikó) is run by the lovely, multilingual María Kanelópoulos and her energetic, bouzouki-playing husband Yíorgos (tel 27310-82671 or 27310-22938, mob 698-7101555, 698-7128554 or 697-9118855, https://kaneltrekking.gr). With help from locally resident Swiss expat Rolf Roost, Yíorgos oversees the whole E4 Peloponnese route; he can help with route queries and reservations at the Taïgetos refuge, or possibly drive you there in his old jeep if it's still in one piece.

Visiting Mistrás site

You can either take a bus or taxi from Mistrás village to the upper (castle) gate or, if you set off early, walk up a mini-gorge to the upper gate.

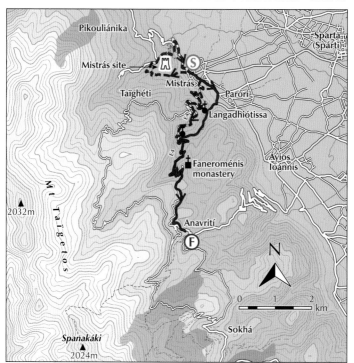

If you choose to walk: from the plane tree in the village centre, follow the road NW towards the site. At the fork in the road with the statue of Constantine Paleológos in the middle (**2min**), fork L and keep L up Steven Runciman Street (named after a prominent British Byzantinist). The lane bears R. In front of a large church (**5min**), turn L up towards the mountains and, at the end of the lane, continue up the cobbled path. At the cypress grove, follow the path R, climbing gently through a mini-gorge where kestrels and falcons wheel from grey cliffs. At the second wooden signpost (**18min**), turn R to reach and cross the stream. On the far side, pick up a jeep track zigzagging broadly NW steadily up among tall plane trees. At the top (**45min**) turn R, slightly downhill, along a dirt/concrete road to the car park by the upper gate into **Mistrás site** (**55min**).

From the upper gate, we suggest that you climb the castle, then wander down through the site past the Despot's Palace to leave through the lower (main) gate and down the road back to Mistrás village.

Mistrás village with the hilltop castle just visible behind

From the central junction in the village of Mistrás, by a large plane tree and the Mystras Inn, head SE along the asphalt lane towards Paróri and Áyios Ioánnis. Almost immediately, the E4 route turns R up a narrow lane. Those with a fear of heights should follow the E4, snaking SW up the hillside for about 3.5km, then forking L (flat, then downhill) to the chapel of Metamórfosi tou Sotíra (see 1hr point below).

If you choose not to follow the E4, continue SE along the lane to the village of **Paróri** (1km), which has a couple of outdoor tavernas by a series of gushing springs. Continue past these, across the bridge, and immediately turn R up a gravel track (orange triangle; **15min**) up the gorge, where orange-grey crags tower above you on both sides. After 5min, the track ends. Continue along a path next to a water pipe, climbing steadily. After 4min, turn sharp R to visit the serene chapel of **Langadhiótissa**,

Langadhiótissa gorge: the vertiginous section

tucked at the back of a cave. Below you are the narrows of Apothetai, where legend has it the ancient Spartans abandoned their malformed babies.

Return the same way and (**25min**) continue up the clear path. After 10min, join and follow the water channel, walking on its concrete cover. There are two potentially vertiginous passages: the first cut into the cliffside (wire railings help), the second without railings but less sheer. You then enter shady woods, cross a dry stream and climb up to the plane-shaded chapel of Metamórfosi tou Sotíra (taps, concrete benches; **1hr**).

Here, you join the E4 jeep track and follow it L (SE) across the dry streambed and uphill, gently at first, then with steeper zigzags. The 2000m ridge of Goúpata–Neraidhovoúna dominates the skyline ahead (west-south-west); you may spot the three isolated houses of Pergandhéïka in the valley.At the top (**2hr**), **Faneroménis monastery** is on your L (closed 1–4pm).

> **Faneroménis monastery** is a huge building with a triple-arched entrance but only one monk. It was apparently founded in the 1840s by Archimandrite Athanásios Ladópoulos who, guided by visions of the Virgin Mary (*faneroméni* means 'made visible'), found a miraculous icon in a cave and was instructed to build a chapel on this very spot. If the monk – a young, English-speaking man named Ierótheos – is in, he will open the chapel for you to admire this and many other icons.

To continue the route, follow the asphalt road away from the monastery (E4) past the white chapel of Áyios Stratigós, ignoring the green-triangled path forking R towards Pergandhéïka. About 300 metres after this, fork L down a narrow path (E4).

Curious goats on the path below Metamórfosi tou Sotíra chapel

Descend briefly, bear R and climb past the chapel of Ayía Paraskeví to a second chapel, Áyios Yiórgos, under a plane tree (**2hr 30min**). The village of **Anavrití** is visible ahead.

Descend the cobbled path to cross old terraces and a stone bridge hidden by foliage. At the first houses, continue straight (E4), briefly join a concrete lane, then climb to the main asphalt road (**2hr 40min**). Turn L and then, for the 'Arhontikó Guesthoyse', fork R up past the church (**2hr 45min**).

STAGE 12

*Anavrití (810m) to
Taïgetos mountain refuge (1550m)*

Start point	Anavrití
Distance	12km
Difficulty	3
Walking time	5hr
Height gain	1050m
Height loss	310m
Waymarks	Red triangles, then E4

This is a glorious day's walk along the eastern flanks of the Pendadháktilo (five-fingered) ridge of Taïgetos. You climb, mostly in pine and fir forest, to the springs of Lakómata, then contour around the 1500m mark to the mountain refuge run by EOS Spártis (Alpine Club of Sparta). There are dazzling views up to gleaming limestone slopes and down over the verdant plain of Sparta to the distant sea.

You will need to pre-book the refuge (Vasílis Yeoryiádhis/EOS Spártis, tel 27310-22574 evenings, tel 27310-26343 or mob 697-4454079 daytime; alternatively, contact Yiórgos Kanelópoulos: see Stage 11). Ideally you want to time your visit to coincide with another group, to split the hefty fixed cost of the stay. The refuge itself is a simple dormitory (26 bunks, mattresses with blankets but no sheets) with a dining table and woodburner, plus a small kitchen (gas cooker, water tank), but no washing facilities.

From the lower village square and café, follow a small lane W (E4 on wall of raised playground), climbing to a four-spouted spring bearing the date 1987. Here, where the lane descends, fork R up a small track (E4 sign). After **3min** follow the track sharp R at a wooden signpost with red triangle (RT) and E4; 1min later turn sharp L up a path (RT,

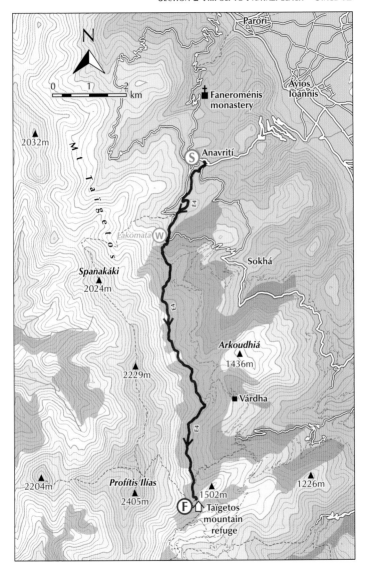

E4). You thread between purple cistus bushes, then cross a metal bridge over a gully. Join a stepped path and pass just beneath a chapel, following RT and E4 marks and ascending steadily.

After **20min**, you emerge on a new jeep track and continue straight/L. After 100 metres, fork L down a path (E4, RT) past the stone-walled spring of Platanítsa (the little plane tree). This must have been named some time ago, for the tree is now huge. Descend to a leafy valley, passing one washed-out section, and cross on a wooden bridge. Climb steeply under pines to a small track (**40min**): turn R and immediately L along the continuation of the path, which bounces off the track. After 2–3min, keep L (E4, 'Lakómata 1hr 15min, Refuge 4hr'). The red-triangled route leads R, to the Spanakáki summit. The path passes atop a concrete-covered water station, contouring towards the main summits. At **55min**, climb steps to the dirt road and turn L (S) along it, by plane trees and a water relay station. At **1hr**, just after a L bend and a dry gully, turn sharp R up a path (E4).

This climbs steadily through pines and firs for 45min to hit a jeep track. Turn L ('Lakómata 10min, Refuge 2hr 55min', E4). At a Y junction, keep R (E4) to reach the spring, stone benches and closed huts of **Lakómata (2hr)**. This is the last reliable, year-round water source until the refuge.

From the spring, follow the path S (E4) threading up through fir-shaded terraces to cross a rocky gully (possible washout; **2hr 20min**). Cut up to a grassy spur among stunted firs (**2hr 30min**) – a good rest spot, as from here it is relatively level. Lovely open stretches lead you broadly ESE, with the stony flanks of the Pendadháktilo ridge soaring up to your R. Pass the weak spring of Kanellákia and, at a big eroded gully, turn sharp L (E4) and down a couple of terraces before resuming S.

The path above Anavrití

Crossing the eastern flanks of Mt Taïgetos

At **3hr**, you pass a lovely picnic spot – the site of an old threshing floor – and shortly after, a sign for Ayía Paraskeví spring (30 metres L). The path crosses the spur of Arkoudhiá and descends gently past Tsagáki spring to the jeep track above the scant houses of **Várdha** (**3hr 40min**). Don't follow the track down, but keep R along the E4 path.

You bear R (SW) across open ground, speckled in spring with harebells, yellow asphodels, pink soapwort and orchids; then cross two eroded gullies and climb to a majestic stand of black pines, whereupon the path improves. Shortly after (**4hr 40min**), the red-squared path from 'Manganiári Spring 1hr' joins from your L; keep straight on towards 'Refuge 15min' (E4). You pass the weak spring of Varvára (**4hr 50min**) and at the top, turn R up a jeep track (E4, red squares) to the **Taïgetos mountain refuge** (1550m; sign 'EOS SPARTIS'; **5hr**). There are signposts up to 'Prof Ilias peak 2hr 45min' and back to 'Anavrití 4hr 30min'.

The ascent of the spectacular 2405m peak, known as **Profítis Ilías** or Áï-Liás, is amply worth it if you have an extra day to play with, and can manage a second night in the refuge. Views from the top – the highest point in the Peloponnese – are breathtaking.

It takes around 5hr hiking time (3hr up, 2hr down), following a small path which twists up steep limestone flanks waymarked with red paint and occasional signposts. There is no reliable spring and no shade, so take lots of water and sun protection, as well as water-/windproof jacket, food, first-aid kit, etc. Cloud can roll in fast, and snowpack remains till mid or late May;

from December to April the upper reaches may require crampons and ice axe.

Every year on 19–20 July, Greek hikers gather at the summit for an overnight celebration, complete with a candle-lit liturgy outside the semi-ruined summit chapel.

STAGE 13
Taïgetos mountain refuge (1550m) to
Árna (780m)

Start point	Taïgetos mountain refuge
Distance	16km
Difficulty	3
Walking time	6hr
Height gain	570m
Height loss	1340m
Waymarks	E4 almost the entire way (+ green squares, red diamonds)

A lovely but tough day's walking in fir forest with majestic stands of black pines, passing the summer forest settlement of Áyios Dhimítrios, before a rough and rocky descent off the high mountain. You return to cultivated land and open views – with glimpses of the Laconian Sea behind Yíthio – before reaching the somewhat ghostly villages of Spartiá and Árna. Here, on the village square, you'll find a couple of tavernas in the shade of a huge plane tree, and a simple pension nearby (Volianíti, tel 27330-24666, mob 697-7923539, mob 697-2772845, info@volianiti.com).

From the refuge, follow green squares (GS), E4 marks and red '32' diamonds (RD) SE downhill, slippery with pine branches and stones, to rejoin the track; keep R. After 100 metres by a L bend, turn R down a path (GS, E4) descending through mixed pine and fir forest to a spring (1400m). The descent steepens to cross a dry gully. Leaving the forest, you look SE to the gulf of Moláï and, below you, the three huts of Pendavlí which, unfortunately, you need to descend to.

At the lips of a small cliff (**30min**), with a sign (R) prohibiting 'the simultaneous crossing of more than 10 persons', you descend a metal ladder (one by one!) and cross a boulder-filled gully. Above you, water gushes from five holes in the cliff face. Find the continuation of the path, a few steps higher, next to a big black hose (E4, RD). It winds down through old walnut terraces; keep your eyes peeled, as it heads further L than

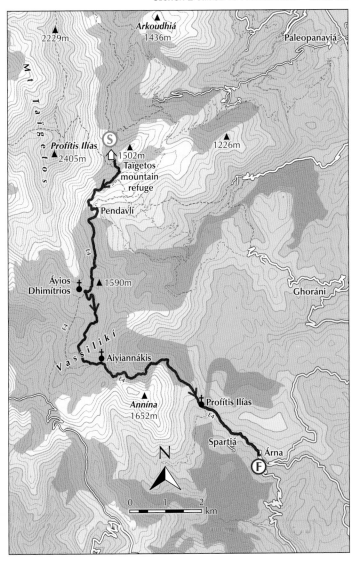

The crude shelter at Pendavlí

expected. At **50min** you reach the huts of **Pendavlí** (1200m).

Pendavlí makes a decent campsite, with a water tap and, on your right, a crude roofed shelter, jokingly called the ΔHMAPXEIO (DHMARXEIO, or town hall) where you could sleep if necessary, but, having no door or windows, it will be chilly. We surprised some (friendly) wild pigs here.

Turn R (E4, 'Agios Dimitrios 1hr 15min', etc) and, after 30 metres, R again, up two terraces and slightly L. Enter the fir forest by a small pond (E4, RD) and climb quite steeply for 5–10min. Around 1300m, you cross a dry gully and the gradient eases. At **1hr 25min** the path bends R in front of a big fallen tree and steepens again. At **2hr**, after a rather relentless final push, you reach the saddle of Sóros (1560m, the day's high point) by some century-old black pines. Look back north for views, clouds permitting, of the pyramidal peak of Profítis Ilías (2405m).

Follow the stony path straight over (S), descending steeply into the forested bowl of Vassilikí, with the flat-topped summit of Mavrovoúni (1909m) ahead. Keep your eyes peeled for cairns and waymarks. Pass above a new stone chalet (**2hr 13min**) and descend to the **chapel of Áyios Dhimítrios** (**2hr 15min**), with a spring flowing from beneath it. In an emergency, you could sleep here; it is normally unlocked.

At the chapel, ignore the E4/RD signs pointing R (SW) and instead follow the dirt track L (SE), descending gently. Ignore a R fork (**2hr 27min**). At **2hr 50min** the track bends L (E) and 5min later (**2hr 55min**), at a R bend, you turn L (E) up an easily missed path in a shallow gully, heading away from Mavrovoúni. Yellow-and-black waymarks show that you have rejoined the E4, heading now towards the villages of Spartiá and Árna.

If you're self-sufficient, you could skip these villages and take a **shortcut to Panayía Yiátrissa monastery** (Stage 14). For the shortcut, remain on the dirt track, ignoring three turn-offs to the right and climbing past Vassilikí forest station (possible camping) to a 1400m crest and road junction; here, descend left to rejoin the route at the clearly visible monastery of Panayía Yiátrissa. It is not the most exciting route, but it is much quicker and there are long, serrated views south to distract you.

The wayside chapel of Aiyiannákis

For Árna, continue up the shallow gully (rough underfoot but plenty of E4 signage). After 15min (**3hr 10min**), you reach the 1350m watershed by the crude stone **chapel of Aiyiannákis**. Ahead is the rugged peak of Annína (1652m), whose sheer northern flanks you will shortly traverse. The path bears R, initially contouring across two small spurs, then descending, at times knee-jarringly, downhill. Be prepared for fallen trees, and take care across a slope of semi-loose boulders (**4hr**). Eventually the path levels out, crosses a small gully and follows a natural limestone shelf to reach some slabs which cry out to be rested on (**4hr 30min**).

Bearing R (SE), the path crosses the E flank of Annína before leaving the forest to cross scrubby hillsides, with the red roof of **Profítis Ilías chapel** ahead. At the saddle next to this chapel (**5hr 10min**), bear L alongside a fence (E4), through a gate and along a track. At a five-way junction (**5hr 20min**), keep R/straight down a concrete road. Looking right (south), you may see Panayía Yiátrissa monastery, tomorrow's highpoint, on a ridge between two wooded hills.

Pass above the main part of **Spartiá** village (**5hr 30min**) and, by the plane tree and bus shelter, keep straight along the road. Entering **Árna** (**5hr 50min**), at a L bend, go down to the R of the church, then curl back L and into the main square (**6hr**). Taverna Anna is on your L; Pension Volianíti is 100 metres beyond.

STAGE 14

Árna (780m) to Pantazí beach (0m) via
Panayía Yiátrissa monastery (1035m)

Start point	Árna
Distance	19km
Difficulty	3
Walking time	6hr 40min
Height gain	770m
Height loss	1550m
Waymarks	E4 to monastery

The route for the final day takes you back over the Taïgetos watershed, crossing at the forbidding-looking monastery of Panayía Yiátrissa and westwards down into Messinía, along the ancient (sometimes overgrown) footpaths which linked this region's pretty stone hamlets. It's a long day, with a lot of downhill on stony paths, but you pass through some lovely deep valleys cloaked with maquis, wildflowers and ancient stone hamlets typical of the Outer Mani region. You end at the small beach of Pantazí, where you can reward yourself with a well-earned swim, before continuing either on foot or by bus or taxi (www.taxistoupa.com) to one of the lovely, lazy villages which dot this west-facing stretch of coast.

The nearest are Áyios Nikólaos (known locally as Selinítsa) and Áyios Dhimítrios, both of which have a few small hotels and tourist-friendly tavernas; the former also boasts a picturesque fishing harbour. You can reach either of these on foot. But my personal favourite is Kardhamíli, 13km to the north, partly because of its tasteful, arty vibe, and partly because it is the hub – should you still have the legs and the lust – for several short day hikes into the stunning gorges, villages and historic chapels of the western foothills of Taïgetos. The Sunflower guide *Landscapes of the Southern Peloponnese* has details; or you may be able to manage with the Anávasi *Exo Mani* map. Whichever you choose, make sure to book your accommodation well ahead, as the area is deservedly popular with the Hellenic cognoscenti.

Of course, if you prefer to follow the E4 trail down the eastern valleys of Taïgetos to Yíthio, this is quite possible and does allow you to link up (via the Yíthio–Kíssamos ferry) with the onward E4 trail across Crete. But bear in mind that it takes two days, with a fair amount of (increasingly warm) road-walking. The second day may be re-routed to reduce road-walking; check the E4 website (www.e4-peloponnes.info) for latest. Yíthio is a bustling little harbour town with handsome neoclassical houses and no shortage of hotels and restaurants.

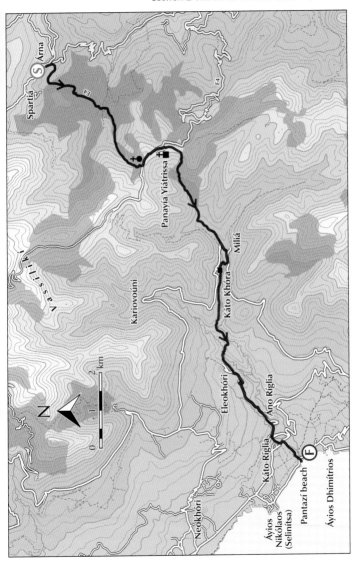

Árna

From the tavernas on Árna's central square, with the huge plane tree ahead, go a few steps L (E) and then fork R down an asphalt road (faded E4 on pole, also 'PHGH AGIAS MARINAS'). After about 200 metres, turn R down a small concrete lane (E4) and, after 100 metres, R again down a stepped path to rejoin the road and turn R. Where the road bends L (**7min**), continue straight/R along a concrete lane which becomes a farm track descending steadily among olive groves. Where this levels out (**15min**), with a white hut ahead/L, turn R (easily missed) onto a small path (E4) which crosses the gully and traverses the R flank, climbing steadily to cross a spur. At the second spur (**36min**), with Panayía Yiátrissa monastery visible ahead like a fortified observatory, descend carefully (loose stones). You briefly enter a shallow, oak-shaded dip before bearing R and then descending in earnest right down to the valley floor. Here (490m; **50min**), cross the dry streambed with a big plane tree on your L and bear L to a mossy-bouldered side gully.

For the next 1hr 30min, the path climbs SW up this cool, shady side valley, sometimes in the streambed, sometimes up one or other bank, with occasional stone-built sections, all the way to the 1010m watershed. A couple of pointers: after 20min (**1hr 10min**) it climbs the L bank for 15min before traversing R to the streambed. At **2hr** it bears L (S) into the firs and steepens.

At the top (**2hr 20min**), with the stone **chapel** of Áyii Apóstoli on your L (wooden signpost), turn L along the dirt road. On your right, down in the valley, the village of Miliá comes into view and behind it the Messinian gulf and Methóni peninsula. After passing an optimistic car park (apparently it does fill once a year, on 8 September, for the Virgin Mary's Nativity feast), you reach the **monastery of Panayía Yiátrissa** (**2hr 30min**).

Panayía Yiátrissa monastery is open from 7am–1pm and from 4pm till sunset. It is home to two monks and two cats. If the former are in, they can open up the church, painted with hundreds of saints and boasting a miraculous, silver-leafed icon of Mary 'the Healer' (Yiátrissa). This was reputedly left by a pious

Panayía Yiátrissa monastery

man named Ilías Panagoulákos in 1863, after he contracted tuberculosis and, spurning his doctors' advice to seek treatment in a Swiss sanatorium, came instead to this spot. For many months he prayed daily and filled his lungs with fresh Taïgetos air, before making a full recovery.

The path continues behind (S of) the monastery. We found it easiest to go round the L side, through a small gate/gap in the fence, and along an ankle-prickling path just L (E) of the ridgeline. About 5min from the monastery, at a slight dip, bear R along a stony path (cairns, faded blue waymark), descending gently SW into sparse firs. After some messy sections, you pass the spring of Libovísia (**3hr**) in the shade of a fig tree. A further 50 metres below this, the path contours L and over a fallen tree, descending quite steeply. Keep your eyes peeled for blue or red paint dots, and occasional cairns. After a couple of bends and a stone-edged section, you zigzag down towards the gully and then alongside it. At **3hr 25min**, cross to the R bank for 8min before zigzagging back down.

The path now stays near (or occasionally in) the dry gully: L, R, L and finally R, to pass above a smelly goat shelter with a corrugated plastic roof (**3hr 50min**). Go through the gate (red sign to 'ΠΑΝΑΓΙΑ ΓΙΑΤΡΙΣΣΑ', PANAGIA GIATRISSA, on the fence) and follow the track for 100 metres. At a R bend, turn L (two red arrows painted on the rock) down a path which soon runs right next to the gully. A walled path joins from your R; you pass a small chapel and cross a stone bridge onto the L bank. Another path joins from your L; olive groves appear on your R. At **4hr 6min**, you join a concrete track by a red sign to 'Monastir' and continue straight/R. At the asphalt road (green sign to 'Monastery of Virgin Mary the Healer'), continue L/straight up to the main part of **Miliá** village (**4hr 10min**).

Follow the paved road WSW through the square (lovely Maniot stone church and seasonal café) and out of the village. After 300 metres (**4hr 14min**), between a cypress tree and a 'road narrows' sign, turn R down a stepped path past an old school. Now overgrown, the path winds down to the valley floor, across a stone bridge and along the R bank. Join a concrete track and continue gently up to the satellite hamlet of **Káto Khóra** (**4hr 23min**). Some 30 metres after the square with three plane trees, turn L (green sign to 'Elaiochorio') along a walled path. Ignore the L turn down to 'Gorge Tepeni'. Pass a chapel inscribed '1975' (**4hr 28min**); ignore a R fork.

The path now climbs gently for a good 20min through prickly kermes oak bushes half decimated by caterpillars in 2015–16, until you see, ahead of you, a rocky spur dividing two gorges with a tiny inaccessible chapel atop the right-hand hump. The path then descends past a stone ruin and gains a wall on its L side. Here (**5hr 10min**), follow the path round to the R, descending the far (N) side of that rocky spur. At the dry streambed (big step; **5hr 23min**), go 10 metres up (R) and pick up a small path on the far side. You emerge on a farm track and turn R (uphill), climbing through olive groves. About 7min along this track, at a R bend (**5hr 30min**), shortcut L onto an overgrown path climbing W, with plunging views over the gorge on your L.

At the concrete lane just below the village of **Eleokhóri** (green sign pointing back to Miliá; **5hr 45min**), turn L down the lane, winding between olive groves. At the first houses of **Áno Ríglia** (meaning 'Upper' Ríglia; **6hr 15min**), by a L bend, fork R down a narrow lane between flower-covered walls and pretty cottages, to rejoin the lane at the bottom of the village. At the first L bend, by the first houses of **Káto Ríglia** ('Lower' Ríglia), again turn R ('Anaxo Resort'), cross the gully and follow the lane L (SW) through the village. At the small village square, fork L past the café to reach the main Kalamáta–Areópolis road (**6hr 30min**). Here, you could hail a bus (four daily) or call a taxi to take you to Áyios Nikólaos, Stoúpa, Kardhamíli or wherever you've decided to rest and recuperate.

If, like me, you want to complete the walk from ocean to ocean and reward yourself with a plunge, turn L and after 100 metres R (blue sign to 'ΑΓΙΟΣ ΔΗΜΗΤΡΙΟΣ / ΤΡΑΧΗΛΑ', AGIOS DIMITRIOS / TRAHILA) down a paved lane. After 800 metres you reach the beach of **Pantazí** (**6hr 40min**), with a seasonal café and clear blue waters. After the hot, pounding descent, it feels magical to swim and take the weight

Pantazí beach

off your feet – and it no longer matters if the Compeeds come unstuck! From here it is about 1.2km/15min walk along the coast road either to Áyios Nikólaos (R) or Áyios Dhimítrios (L).

PART 2
THE PÍNDOS WAY

The path from Anifóra to Epinianá (Stage 11)

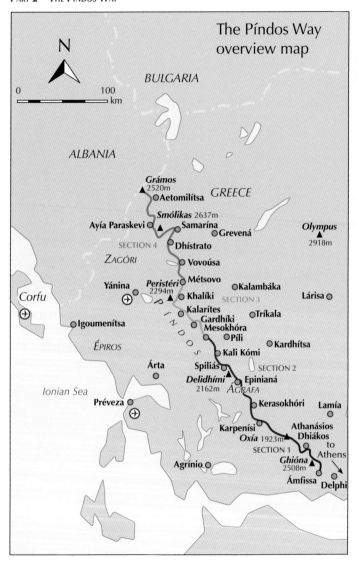

View of Ágrafa village from Epiniana

At roughly 30 days hiking, the Píndos range accounts for a good two thirds of our traverse of Greece's mountain backbone. It is also the tougher part: because it is more continuously mountainous and more remote, navigation is more difficult and it is less well supplied with places to stop and stay. You will of necessity have to carry camping gear. At the same time, the wildness and remoteness add greatly to the drama and the charm of the hike and to the sense of achievement. It is wilderness but an intimate, unintimidating kind of wilderness, shaped and used by centuries of pastoralism. We have divided it into four sections, each requiring about a week to complete. For additional photos, snippets of information, anecdotes and news, check out our website, www. thepindosway.com.

It begins in the small provincial town of Ámfissa just west of Delphi, seat of the famous Oracle, and close to the shore of the Gulf of Corinth, which divides the Balkan 'mainland' part of Greece from the Peloponnese. Of the four sections of the Way, this is by far the most accessible. If you only have time to tackle one section, this would be the one to choose. Karpenísi and Métsovo, the starting points for Sections 2 and 4, also have frequent bus services; it is just that the further north you go, the longer it takes to get there. Mesokhóra, the start of Section 3, is the only starting point without a regular bus service.

SECTION 1 ÁMFISSA TO KARPENÍSI

Descending the northern flank of Sarádena (Stage 7)

This section of the route does not present any technical difficulties and navigation is relatively straightforward. As always in the Greek mountains, the going is arduous: plenty of up and down and no creature comforts. The route begins with the ascent of Mt Ghióna via the beautiful Reká ravine, followed by the crossing of the Vardhoúsia massif which leads into a two- to three-day ridge walk, on grassy rounded tops between 1400m and 1900m.

Athanásios Dhiákos/Áno Mousounítsa is the only village where you can count on a bed and a decent meal, although you can certainly get something to eat in Sikiá as well. You pass three refuge huts – all locked, as is unfortunately usual in Greece; the

locations, however, make good campsites, with water. You will need to camp most of the time and carry water, the springs being less reliable than they used to be. The reward, however, is wonderful wild unspoilt country.

LOCATION

Ámfissa is approximately 200km north and west of Athens, about midway along the north shore of the Gulf of Corinth and a dozen kilometres from the sea, at the point where the Píndos mountains, themselves the southward extension of the Julian and Dinaric Alps, descend into the sea. It is roughly 2hr 30min by road from Athens airport.

MAPS

- Anávasi Topo 50 (1:50,000) Central Greece 2.3 *Giona, Iti, Vardhousia*
- Anávasi Topo 50 (1:50,000) 2.4/2.5 *Mountains of Evritania*

BASES

Ámfissa has banks, shops, restaurants and the Hotel Amfissaeum (tel 2265-022161, www.amfissahotel.gr). If you have left anything behind, you will not find sophisticated outdoor gear here, but you will find food, batteries, phonecards and other everyday things. Stock up, for there is nothing else before Karpenísi.

Athanásios Dhiákos/Áno Mousounítsa has the Ravánis *magazeé* and rooms (tel 2265-063214). In **Karpenísi** you will find banks, shops (including outdoor gear), restaurants and hotels, including the Hotel Ánesis, Zinopoúlou 50 (main street leading to town centre; tel 22370-22840, info@anesis.gr, www.anesis.gr).

REFUGES

All are locked, but the sites are good for camping, with water nearby:

- Ghióna: Láka Karvoúni
- Vardhoúsia: two in Pittimáliko meadows, south of Stavrós col
- Sarádena: on the col above Graméni Oxiá village

ACCESS

There are several buses every day between Athens and Ámfissa and between Athens and Karpenísi. Both services operate via Athens Odhós Liosíon terminus.

Karpenísi (Stage 8)

STAGE 1

Ámfissa (175m) to
Víniani (500m) and Reká ravine

Start point	Ámfissa
Distance	15km
Difficulty	1
Walking time	4hr 30min
Height gain	650m
Height loss	200m
Waymarks	None

For a quick start you could take a taxi from the square in Ámfissa to Víniani: about 15km by the taxi route. Our preferred start is to take the old road via the village of Prosílio. It is slightly shorter, has pretty views and the first half at least is do-able by path.

To walk the whole way, leave Ámfissa by the street leading N from the main square, passing R of the church that appears to block the way and continuing uphill towards the E end of the pine-clad castle bluff. You come to a second church – Áyios Thanásios. Bear R again and L. In 5min, through narrow back streets, (**20min**) you have reached the last houses. On the R, a scruffy concrete bridge crosses a stream with the ominous name of Cat-drowner (E00358073 / N04266240; 219m). Cross over and head diagonally L, leaving a fenced enclosure on your L. Pass through a bit of scrub and come to a rough track by an electricity pole.

Turn L on the track and follow it along the edge of an olive grove at the foot of a steep scrubby slope rising on your R. Pass another fenced enclosure with barking dogs and in 10min (**30min**) you come out on a narrow tarmac road with a wrecked concrete hut on the other side (E00357484 / N04266969; 273m). In front of you, blocking a dry gully, is a sort of gritty scree of rubble from the construction of the road. Go up the R side on a sort of path to join the road again at the top (E00357516 / N04267223; 340m; **40min**). Turn R on the road for 30 metres, then sharply back L on to a sort of ramp/ledge that climbs up the R side of the gully. Where the vegetation thickens, bear L across the gully and back L a bit further to climb up the bank on the road (E00357357 / N04267379; 369m; **1hr**).

Turn R on the road. Continue round a bend and past some tin goat pens below the road. On the L of the sharp R bend immediately after, there is a big fibre-glass cylindrical water tank (E00357161 / N04267690; 426m; **1hr 5min**). Turn L off the road here

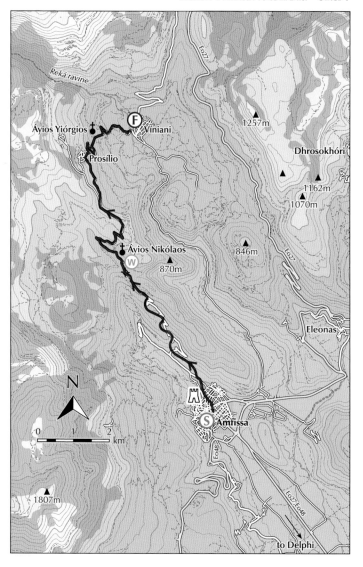

Áyios Nikólaos spring

and follow up the bottom of the shallow gully (in fact the continuation of the gully you have been following most of the way) heading NW. There is no single path, but sticking close to the gully bottom it is easy to make your way up through the crumbling terrace walls. There are scattered prickly oaks and low thorn bushes on the ground but they are not a problem. There is a clump of conspicuous cypress trees ahead to the R and another on a low shoulder to the L of your gully. As you draw nearer, begin to aim diagonally L up the L side of the gully towards this latter clump. There are clear remains of old path. When you reach the cypresses (about 30min from the water tank), there is a clear stony path leading straight uphill through the scrub to rejoin the road just short of a tin shrine (E00356522 / N04268540; 615m; **1hr 45min**).

Head up the road for 15min, crossing the ridge between conspicuous tooth-like rock towers. 20min later, after crossing a bridge over the next stream gully to the E, you come to a beautiful roadside spring under a plane tree (**2hr 20min**), with the tiny chapel of **Áyios Nikólaos** just out of sight among the rocks behind it. You could camp on the terrace. If the spring is dry, the powerful all-year Kría Vrísi is 200m up the road on the L.

From here it is about 2km uphill on the tarmac to the high point at 900m, followed by a descent of 3km to **Prosílio** (**3hr 30min**). The centre of the village is beautifully shady, but deserted for all but three months in the summer. Fill up with water at the fountain, especially if you are planning to camp in the Reká ravine; the next sure source of water is at Mílos 4hr away.

Turn down sharp R from the square, on the tarmac again. Descend through tight hairpins for about 25min to the little modern chapel of **Áyios Yióryios**, built on a small mound on the L of the road. There is a spring with a tap at the back; so there should be water. You could camp here.

Behind the chapel you can see the mouth of the **Reká ravine**. Descend into the gully below it and follow it down to the mouth of the ravine (**4hr 30min**); a number of goat paths lead down through the open scrub. You could carry on down to Víniani village, but there is little point. There are no shops, not even a café.

REKÁ RAVINE

Reká ravine above Mílos

In Greek the name of the ravine is *to farángee tis rekás*. The word *reká* comes from the Slavonic word for river, as do so many of the village names and other toponyms all through the Píndos range, the legacy of early medieval invasions by Slav-speaking peoples from further up the Balkans. Not many of these names survive on contemporary maps because the 1930s dictator, General Metaxas, carried out a widespread campaign of purifying Greece from all traces of foreign cultural 'contamination'.

Older generations of locals continued to use the old familiar names until quite recently, and in some cases they still do. For example, in a couple of days you will reach the village of Áno Mousounítsa, whose official name is now Athanásios Dhiákos.

STAGE 2

Mt Ghióna: Víniani (500m) to
Láka Karvoúni refuge (1750m)

Start point	Víniani
Distance	11km
Difficulty	3
Walking time	5hr 15min
Height gain	1250m
Height loss	0m
Waymarks	Red paint, E4

If you have arrived in Víniani by car, head NW from the village along the track that follows the dry riverbed. Where the riverside meadow ends, the **Reká ravine** begins (20min from the village); you cannot mistake it.

Occasional red paint marks show the way, although there is no real need as the ravine guides you for the next four hours. Soon you are enclosed within a narrow trench some 300–400m deep. Trees and shrubs lean out precariously from the nearly sheer walls. It is hard going, with the loose gravel shifting under your feet. The ravine twists and turns, climbing all the time. You realise how quickly you have been gaining height by the presence of firs right down at the edge of the riverbed.

About 2hr in and just past a series of bends, the ravine opens out a little with a terrace of flat firm ground on the R with fir trees growing along it. Some 20min later (**2hr 20min**) you come to a wide bowl-shaped opening in the ravine with a narrow wooded defile ahead known as Pórtes (Gates) and a steep tributary gully running down off the heights R (campsite).

> The locality is called **Mílos**, after a long-vanished water-powered sawmill. There is a wooden picnic kiosk (of the type beloved of the Greek Forestry Board), to which the once deliciously cold spring has been conducted in an exposed pipe, thus ensuring the water is hot on sunny days. But do not spurn it as the next sure source is by the refuge, 2hr 30min away.

Follow the path into the defile ahead, crossing to the L side of the gully and zigzagging steeply up an open stony slope. At the top it levels out and you find yourself once more trudging along the gravelly riverbed under the firs. About 50min later (**3hr 35min**) there is a great red cliff L, dripping with water and verdant with hanging plants. Clamber up the scree to its base and you will find plenty of water, at least until early summer.

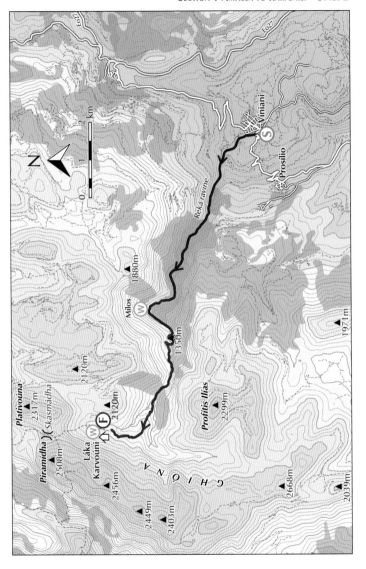

Start of the path from Reká ravine to Láka Karvoúni refuge

At **3hr 55min** you emerge from the trees into a wide open space where the riverbed describes a substantial curve to the L. Do not continue up the main river. On the R of the bend is a hard flat terrace where the path for the refuge bears off R, clearly marked by E4 signs, up a steep spur into the firs. It has been refashioned by machine, which makes for a rather unnatural gradient. A 30min climb brings you out above the treeline in a patch of meadow where there is another picnic kiosk (**4hr 25min**).

From here, a clear path bears R and N pretty much on the contour all along the base of the summit ridge and close to the treeline. The pink-roofed building that is in view all the way is the **Láka Karvoúni refuge (5hr 15min)**. There is water from a spring 15min along the path due N. The refuge will be locked but there is flat grassy ground to camp on.

STAGE 3
Láka Karvoúni refuge (1750m) to
Sikiá (720m)

Start point	Láka Karvoúni refuge
Distance	9km (11km including Piramídha summit)
Difficulty	3
Walking time	4hr 40min (6hr 10min including summit)
Height gain	450m (857m including summit)
Height loss	1500m (1857m including summit)
Waymarks	Red paint, E4; fairly frequent to summit

Above the refuge, the summit ridge rises to its highest point in the Piramídha peak (2508m), before dropping north into the col of Skasmádha (*to dheeyáselo tees skasmádhas*), then curving east to terminate in the lower peak of Plativoúna. These two peaks and the col together enfold the corrie or *láka* which lies directly behind the refuge.

To proceed to Skasmádha col from the refuge, follow the path N (E4 signs). It bends up R towards the end of a visible track, where there is a sheepfold and another picnic kiosk. Turn L to the kiosk, pass it and work R up a grassy rounded spur towards the R end of the crags above (**30min**), passing big whitish boulders. Angle up L following the base of the crags across the scree. The path to **Skasmádha col** is fairly clear.

Optional ascent of Piramídha
From the Skasmádha col, bear quite sharply L or W, then SW, climbing steadily up a rocky slope to hit the ridgeline just S of the summit (2508m; **1hr** from the col). The view is superb, with Mt Íti to the north, the distinctive conical shape of Mt Veloúkhi far off to the north-west and the heights of Ágrafa beyond, the merest fudge of blue at this distance. To the west, you look sheer down into the valley of the Mórnos river with the long craggy ridge of the Vardhoúsia massif opposite.
    Return to the Skasmádha col the same way (**1hr 30min**).

Cross the col (2150m; **1hr 15min**) and keep N down the R flank of the gully opening in front of you (waymarks), with the Piramídha peak and the deep grassy hollow of **Vathiá Láka** at its foot to your L. At the bottom of the slope below Vathiá Láka, you come to the copious **Khalíki spring** (E00348554 / N04279876; **1hr 45min**). With your back to the spring, bear L up the slope opposite on to the top of the spur. You will see

Piramídha summit and Vathiá Láka

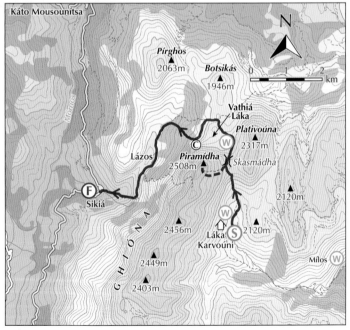

the collapsing walls of the old Nisí sheepfold in front of you (E00348270 / N04279801; **2hr**).

> The **Nisí sheepfold** makes a good campsite and is relatively dog-proof, if – increasingly unlikely – there is a summer sheepfold in Vathiá Láka. You will, however, need to bring water up from the Khalíki spring.

Continue W along the L flank of the gully that opens beneath Nisí. Pass just below the barrier of boulders in among the uppermost of the scattered fir trees that lie ahead of you. Do not go down into the gully. Maintain your level and bear sharply L and S round the end of the rocky spur whose flank you have been traversing. There are occasional small cairns. Follow the sheep path along the contour until you reach a large **cave**/overhang (E00347880 / N04279593; 1799m; **2hr 50min**).

From the cave, make your way down the R flank of the gully beneath, over turf and stony ground, and cross to the L flank after about 100 metres. The not very clear path follows the more or less open ground towards the top of the L bank of this gully. Square yellow waymarks appear on the fir trees. Keep your eyes skinned, for lower down the path veers R and descends through the fir trees towards the stream bank, which it follows downhill (remains of old terrace walls under the trees; **3hr 20min**) to the junction with the Lazórema stream (**3hr 25min**). It then bears L, still in the trees, following the united streams down to the open meadows at **Lázos**, passing one sheepfold directly on the line of the path after 200 metres and a second beside the stream 10min later (E00346513 / N04279757; 1192m; **3hr 40min**). This is a good place to camp. If the sheepfolds upstream are unoccupied, you can drink the stream water.

On the descent to Lázos

From here the path continues SSW across levelish grassy ground (where once the villagers of Sikiá cultivated fields) above the steadily deepening Lazórema stream gully on your R. You come to a distinct saddle before dipping steeply down the flank of a big dry gully cutting into the rocky W flank of Mt Ghióna on your L. At the bottom, turn sharply R or W across the opening of the Lazórema ravine, passing the old water conduit and bearing L down the R bank of the plane-lined Lazórema stream to reach the **Sikiá** village street by a stone-walled spring (**4hr 40min**). Turn uphill to the L for 50 metres for the *plateéya*, church and *magazeé*. There are no shops but the *magazeé* will produce a meal and would certainly help you find a place to sleep if necessary.

Sikiá is a tiny village on the eastern flank of the Mórnos river valley, about 17km north of the little town of Lidhoríki (walkable, but tarmac all the way) where the river has been dammed to create a reservoir supplying water to Athens 245km away. The jagged height opposite is Mt Vardhoúsia.

STAGE 4
*Sikiá (720m) to
Athanásios Dhiákos/Áno Mousounítsa (1050m)*

Start point	Sikiá
Distance	11km
Difficulty	2
Walking time	4hr 15min (5hr 40min following the riverbed)
Height gain	350m
Height loss	70m
Waymarks	E4 on Daoút section

For the moment the surest route is to follow the tarmac out of Sikiá for the 7km to the **Daoút bridge** over the river Mórnos (**2hr**). Turn L at the first tarmac junction down past a powerful spring.

Route following the riverbed
A much more interesting and perfectly do-able route involves following the riverbed. Should you be tempted, head N out of Sikiá on the tarmac. At the second L turn, just after a big concrete water tank on the R and a flat grassy area with benches, turn L down a zigzagging track to the village cemetery (**45min**). The track continues for another few hundred metres and ends on the edge of the plane-covered shingle banks of the river Mórnos (**1hr**).

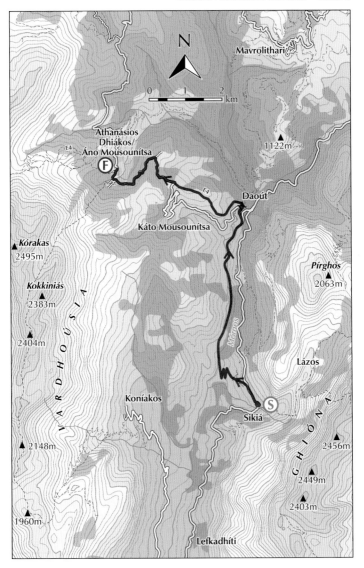

Make your way R through the trees to come out on the open shingle of the river bank and head N upstream. There was a path on the opposite (true L) bank, which we have not yet explored, but which followed the open spaces close to the river before burrowing in and out of the scrub that has now grown up. The water is never more than a foot or two deep in summer.

To be safe, stick to the riverbed until you reach the point I reached with my saw coming the other way (E00344196 / N04280872; 570m)! It is about 1.5km, on the W or true R bank; you should reach it within 40min. There turn into the plane trees which cover the flat ground behind the shingle and head R (N/upstream) for 5min (**1hr 45min**). L is an earth bank leading to open 'fields' (E00344235 / N04281060; 578m). Clamber up and turn R across the grass. 5min later you cross more 'fields' (E00344232 / N04281154; 582m), keeping on the contour, and enter a stretch of scrub which a clear path tunnels through. The river all the while is only 40 or 50m below you. Cross a further patch of 'fields' (**2hr**), keeping along the top edge. At the end on the R is a big rock (E00344082 / N04281570; 597m). Enter the scrub and a few paces later cross

Daoút spring

a stream gully. A moment later, on what looks like the remains of a path (E00344075 / N04281605; 597m; **2hr 10min**), leave the clear path you have been following and bear R down towards the river. You have to push through the trees the last few metres to reach the river bank (E00344074 / N04281692; 588m).

Cross and turn upstream for 80 metres. Just before you get to a big rock jutting out and blocking the way ahead, on the R by a plane tree (E00344079 / N04281748; 591m; **2hr 30min**), a path climbs L up a gritty bank and into the scrub, heading N on the steep E flank of the valley. The line of the path is clear. In 20min it brings you to a grassy track by a judas tree and a patch of brambles (E00344156 / N04281979; 624m; **2hr 50min**; good campsite, if you have brought water). The track ends 50 metres to the R. Turn L and follow it along the contour – easy going – to meet the tarmac road from Sikiá (**3hr 15min**). The copious spring is 5min uphill to the R. Turn L for **Daoút bridge** (**3hr 25min**).

At the end of the bridge a ramp leads sharply R down to the river where there is an E4 post (E00344679 / N04283749). Keep along the riverbank for 60 metres to a plane tree with an E4 yellow diamond. Turn L up the wooded bank into the remains of a scrubby field. Some 15 metres ahead is a bit of broken wall. Go round it L and come to another E4 post (E00344624 / N04283796; **2hr 6min**). Turn 90° L. A clear path leads uphill at a steady gradient, marked with occasional signs and streamers, to the bottom R corner of a patch of meadow known as Kostínga (E4 post; E00344286 / N04283882; **2hr 26min**). Bear up the slope at 330° to the top L corner (E4 post at E00344266 / N04283970; **2hr 31min**). Here the gradient increases. Climb steeply up the nose of a gritty spur among scattered firs. The path – although it hardly deserves the name – follows various rain gullies. Keep your eyes skinned for the markers. The trees thicken as you gain height, sometimes barring the way with fallen trunks. The direction is between 250° and 270°.

At **3hr** there is an E4 sign on a tree near a small oak (E00343952 / N04283980; 859m). A few metres above there is another attached to a fallen tree, above which the path is blocked by a thicket of broom which you are forced to go round. You can see the remains of wooden steps going through the middle. The top of the steps is at E00343873 / N04283949 (**3hr 10min**). Gradually, the gradient eases and you reach the edge of a clearing with scattered juniper bushes (E4 signpost; E00343830 / N04283954; 920m; **3hr 20min**). From here, for the first time, you can see the peaks of Mt Vardhoúsia ahead of you.

E4 to Áno Mousounítsa

Keep along the upper R edge of the clearing and, sticking to the spine of the ridge among the firs, you come to the road in about 10min (**3hr 40min**). Turn R and follow the road into the village of **Athanásios Dhiákos**, known locally as **Áno Mousounítsa** (**4hr 15min**).

The road enters **Áno Mousounítsa** at its upper edge. The church and plane-shaded square are just a few metres below to the right, where there are several tavernas – and a drinking fountain. Ravánis at the bottom right corner (tel 2265-063214) has rooms; some of the family speak excellent English.

STAGE 5

*Mt Vardhoúsia: Athanásios Dhiákos/Áno Mousounítsa
(1050m) to Yiourtáki sheepfold (1600m)*

Start point	Athanásios Dhiákos/Áno Mousounítsa
Distance	9.5km (15km including 2495m Kórakas summit)
Difficulty	3
Walking time	3hr 25min (7hr 25min including Kórakas summit)
Height gain	670m
Height loss	120m
Waymarks	E4 to Skasméni

It takes another three to four days to reach Karpenísi, the end of the first section of the Píndos Way, most of the time following the crest of grassy rounded ridges with magnificent views. Camping is unavoidable and you will need to carry all your provisions, as there are no villages or shops on the route until you reach Miríki in sight of Karpenísi. The going, however, is fairly easy once you have gained the initial height.

The first obvious place to stop is the Sarádena refuge, which is 14 hours away if you take in the Kórakas summit of Vardhoúsia – and there is always the possibility that navigation problems will extend this time. So we have presented this as two stages (5 and 6). You could even eliminate Stage 5 by engaging someone to drive you to the Yiourtáki sheepfold.

The first objective is the col of Stavrós, the obvious gap in the ridge directly above Áno Mousounítsa. The path, marked with standard E4 yellow-and-black signs, begins in a tree-lined gully L of the road as you came into the village, just before the turning into the *plateéya*.

> There is a **shepherds' track** up to Stavrós. It starts about 1.5km N of Áno Mousounítsa. It is considerably longer than the E4 path, but you might get a lift up with the shepherds if you ask around in the square the night before.

The E4 winds up through open firs to meet the shepherds' track just past the remains of old fields at Yiatákia (E00340370 / N04284869; **40min**). Turn L and follow the track to the first sharp R bend. Here the path branches off L (E00339938 / N04284865; 1309m) and zigzags steeply up above a deep stream gully to a grassy

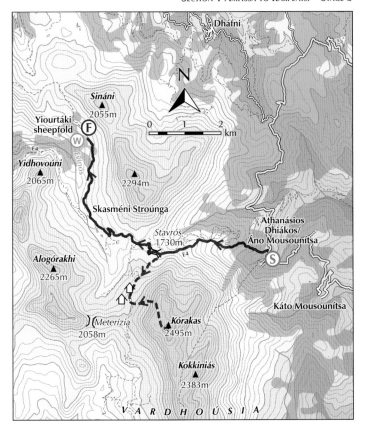

level clearing close to the track, where there is a small stone shrine dedicated to Profítis Ilías (1380m; **1hr 15min**).

> The grassy level clearing makes a good **campsite**, although you'll need to bring your own water because the spring here seems to be dry nowadays. There is water higher up the track but you don't want to camp too close to the sheepfolds at Stavrós because of the dogs.

After Profítis Ilías, the E4 leaves the track and heads L up a grassy spur to rejoin it on an eastward loop after 30min (E00338944 / N04284830; 1589m). Thereafter stay on the track. Ignore a first L turn (path leading S to the Vardhoúsia refuges) and a short distance later you come to a second: this is **Stavrós** (**2hr 15min**).

> From **Stavrós**, the ground slopes away to the west and north, reaching its lowest point in the pasture known as Skasméni. There, the Kariótiko stream, which rises in these pastures and later becomes the river Evinós or Fídharis (Snake river), plunges into a ravine which leads out of the north-west corner of the massif.

Optional ascent of Kórakas

If you want to follow the track up to the two Vardhoúsia refuges (not likely to be open), turn up L here at Stavrós. If you prefer to stick to the grass, turn up L at the junction before Stavrós (mentioned above) and walk up the rounded spur which leads nearly due S to the refuges. There is a strong spring in the stream gully just below the first refuge (1960m; **25min**) and another signed just past the second (2000m; **35min**). Both refuges stand right on the crown of the spur dominated by the western flank of Kórakas.

The clearest route to the summit starts from the upper refuge. At the edge of the track below the S end of the building there is a rock with a blob of red paint (E00337308 / N04283296). Ignore the prominent red arrow, which points to a nearby spring.

Standing by this rock, aim for a point on the ridge above at 82°, not the gap further R (a shallow couloir, which makes a nice easy ice climb in winter). Head up the steepening scree slope at 110° for about 200 metres, then at 50° towards a rain-scoured channel marked with big red arrows. The scree gives way to more solid rock. Towards the top, step L over a rib of rock and finish the climb in a steepish rocky couloir. It is a very mild scramble with plenty of red paint marks and solid footholds.

Emerge after about an hour (**1hr 30min**) at the top, on the rim of a wide grassy hollow, Mégas Kámbos. The summit is to your R. Cross the intervening hollow on to the ridge and across a narrow rocky bridge to the **Kórakas summit** in about 45min (2495m; **2hr 30min**), with fantastic views all round and south towards the sea. Return to **Stavrós** by the same route, in about 1hr 30min (**4hr**). There is a wonderful but arduous ridge walk S from Kórakas, descending SE towards the Mórnos valley, then N to the village of Kóniakos, in around 7hr.

Continue down the track from Stávros for about 45min (**3hr**) to the second L fork. The area is known as **Skasméni Stroúnga** after the sheepfold across the river. The E4 turns down at the L fork and crosses the river, heading for the village of Artotína. Ignore the L fork and bear R along a track that runs almost due N along the 1600m contour for about 1.5km until you come to a large cattle trough and copious spring among tall scattered firs (E00336317 / N04287188; **3hr 25min**). It is a perfect campsite. The now abandoned **Yiourtáki sheepfold** is actually a few minutes further up the track, but the spring, for obvious reasons, makes the better campsite.

Skasméni Stroúnga and Yidhovoúni peak

STAGE 6
*Yiourtáki sheepfold (1600m) to
Mt Oxiá/Sarádena refuge (1650m)*

Start point	Yiourtáki sheepfold and spring
Distance	15.5km
Difficulty	3
Walking time	6hr 25min
Height gain	830m
Height loss	780m
Waymarks	None

Looking up ahead you can see a low grassy col just clear of the forest: this is what you are aiming for. A few minutes past the spring, the track ends in a grassy clearing with some abandoned shepherds' huts (**5min**), known as the Yiourtáki sheepfold. Go straight ahead past the huts and enter the fir forest (E00336138 / N04287188; streamers on trees).

The path is reasonably clear to start with. Pass through a grassy clearing (E00335932 / N04288206 to E00335798 / N04288283), along the top side of a rocky clearing (E00335789 / N04288457) and across a fairly open scree slope (E00335817

119

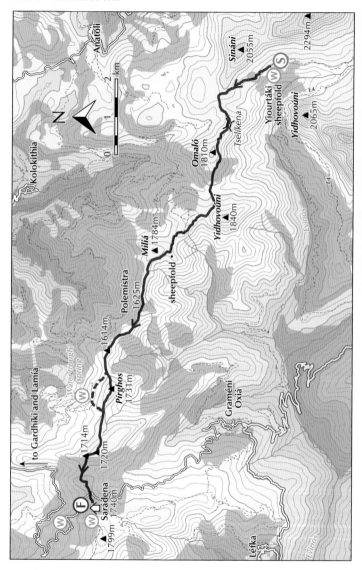

Approaching Tselíkena col

/ N04288567). Navigation gets more difficult as you re-enter the trees. The general bearing to follow is 330°. You are climbing slightly, towards the grassy col that was visible from the spring and cattle trough before the huts. There is an occasional red paint mark (E00335747 / N04288690; 1638m). Try to keep to your bearing as you push through the trees. A 15-minute struggle (E00335695 / N04288786; E00335665 / N04288822; E00335615 / N04288847) brings you clear of the trees into grassy open slopes (E00335584 / N04288872; 1681m; **1hr**). Keep bearing 330° and 5min later you reach a point on the spur ahead by a lone juniper, where you can see down the further side into a deep gully (E00335502 / N04288962; 1709m; **1hr 5min**).

In front of you and a little lower down at the very head of this gully is a narrow grassy 'bridge' – **Tselíkena** (E00335295 / N04289330; **1hr 18min**) – linking to the next grassy height to the NW. Cross it and climb the ridge line to the **Omaló** peak in 17min (E00334715 / N04288996; **1hr 35min**). The Anávasi map shows the path rounding Omaló some way below the ridge to the S, but there is no trace of it on the ground. Best to stick to the high ground – which is true all the way on this route.

Coming down from Omaló, you reach a 'bridge' (1595m) to the next summit, **Yidhovoúni** (**2hr 5min**). Cross and keep straight up the spur to around 1650m before bearing R across the slope through the firs. The old path is clear in places, but not easy to find; don't bear off R too soon or too low, where a path seems to lead. You need to come out on the ridge at the N end of Yidhovoúni (about 30min after crossing the 'bridge'; **2hr 35min**), where it levels off at around 1720m – quite narrow here. There is a lone fir tree at the head of a small gully, with a spring about 120 metres below, on the W side. This seems to be the only water hereabouts, so do not miss it. The springs marked on the Anávasi maps are not easy to find.

Keep along the broad grassy ridge top in a NW direction (plenty of flat ground for camping hereabouts). There are the remains of a vehicle track as you descend. Pass a **sheepfold**/shepherds' hut on a knoll to your L (W) above a little shoulder below the 1784m **Miliá** peak (around **3hr 15min**). About 15min further, past two or three dry springs, you come to a grassy hollow, beneath the W ridge of Miliá (campsite, without water; about **3hr 30min**).

Continue WNW along the ridge to a narrow neck marked **Polemístra** on the map (E00329660 / N04291639; 1625m; **3hr 45min**). In front are beech woods climbing to a narrow grassy ridge. The path goes down to the R of a rocky outcrop, then follows the upper edge of the beech wood. Descend from the high point of the ridge, always above the trees, to a wide grassy spur (**3hr 53min**) below the 1604m trig point marked on the Anávasi map, with scattered fir trees.

Continue along the top of the ridge to the **1614m trig point** (**4hr 10min**) and descend quite steeply to the next 'bridge' at the foot of Pírghos. The direct route is straight ahead up the E spur and down the W (**4hr 50min**); but, if you need water, you could take the following detour to a strong spring.

Detour for water
Bear R on the contour, across the dry gully which stems from the connecting 'bridge,' to meet the end of a rough track (about 20min from the 1614m trig point), where there is a **water trough** and a strong **spring** (E00327779 / N04293061).

To rejoin the main route, continue along the track, leaving it before it begins to bear away R and downhill (another spring), and climb L (S then SW) up the grassy spur (do not lose height dropping into the large gully to your R). At around 1610m, you reach the 'bridge' at the foot of the W spur coming down from Pírghos (just under an hour from the 1614 trig point – a little longer than the direct route over the summit) and rejoin the direct route.

From the W spur of Pírghos, there are rising grassy slopes ahead, rather featureless, topped by a long grassy ridge with two or three summits. Aim towards the R end, not towards the more obvious cairned summit at the L end, bearing just slightly N of W. Follow the terrain, keeping to the spurs between gullies, and zigzag up the slope; there are traces of the old path. You reach the ridge in 30min (1720m; **5hr 38min**).

> The **views** from the ridge take in the pink-roofed Sarádena refuge below you to the west, with the Sarádena peak rising behind, as well as much of the route beyond to Karpenísi. The conical peak in the distance is Veloúkhi.

Go down the ridge to the R, to the **1714m trig point**. Facing the refuge, you can see the grassy open ground you need to reach below you. Retrace your steps a few paces S along the ridge from the trig point. There is a fallen steel mast lying on the ground (E00325856 / N04293175). Begin to descend R (W) towards the uppermost beech trees and then the easier ground of a spur. Go carefully. The ground is very friable

Approaching the 1714m trig point

and a steep deep gully opens below to the L. Past the first beech tree (E00325783 / N04293177), a faint path (E00325749 / N04293187) bears diagonally R away from the gully and across the open back of the spur to enter a denser beech wood at E00325667 / N04293205. Exit from the wood (E00325621 / N04293225; 1606m) into the top corner of a sloping 'field.' Go straight ahead, aiming for the top L corner of this field, passing a kind of shooting butt (E00325458 / N04293298) on the north-facing flank of a conical knoll in the middle. Shortly afterwards (E00325243 / N04293353), bear 45° L through the bracken-filled gap between the wood on your L and the next clump of beech in front of you.

In 200 metres you come out on the open grassy top of a spur (E00325166 / N04293146; 1625m) with a wide view over the Evinós valley opening in front and a thick beech wood on your R. Bear downhill and slightly R round the edge of these trees. You pick up the old path and enter the wood at E00325092 / N04293125. In a few moments (35min from the 1714m trig point; **6hr 13min**), you come out on the col on the dirt road from Graméni Oxiá to Gardhíki, which leads eventually to Makrokómi in the Sperkhiós valley on the main Lamía–Karpenísi road. Before reaching the col, look out for an ancient much-inscribed beech tree known as fagu scriptu, its Latinate name evidence that Vlach-speakers must once have summered up here.

The **Sarádena refuge** (1650m) is about 10min further, straight up the track opposite, at the upper limit of the beech woods (**6hr 25min**).

You will find the **Sarádena refuge** locked, but there is a spring in front and a beautiful grassy area for camping, with a magnificent view south-east to Vardhoúsia. There is a concrete veranda along the front of the building, but no shelter.

123

The nearest alternative source of water is about 2.5km down the road (north) towards Gardhíki by the chapel of Metamórfosi tou Sotíra. The pretty village of Graméni Oxiá lies 8km south by the dirt road (downhill all the way), with a *magazeé* and the possibility of a room.

STAGE 7

Mt Oxiá/Sarádena refuge (1650m) to Kokália obelisk (1431m)/Rákhes Timfristoú

Start point	Sarádena refuge
Distance	17km
Difficulty	2
Walking time	5hr 30min
Height gain	220m
Height loss	370m
Waymarks	Occasional cairns and red paint

Go straight up the hill behind the refuge, then up the next grassy height, following the vehicle tracks. Keep along and down the ridge, bearing slightly R. The grassy bulk of Sarádena rises directly ahead. Start climbing; you can see the line of the path, keeping L of the beech woods on the NE slopes. (There are beech woods to your L as well.) The view stretches away to the Sperkhiós river valley.

After **1hr** you come to a lone beech tree on the path, just detached from the wood (1810m). Continue up the ridge a short way. An arrow on a rock points straight up for the summit. Bear R, skirting Sarádena peak to the east, pretty much on the 1800m contour. A clear path contours round grassy slopes, across gullies, to reach the main ridge again with a view down the other side into a deep enclosed gully. Follow down the spur line to cross a track at 1705m (**1hr 35min**). The way ahead is grassy and rounded as far as the eye can see, with the conical peak of Veloúkhi visible to the north-west.

Cut off the loops, heading down to a broad saddle, the lowest point, with a lone hawthorn tree at 1639m (**1hr 45min**). Continue along the high ground L of the track. After 20–25min come down to a track junction (cattle trough below the track R; **2hr 10min**). Continue along the track on the R flank of a green gully with another cattle trough over to the L. At the top of the climb, the track bends L (1640m). Continue downhill to a R bend on a low saddle at 1625m (**3hr**). For the first time since the track junction, you can see down both sides of the ridge.

Ahead, you can just detect the shadow of the old mule road zigzagging up the grassy slope in front, bearing L. Leave the track here and follow the old path. Over the first skyline, bear R across a grassy slope, heading 350° to a stone cairn (**3hr 10min**);

Camping near Kokália obelisk

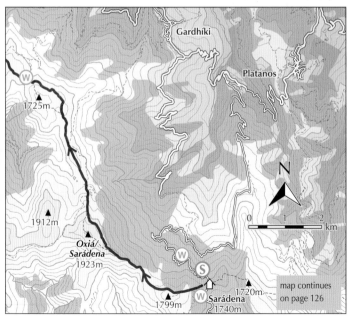

map continues on page 126

125

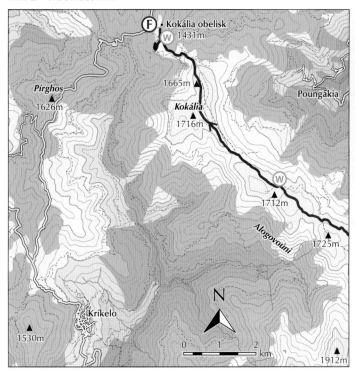

3min later you can see over the grassy ridge to Mt Veloúkhi again – a short iron spike in the grass marks the high point here. Descend towards a large cattle trough in a hollow below the track end (**3hr 35min**). There is a red square on a white background on the end of the cattle trough.

Continue up a shallow grassy 'funnel' behind the trough, in the direction you have been following. Immediately over the first top (a few minutes), you find yourself descending gently down a long shallow vale with distinctive cairns on ridges to either side. There are vehicle tracks in the grass; follow them, to the lowest point of the whole route at 1560m (**3hr 55min**).

Proceed straight up the rising ridge ahead of you to the **Kokália trig point** at 1716m (E00316822 / N04301585; **4hr 25min**). Continue N across a broad grassy plateau to a weather mast; bear slightly NW at 320° to the **1665m trig point** (**4hr 45min**), then straight down the grassy slope below at 330°. Cross a bulldozed track; meet it again

Kokália obelisk with Mt Veloúkhi in the background

and keep straight on down, bearing L on a lower track to a low grassy col (E00316025 / N04303177; 1461m; **5hr 15min**). There is a stone shepherds' hut L.

Bear up R on a broad grassy ridge to a wooden drinking trough and spring. Bear 295° over open grass on a faint track among juniper and young firs to reach a concrete cattle trough (**5hr 25min**; campsite). Here, the track bears 350° through firs and L down to a spring and the **Kokália obelisk** (**5hr 30min**). This stone pillar commemorates a victory over Celtic invaders in 278BC.

STAGE 8

Kokália obelisk (1431m)/Rákhes Timfristoú to
Karpenísi (960m)

Start point	Kokália obelisk/Rákhes Timfristoú
Distance	14km (to Karpenísi town centre)
Difficulty	1
Walking time	3hr 30min
Height gain	30m
Height loss	500m
Waymarks	None

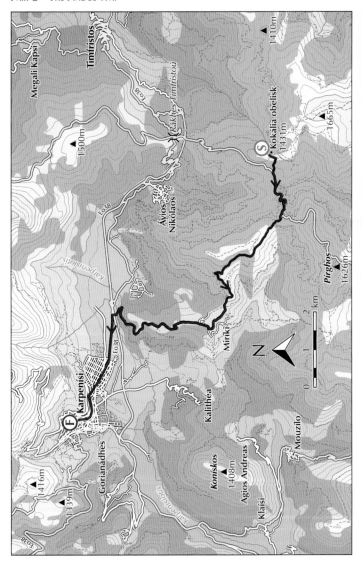

You now have two options. Either turn R on the road and hope for a lift into Karpenísi – an altogether reasonable prospect. It is roughly 4km to the crossroads at the **Rákhes Timfristoú col** on the old main Lamía–Karpenísi road, which now has a tunnel underneath it and where the prospect of a lift is slightly better. Or you can leg it all the way by tarmac and dirt road via the village of Miríki, most of the way in fir forest.

In either case, take the track from the monument and bear R at the junction to reach the Kríkelo–Karpenísi tarmac road in **15min**. For Miríki, turn L along the tarmac for about 1km and take the second turning R, on a L hairpin (**30min**), down a broad descending dirt road. Ignore two L and three R turns.

After 4km you pass the Profítis Ilías chapel in a kind of park on the R (**1hr 30min**). Another 1km brings you to the tarmac road to Karpenísi (**1hr 45min**). A L turn takes you into **Miríki** village where you could ask the *magazeé* to call a taxi. A R turn takes you down to the E edge of **Karpenísi** (5km; **3hr**), with another 2.5km to get into the town (**3hr 30min**). The Hotel Ánesis, which we recommend, is on the L as you approach the town centre.

SECTION 2 KARPENÍSI TO MESOKHÓRA

Asprórema: the valley leads to the Delidhími col (Stage 12)

This section of the Píndos Way encompasses the part of the Píndos range known in Greek as *ta ágrafa*, which, literally translated, means 'the unwritten places', in other words they are unrecorded. One day on foot in this terrain is enough to tell you why. Before the roads, and they only began to be bull-dozed post-World War II, it was almost impenetrable for outsiders and easily defensible against the troops of the Turkish overlords who ruled the country for so many centuries. Even in the 1970s, when I first explored the region, there were villages 10 hours on foot from a roadhead.

Inaccessibility made the region a sanctuary for rebels of all sorts, half-brigand Robin Hoods, Greek nationalists seeking freedom from Turkish rule, wartime Resistance fighters against German and Italian occupation, Communist partisans during the post-World War II Civil War. Life was hard, of course, and people were very poor. The geology is rocky, contorted and very friable, the terrain so steep you wonder how they managed to produce any food beyond what their livestock could provide.

Villages tend to be high up the valley sides, towards the treeline, all seriously depopulated now, if not actually abandoned. Beside stream gullies, on any vaguely level grassy place, you come upon the ruins of scattered houses, where people once struggled to make a living. Ancient packhorse bridges and stretches of beautifully cobbled stairways, all now overgrown, suddenly appear under your feet, testimony to the extraordinarily dense life that once went on here. There is a certain melancholy as a result, especially if, like me, you once knew some of these places as living settlements. It is a fascinating and beautiful place nonetheless and in summer at least there is still life when the flocks return from the winter lowlands and the grandparents return from a more comfortable winter in the lowland towns, bringing their grandchildren with them.

There are some wonderful stretches of path still surviving, especially before and after Epinianá. There is also more road-walking than in other sections, as so many footpaths are no longer used or maintained. But don't let that put you off. These roads are largely bulldozed unsurfaced forest tracks, really only distinguishable from paths by their width and their gradient designed to accommodate wheeled vehicles, and there is no traffic beyond the occasional shepherd's pick-up.

LOCATION

Karpenísi lies 292km from Athens on the most southerly of the two main routes crossing the Píndos range. It is just over an hour by road from Lamía on the main Athens–Thessaloníki National Road. If you are travelling by car, take the time to stop at Thermopylae, signposted just off the motorway a few miles short of Lamía. A statue commemorates the battle where Leonidas and his 300 Spartans made their legendary last stand to hold the pass against the vastly superior Persian army that invaded Greece in 480BC.

MAPS

• Anávasi Topo 50 (1:50,000) 2.4/2.5 *Mountains of Evritania*

• Anávasi Topo 50 (1:50,000) 4.1 *Northern Ágrafa: Plastíra Lake*
• Anávasi Topo 50 (1:50,000) 3.2/4.2 *South Píndos: Tzoumérka, Peristéri, Kóziakas, Avgó*

BASES

Karpenísi has banks, shops (including outdoor gear), restaurants and hotels, including the Hotel Ánesis, Zinopoúlou 50 (main street leading to town centre; tel 22370-22840, info@anesis.gr, www.anesis.gr). There are no other shops after Karpenísi until you reach Métsovo at the end of Section 3. Apart from providing meals, village *magazeé* will always help you out, with bread and cheese and simple things, but you will not be able to stock up with provisions.

Rooms are available in **Sténoma**; and there's a good chance of a room in **Kerasokhóri** too, especially during the school summer holidays: ask at the cafés. Alternatively, there is the Hotel Mákkas at **Kréndi**, 3km along the road to the west (tel 22370-31350).

The Panórama in **Epinianá** is a very attractive and truly welcoming guesthouse/restaurant run by Kóstas and Yióta Gantzoúdis (tel 22370-94122, mob 697-2330058). Here, in the heart of Ágrafa, you will find good food and a magnificent view. It is a great place for a day or two's rest.

Dormitory accommodation is provided at **Moní Spiliás**, a beautiful old monastery in a spectacular position, perched on a crag above a deep ravine; two monks are in permanent residence. You can eat in the refectory. If you prefer more comfort, both culinary- and sleepwise, go to Váïos Pózios' taverna and

Approaching Mégdhovas bridge. Keep a sharp eye for E4 signs (Stage 10)

very comfortable rooms at Ta Ragázia, on the road about 30min walk below the monastery (tel 24450-32020 and 24450-41140, mob 697-9728262) – another very welcoming place.

The Hotel Alkiviádis in **Kalí Kómi** is a great place for a rest (tel 24450-31511, mob 697-1617644, mob 698-0868455, mob 698-0718584, info@alkishotel.gr, www.hotell-alkiviadis.no/eng): wonderful landscapes, beautiful river nearby, good food. And it is run by a Welsh woman, Jeannette Skylas, and her Greek husband, so no language problems. **Mirófilo** has a small guesthouse.

In **Mesokhóra**, the Hotel Akhelóös (mob 697-7803074) is just down to the right from the *magazeé* in the centre of the village. It is open all year.

ACCESS

Daily buses run from Athens (Odhós Liosíon terminus) to Karpenísi. There is one bus a day (excluding Sunday) from Karpenísi to Kerasokhóri, going on to Kréndi and Dhitikí Frangísta. For further information, consult KTEL Karpenísi (www.ktelevrytanias.gr).

A minibus runs from Ágrafa to Kréndi (Monday and Friday), with a bus connection (Wednesday) on to Karpenísi and to Kardhítsa in the plain of Thessaly. You can pick it up on the road in the valley bottom; ask Kóstas and Yióta at the Panórama guesthouse in Epinianá.

From Mesokhóra, a bus runs every day in summer (or Monday and Friday at other times of the year) to Píli and Tríkala for onward journeys to Athens.

STAGE 9

Karpenísi (960m) to
Kerasokhóri (1000m)

Start point	Karpenísi
Distance	31.3km
Difficulty	2
Walking time	9hr 15min
Height gain	1040m
Height loss	1000m
Waymarks	E4 signs fairly frequent on E4 sections, otherwise none

The route for this stage for the most part follows one of the better signed sections of the E4. Broadly it heads north-west from Karpenísi over the shoulder of Mt Veloúkhi, the peak towering above the town, crosses the valley of the river Mégdhovas and begins to climb into the foothills of the Ágrafa region. There is more road work than footpath, but much of that is scarcely used track and even the tarmac sees little traffic.

It is most comfortably done in two parts, but there is no obvious break. The only chance of a bed is in the village of Sténoma, which involves continuing down the tarmac from the 4hr point for 3km. You would then rejoin the E4 the next day at the 4hr 40min point where it crosses the Sténoma–Mégdhovas track, thus adding about 8km to the overall distance. Alternatively, you could camp by the Mégdhovas river bridge at the 5hr 25min point or continue to Néa Víniani village (6hr 30min).

Leaving Karpenísi, head up the main shopping street through the central *plateéya* and bear L round the top of it, passing the town hall (*dheemarkheéyo*), the Hotel Mont Blanc, then the police station. Where the main road bends L, head straight uphill on Karaïskáki Street and follow it all the way to the top where it joins another road. Keep uphill to the R. The houses become sparser. There is a plane-lined stream gully L and the remains of old fields.

On a R hairpin by a lone tree-shaded house, a gravel track heads off L by an E4 sign. There is a confusion of tracks at the beginning: keep straight ahead. In **10min**, bear 90° L by a big concrete weir designed to hold back the stones in the streambed (yellow-and-black paint signs) and begin to climb W on a rough vehicle track. In 20min (**30min**), you pass two small houses in a cultivated enclosure L. A few moments

133

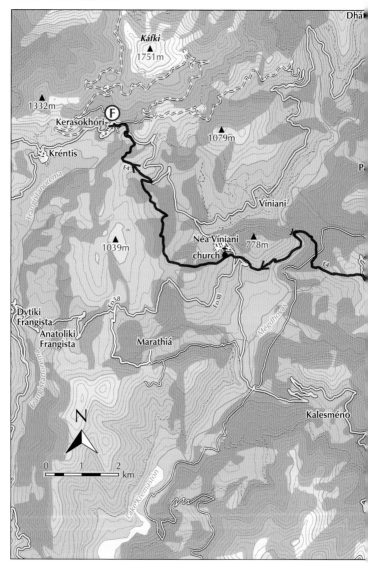

later the track bends R across the stream. Before the bend, on the L bank of the track (E00306638 / N04311477), a path goes up through the fir trees (yellow paint and E4 sign) and bears NW, becoming a little unclear in a grassy open gully. Keep to the R side of the gully. An E4 diamond sign is visible on a tree up ahead. At the top of the slope, you emerge on to open level grassy ground with a wide view ahead and to the west (E00306379 / N04311497; **50min**). The path – reasonably clear and signed – follows the 1400m contour through the firs just above the tarmac road, which it joins by the chapel of **Áyios Thanásios** (**1hr 30min**).

Turn R and continue along the tarmac for about 10min, then take the E4-signed track dropping L down into the trees. The track passes to the L (W) of a thickly wooded ridge, whereas the tarmac, which it rejoins after 3km (**2hr 30min**), passes to the R (E). Both routes are beautiful. The tarmac is slightly shorter and involves less of a climb, if you do not mind the hard surface. There is hardly any traffic.

There is no escaping the tarmac – mostly downhill – for the next 5.5km until you reach a **white roadside shrine** a bit like a bus shelter on the R (E00302469 / N04315425; 860m; **4hr**). For overnight accommodation in Sténoma, continue down the tarmac for 3km. Smack opposite, a red gritty track leads up L and almost immediately forks, by a cattle trough with E4 markings. Take the L fork, descending steadily on red grit for the first 15min or so, with a view south over the Mégdhovas river valley, till the track turns into the old footpath, still pretty clear and signed (E4 diamond on tree at E00301480 / N04315497; 709m). It descends through the prickly kermes oak (*poornárya*), bearing gradually N and E to meet the track (E00300886 / N043150907; 560m; **4hr 40min**) descending from Sténoma village to the Mégdhovas river. If you are coming from Sténoma, you will rejoin the E4 at this point.

Cross the track, bearing R for a few paces, and bear L down the far bank into the oak trees (frequent E4 signs). After 10–15min (**4hr 55min**), cross a narrow but deep stream gully by the ruins of a very small stone bridge and emerge into a grassy open clearing where the way ahead is not clear (E00300998 / N04316256; 560m). The most obvious path appears to bear R over the nose of a grassy spur and head off into the woods again. This is wrong. As you emerge into the open grassy space with the stream gully below to your L, keep straight ahead on the L or south-facing flank of the spur for perhaps 100 metres. There are a couple of painted rocks lying in the grass which are easy to miss and two large oaks directly in front of you with E4 diamonds on their trunks. Pass between them. Bearing N and then W, you descend on a clear path to the old arched **packhorse bridge** over the river Mégdhovas, now officially known as the Tavropós (E00300593 / N04316744; 362m; **5hr 25min**). This is a beautiful spot for camping, although you might prefer to bring water as there are a few small villages upstream.

From the far bank a track climbs SW above the river to the village of **Néa Víniani** in about 1hr (**6hr 30min**). Just short of the tarmac road, a very rough track branches steeply up R; take it. There are no shops but the *magazeé* is a couple of minutes along the tarmac to the R and would help you out with food. You could camp on the village green or anywhere hereabouts.

> During World War II, ELAS, Greece's biggest and Communist-led Resistance movement, set up its HQ in the old village of **Víniani** and declared this area Free Greece. **Néa Víniani** – New Víniani – looks remarkably like an English housing estate. And that essentially is what it is: it was built to rehouse people from the old village, which, although it still exists nearby, was seriously damaged by an earthquake in the 1960s. About 3.5km to the north, the very pretty ruins are well worth a visit if the opportunity arises.
>
> For the onward route to Kerasokhóri, there are two options. One – slightly shorter at 7.5km – is to continue along the tarmac. The other is a track used only by farmers: it is longer but prettier and shadier, contouring, after the initial climb, along the opposite side of the valley from the road.

To continue to Kerasokhóri via the farmers' route, take the track which begins opposite the point where you entered Néa Víniani, passing above the blue-domed **church of Ayía Konstantína**. Head W for the first couple of kilometres, ignoring the first R turn, but bearing R at the next fork, down past a small chapel (**7hr 15min**). A few minutes later the track swings N, looping in and out of the re-entrants but sticking pretty much to the contour. Ignore a track climbing to the L after about 20min.

At **8hr 15min**, the track doubles back R across a dry gully to meet the main tarmac road on a R hairpin. Just short of the road, a clearly signed section of E4 starts up the bank on your L (E00296476 / N04318132). For 20min it climbs straight and clear

Mégdhovas bridge

diagonally across a scrubby hillside. The scrub begins to thicken noticeably and you come to the lower R corner of an open sloping grassy field (**8hr 35min**). Turn 90° L along the bottom edge of this field (E00296166 / N04318507), ignoring a steep goat path leading down into the gully below L. A clear path begins again after some 40 metres and climbs diagonally through the trees. After 5min it turns into a grassy path following the fence of a field.

Bear L round the field and come to a track (**8hr 45min**). Ignoring a short spur turning down L to a stable, continue along the track, bearing R on to a fir-covered ridge with wide views, past a chapel on the col, then on to the road by a stream gully and into **Kerasokhóri** (**9hr 15min**). Go up the ramp R into the village square where you will find a couple of *magazeé*.

STAGE 10
Kerasokhóri (1000m) to Varvariádha (400m)

Start point	Kerasokhóri
Distance	19km
Difficulty	2
Walking time	6hr
Height gain	200m
Height loss	1000m
Waymarks	None

The geography of the Ágrafa is extraordinarily complicated. It is bisected north to south by the deep narrow gorge of the Agrafiótis river, whose flanks in turn are cut by countless side streams, themselves branching into numerous gullies. Scattered among them, in addition to the main villages, were countless hamlets and tiny settlements where people sought to exploit every moderately cultivable patch of ground. The extensive network of paths that once connected them has largely fallen into disuse or been destroyed by the new EU-funded roads, now gradually being tarmacked. We have consequently had to change our route into the Ágrafa region several times over the years and we are doing so once again.

For the moment, the best route north from Kerasokhóri is along the forest track that keeps just west of the eastern Ágrafa watershed. You are in fir forest (*élata*) all the way. The going is earth and stone, not much different from a footpath, with no traffic beyond the occasional shepherd.

In the old days **our route into the Ágrafa** used to go to Kréndi and then down into the Agrafiótis ravine to the tiny hamlet of Varvariádha, the furthest point accessible to wheeled vehicles. Here, the mountain people used to park their mules and ponies beneath the planes by the spring while they went into town by vehicle to deal with officialdom, go to court, make their purchases. There was an old stone-tiled *magazeé* where everyone met. It is closed now and a plaque commemorates the family that used to run it.

It is many years now since a road was driven all the way up the ravine, completely destroying the beautiful old path. As of May 2017 it had been tarmacked as far as the bridge at Karvasarás, 4km upstream from Varvariádha; and, for the moment at least, there is no way to avoid this last stretch.

Do not be tempted by the path, marked on the Anávasi map, which leads down from Márathos. There is a serious landslip about 40min above Karvasarás. It is just passable for the very sure-footed. The consequences of a fall would be nasty.

To get to Varvariádha, go straight through Kerasokhóri's *plateéya* and bear R up the narrow concrete street leading N out of the village and into the fir forest on the slopes of Mt Káfki. Cross a deep stream gully, bearing W to join the main track where you turn up R. Bear L at the next junction, where the track doubles back L, and keep R at the following one. Soon after, the track straightens and levels out around the 1300m contour for 5–6km, with magnificent views of the peaks of west Ágrafa.

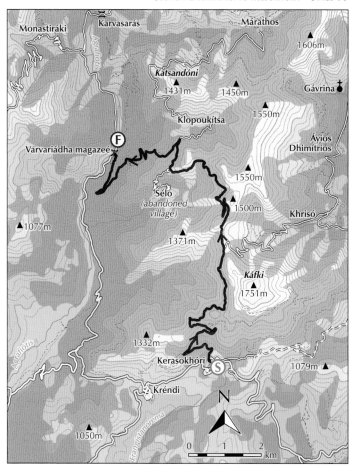

Ignore the R turn for **Khrisó** where the track crosses briefly to the E side of the watershed on a narrow col. Bear NW and W to pass the turning for the deserted village of **Sélo**. You are beginning to lose height now.

About 1km later, turn sharply down to the L on a very poor track that veers largely SW before, close to the valley bottom, doubling back N through the riverside planes to **Varvariádha (6hr)**. There is plenty of room to camp on the riverbank behind the old *magazeé*.

Spring by the old magazeé in Varvariádha

STAGE 11
Varvariádha (400m) to Epinianá (950m)

Start point	Varvariádha
Distance	12.5km
Difficulty	3
Walking time	6hr 25min
Height gain	1150m
Height loss	200m
Waymarks	Rare

Cross the concrete bridge just upstream from the spring and the old *magazeé*, and follow the road upstream on the W bank. Just after the steep L turn to **Monastiráki**, there is a *magazeé* beside the road at the place known as Kotsísta (possibility of refreshment). After a further 1km, just before the road bends sharp R to approach the **Karvasarás bridge**, take the rough track climbing steeply up the scrubby bank to your L (**1hr 30min**).

The track bends back R crossing a stream among plane trees, rounds the rocky spur above the bridge and comes to an end at a sizeable shed housing sheep and goats in a grassy terraced clearing called **Makrí Kámbi** (E00292433 / N04329728; **2hr**

140

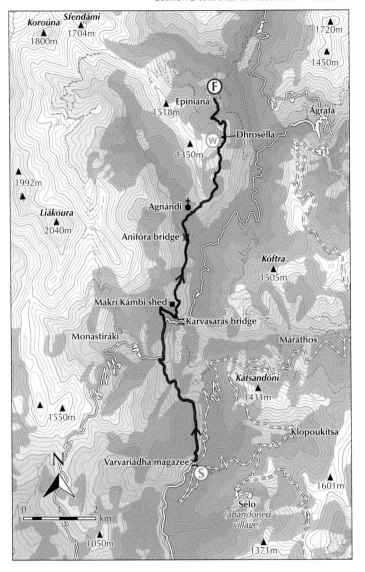

141

Makrí Kámbi: follow the middle-level terrace to the right into the trees and on to the scree

15min). As you approach it, you can see beyond, on the far side of a tree-filled gully, a long run of scree (marked on the Anávasi map as *sára*, the Greek for scree) which is where your route continues. Finding the beginning of it is tricky, but remember that the path across the scree is on a level with the shed, although you cannot see it until you are practically on it.

Pass below the shed and, keeping on this level, follow the terrace to its end at the edge of a steep and thickly wooded gully (evergreen oaks). There is no very clear path. Descend a couple of metres and bear L, traversing along the steep flank of the gully, deep in dead leaves, until you hit the bed of the almost certainly dry stream where even the semblance of path peters out. Clamber across carefully and bear R slightly up and L round a stony intervening spur, across a second gully and on to the edge of the scree (**2hr 30min**), where you can see the trace of a path crossing the rocks just above a small lone Judas tree. Go carefully on the far side (**2hr 35min**) where in two or three places the path has washed down the friable reddish earth and there is nothing much to hold on to.

After climbing for about 40 metres, curl L round a blue metal shrine and descend along a clear path to a second, much smaller scree slope (E00292624 / N04330745; **3hr**). Cross it diagonally R to the bottom corner by a very large evergreen oak to find the continuation of the path. About 5min later, you pass a small tin shrine beside the path in a bit of open ground. The path bears L round a corner and gradually down in the direction of the river Agrafiótis. After passing through a patch of plane trees whose fallen leaves obscure the way, turn down R to the riverbank and follow it across what must once have been a grassy field, passing below a ruined cottage to arrive at a lovely arched stone bridge, **Anifóra bridge**, across the Ftéris stream, by its junction with the Agrafiótis (**3hr 30min**).

Cross the bridge. Ignore what appears to be a clear path immediately L on a stone embanked ledge at the foot of a very rocky spur barring your way. Turn R off the bridge and hard L round the end of this spur, and immediately on the L you will see the beginning of a beautifully made cobbled path zigzagging up the spur. It crosses L of the spur and begins to climb more gradually up the R flank of the Ftéris stream valley through *poornárya* scrub and oak, passing some totally collapsed cottages under big planes at E00292698 / N04331495 and another better preserved ruin at E00292619 / N04331623 (**4hr**) before turning sharply R and up. These are the ruins of Anifóra (locally called Tsórtia). Once large enough to warrant a primary school, this scattered settlement was abandoned 40–50 years ago.

Climb steadily through dappled oak shade. (The path is no longer very clear here, although we did our best to mark it in 2017.) At **4hr 45min** you pass crumbling walls L and the path bends L. A few minutes later you reach more substantial ruins at the edge of a flattish grassy plateau. There are great views here – a good rest spot after an hour of climbing.

At the uphill end of the 'fields' lies a steep, rocky spur which you need to climb, passing some defunct telephone poles, before veering R at its top. There is an old path but it is covered in loose rocks and not always clear. It starts just R of the spur line, zigzags once, then clambers up the stony slope before bearing L of the spur line. It then switches back and forth up the spur among scattered kermes oak (E00293015 / N04332219) before finally bearing R to pass just above a small white **chapel** at the

Goats at Dhrosélla spring

spot once known as *élatos* (fir) or **Agnándi** (viewpoint) (E00293158 / N04332297; **5hr 30min**).

A couple of minutes later, pass through a crude gate by big boulders (1050m) and the ascent is over. The path descends gently NE through firs, with a steep drop R straight down to the Agrafiótis narrows known as the Trípa, and turns into a track by a tumbledown hut R. The track leads N past terraced fields and the plane-shaded spring of **Dhrosélla** L. Ágrafa village comes into view across the ravine to the right, with flat-topped Karnópi (1970m) behind. At **6hr 10min** ignore the L fork up to the chapel of Áyii Anáryiri. The track curves L, then R to reach **Epinianá** about **6hr 25min** from Varvariádha.

> In **Epiniána**, one of the first houses you reach (on the left) is the delightful and welcoming Panórama guesthouse (tel 22370-94122, mob 697-2330058), overlooking the stone-paved section of road that leads up left to the fountain and *plateéya*.

STAGE 12
Epinianá (950m) to Spiliá monastery (850m)

Start point	Epinianá
Distance	25km
Difficulty	3
Walking time	8hr 30min
Height gain	1450m
Height loss	1600m
Waymarks	Occasional

The first half of the route follows the deep narrow wooded gorge of the Asprórema stream, a tributary of the Agrafiótis, pretty much to its source beyond the scattered and now largely ruined hamlet of Asprórema, until recently one of the remotest and most other-worldly inhabited places in Greece. From here, it climbs above the treeline to cross the watershed by the col below Mt Delidhími (2162m) before descending into the much more open country of the Koumbourianítikos river, the next valley to the north.

You could easily break the stage at Asprórema, where the old terraces near the Tsarkórema stream and the first ruined houses make a wonderful campsite.

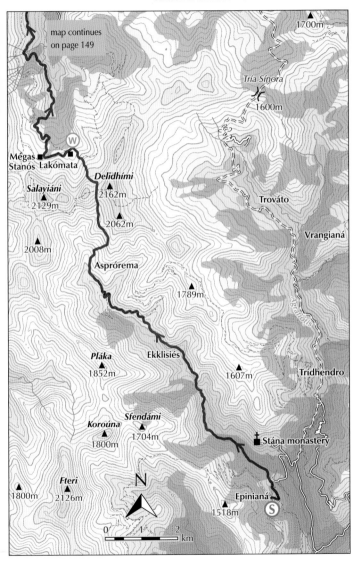

map continues on page 149

1700m

Tría Sínora
1600m

Mégas Stanós
Lakómata Ⓦ

Salayiáni
2129m

Delidhími
2162m

2062m

2008m

Trováto

Vrangianá

Asprórema

1789m

Agrafiótis

Pláka
1852m

Ekklisiés

1607m

Tridhendro

Koroúna
1800m

Sfendámi
1704m

✝ **Stána monastery**

N

Fteri
2126m

1800m

Epinianá
1518m

Ⓢ

0   1   2 km

145

Salayiáni

From Epinianá, follow the main road N out of the village, descending steadily. At the first R bend, by signposts L to Asprórema and Farángi, continue along a beautiful small path into the woods. At around **30min** you emerge from a stand of firs at a wayside shrine.

> There are views upstream to the peaks of **Salayiáni**, and across the river to the buildings of **Stána monastery**, huddled beneath an orange overhang.
>
> Stána monastery, like many in Greece, was supposedly founded when a shepherd discovered a miraculous icon buried here – in this case, that of the Virgin Mary. It had 'walked' here of its own accord from Amfilokhía on the coast when its original church fell to the Turks. The Virgin's birth is celebrated here on 7–8 September, when crowds gather for a night vigil and festival. You can arrange to visit with Kóstas, from the Panórama guesthouse in Epiniána.

After a flat stretch through firs, the descent resumes until you cross a stream tumbling down a striated limestone gully. After another sharp L bend (**1hr 5min**), you can see the meadows of Ekklisiés ahead and 100m higher. At **1hr 30min** you reach a flat-topped grassy spur with a crumbling stone wall L and the single (invisible from here) house of **Ekklisiés** a little higher up. This is a perfect campsite; you can get water from the stream just a few minutes further on.

The path continues beside the wall, dropping down to cross a year-round stream before contouring on through lush oak and hornbeam woods dotted with hyacinths and wild strawberries. Look out for red-and-white helleborines in June, and the distinctive scarlet Heldreich's lily in July.

At **1hr 55min** you reach the start of the stone-built section – not much fun for vertigo-sufferers – with stupendous views over the foaming torrent beneath. Past a shrine on the corner (**2hr 10min**), the path becomes a broad ledge chiselled out of the rock face. After 10min, a second, rusting shrine signals the end of the tunnelled part. On the opposite bank, you can make out the path climbing abandoned terraces to cross the saddle R of a rocky fang.

At a small spur, the path winds steeply down L to reach the junction of the Asprórema stream with its tributary Skilórema (**2hr 30min**). An old concrete footbridge lies a further 100 metres upstream. Make your way up the stony bank to reach it, cross over and continue up the clear path, zigzagging up beneath the rocky fang, keeping the grey scree slope initially on your R. Cross it and climb to the base of the rocky fang, where you turn R and wind up past an obsolete telephone pole to the saddle (**2hr 55min**). Annoyingly, the path now descends – although more gently – passing the moss-covered trunks of evergreen oaks before flattening off slightly. Pass above a field with a fading wooden post pointing vaguely at the Kranoúla spring on the opposite riverbank.

Soon after, you enter a grove of plane trees, cross a side stream and – less clear now – bear L before climbing to some 80m above river level. Cross another rocky outcrop at a saddle with a fir and stone shrine, then plunge back down to river level and keep a stone's throw from the water. Around **3hr 40min** you start to climb R away from the river, up a boulder-strewn gully delta, with only a green metal shrine as a pointer. Pick your way up crumbling terraces and meadows to a grassy flat top (possible campsite) with a ruined house L. The abandoned houses of old Asprórema are visible ahead. Climb a couple of terraces and resume NW to reach a second saddle with a pair of ruined houses. Between these a path descends to cross the Tsarkórema stream, which has water all year. Climb to a modern house (still occupied in summer) beside the shepherds' track from Trováto and Trídhendro (**4hr 15min**).

Asprórema gorge

Coming up from Asprórema to the Delidhími col

Asprórema once had enough families to warrant a primary school, while the older children walked down to Epinianá every day for high school. The last family to quit permanent residence left in 1997. Ironically, it was the arrival of the jeep track, aimed at making life easier, which allowed them to up sticks and move to the town of Agrínio on the coast, where the other villagers over-winter. A couple of families still return to these pastures with their flocks from June to October, when the track over the 1700m Tsoúka Sáka pass is open. But their houses are slowly crumbling.

Turn L on the track that runs behind the modern house. Follow it up to join the main track and continue N for about 25min. You ford a stream and the track begins to climb. Overlooking the first R bend by a stand of fir trees (E00289028/N04340635; 1044m) you come to a once-substantial stone house. Continue along the scarcely used track, passing another more ruinous house, until it comes to an end at E00288704/N04341237; 1152m. Turn R up the bank (E00288770/N04341472; 1301m), then back L. The path is pretty clear, zigzagging up through big open firs to reach the ruined cottages of Sfirí, abandoned a good many years ago. The trees – still big mature firs – are rapidly thinning out here. There are a number of overgrown and aged fruit trees, a sure sign of former habitation, but no sign of a water source.

Keep straight uphill from the ruins for a few minutes. For 20 to 30 minutes from where the trees end the path is very unclear in the unkempt grass and encroaching scrub. You need to get on to the spur directly above Sfirí. The old path seems to have swung out to the L before curving back R above a thicket of young firs and climbing up on to the spur from here. You reach the spur line at E00288922/N04341658 (1417m), clear of all trees. The best thing for the moment may be to clamber directly up on to the nose of the spur from Sfirí, making your way as best you can; it should not take more than 20 to 30 minutes. From here continue up the ridge bearing NE to the 1700m contour (**4hr 30min**).

Turn L or W on the transverse path. Cross a dry gully and bear R along the opposite flank, then up and over a sharp little spur, cutting back L down a good rocky path on the W flank to the shallow gully below. Here, bear R and down to the shepherds' hut at **Lakómata** (E00288364 / N04344572; **5hr**). There is a spring here and it is a good place to camp if there are no dogs in residence.

From Lakómata, follow the track W for 30min beneath the distinctive horn-like peak of Salayiáni, passing a spring on the L, to a second sheepfold with a solid little cottage on a piece of level ground at the locality known as **Mégas Stanós** (E00287091 / N04346821; **5hr 30min**).

> **Mégas Stanós** makes a good campsite too, as long as there are no dogs in residence. A second advantage is that the shepherd who brings his sheep here in summer speaks very respectable English; his name is Yiánnis Makriyiánnis.

Bear R at the fork shortly after. The track contours N along the slope for about 600 metres, before zigzagging precipitously down into the woods at a locality called Niáles. At the bottom zigzag (**6hr**), a disused track comes in from the gully to your R; this is an alternative route from Lakómata, marked on the map but very overgrown with bracken. From Niáles, continue down the track to arrive in **Leondíto** in about 1hr 30min (**7hr 30min**).

Head N along the road from the square with its 900-year-old plane tree. On the L just past a walled spring and opposite the church (R below the road), a track cuts up L to a large new house. Turn R along the path that follows the fence enclosing this new house. You come out in a rough field with a ramshackle hut. Pass it and, bearing L, you enter the fir forest. Do not lose height.

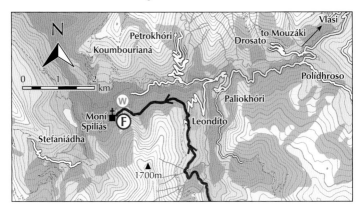

The **path to the monastery** was obviously once a major route for pilgrims. For several years, the word has been that the path is impassable. If anyone tries to tell you that today, pay no attention. We cleared and marked the tricky second half in 2017!

The path improves as you continue in and out of small gullies and over intervening spurs, sticking pretty much to the 900–1000m contour except for the last stretch where, from a natural belvedere at E00286054 / N04349226, you gradually lose about 100 metres in height, dropping below the fir-line down into a deep little gully. Cross over by a large plane tree before climbing back R and steeply up through trees and across an expanse of stable scree. Just before you reach the monastery (**Moní Spiliás; 8hr 30min**), spectacularly perched on a crag above the Koumbourianítikos river valley, you pass a wonderfully powerful spring. Do not miss a visit to the beautiful monastery church.

The **monastery of Spiliá** offers basic accommodation and meals for visitors. There are a couple of monks in permanent residence; you just have to bang on doors until you find them.
    If you fancy a more comfortable and indulgent night, you can make your way down the monastery lane to the tarmac, turn right and walk down to Ta Ragázia, a welcoming, well-appointed *magazeé* right on the road below the monastery crag (Váïos Pózios: tel 24450-32020 and 24450-41140, mob 697-9728262; open all year). It is a 30min walk.

STAGE 13
Spiliá monastery (850m) to Petrotó (700m)

Start point	Spiliá monastery
Distance	12km
Difficulty	3
Walking time	5hr 45min
Height gain	250m
Height loss	300m
Waymarks	None

The recommended route for this stage is along the bed of the Koumbourianítikos river, a tributary of the Akhelóös. The riverbank path has long since disappeared, so you do have to walk in the riverbed, which involves a good many crossings. However, this presents no problems in summer when the water is low. If you do not mind getting your boots wet, there is no need even to stop and change your footwear; and boots dry very quickly under a Greek summer sun. You might prefer to use a pair of Crocs or sandals. The scenery is magical and there is plenty of shade on the banks.

If the water is high, as it might be after a heavy storm, you would have to take the longer (25km approx), more tedious, but easy road route along the western flank of the Koumbourianítikos valley through the villages of Aetokhóri and Sikiá. I have walked the river in April with the water thigh-deep in places, but I would not recommend it, especially not alone.

Looking W from the monastery, you can see an isolated two-storey house on the crest of a steep-sided spur at eye level about 2km away, with a mobile phone relay mast close by. Follow the track from the monastery gate, crossing a gully and keeping L at the junction with the tarmac. At the house (E00284095 / N04348927; 815m), turn off the road R and go down the faint track beside it to the fenced enclosure round the mast. Don't let anyone tell you there is no path and you need to go by the road: I cleared and marked the path myself, with streamers and cairns, in October 2016! Pass along the L side of the fence and keep straight ahead on the path, following the narrow crest of the spur among evergreen oaks.

Spiliá monastery

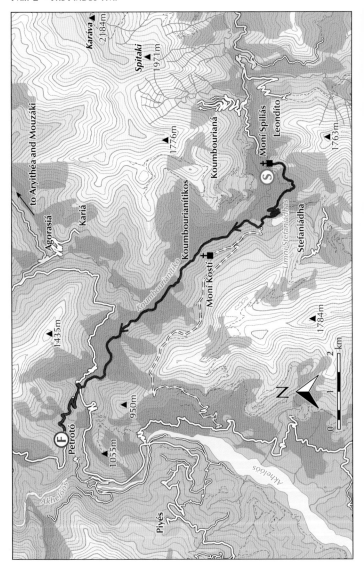

Below, to the left, you get glimpses of the turquoise **Stefaniádha lake**, which was formed in 1963 when an earthquake set in motion an enormous landslip that dammed up the stream. The northern tip of the lake is where you want to get to, where the dirt road to Sikiá runs.

Some 5min from the lone house, the nose of the spur begins to dip steeply down among dark fir trees. The path, the line of which is reasonably clear, here doubles back L to descend along the L flank of the spur overlooking the lake, zigzags again R after passing under the arch of a fallen fir, then back again L. The oaks seem thicker and darker here and the ground underfoot is covered in dead leaves. We built a couple of cairns on this L reach, just before the path disappears into a thicket that was too big for us to clear at the time.

Turn 90° downhill. There is no undergrowth, so you can see clearly under the trees; with luck our streamers will still be visible. After about 50 metres you again encounter the clear line of the path descending on a R-ward reach. Follow it down, round a further sharp L bend and thence steadily down to join the dirt road (E00283854 / N04349261; 664m; **50min**). The lake waters are out of sight, just the other side of the moraine in front of you.

Turn R on the road and bear L round the N tip of the lake – just a few paces. There is a kind of car park space L, and on the R a couple of bulldozed banks of stone and terrace. Climb down to the lower 'terrace' and look over the edge. Between you and the river, which you can see, there is a messy, steep, stony descent, with plane trees either side and more or less open in the middle. There are signs of path.

The L edge of the scree is a bit firmer for the first 50 metres or so; after that you must begin to angle gradually diagonally R. Do not keep straight down or wander into the trees on the L or you will end up on the edge of an enormous red earth cliff. The line is fairly obvious; we left red paint marks and streamers on scattered trees. Towards the bottom R corner of this descent you encounter a sort of gully in the edge of the woods, which you follow more or less straight down for the last 50–80 metres to come out on the stones of the riverbed. The whole descent takes about 20min (**1hr 15min**).

Once in the riverbed, follow the water downstream on the L bank. When the water is low it is easy going. Even in the narrows – where it is deeper and faster – you can generally make your way round on the bank.

The **Koumbourianítikos riverbed** is wide and both banks are lined with plane trees. The valley is deep and traps the heat in the middle of the day, so it is best to make an early start; the bulk of Mt Karáva to your right gives shade until about 10am.

There are few signs of life any more. You see the odd ruined cottage. It is a lovely and lonely spot, the sense of isolation heightened by hearing nothing but the sound of the water, which runs often in two or three channels. You will make well over 20 crossings before you are done.

The riverbed route to Petrotó (photo: Jane Laurie)

After 50–60min the valley widens and you feel less enclosed. At around **3hr 15min** you come to a confluence with another river flowing from the NE along another wooded gorge. Keep L, following the L bank of the combined streams. Not long after, you pass some idyllic summer sheepfolds deep in the shade of the bankside planes.

After 3hr or more in the riverbed, you come to the now defunct works area for one of the tunnels for the Akhelóös river diversion project. Leave the riverbed and climb out on the R bank and up the track to the tarmac road by a fork (**4hr 45min**), where the road for Petrotó climbs steeply uphill R. It is a further 2km into **Petrotó** village (**5hr 45min**).

> In **Petrotó**, the *magazeé* (To Monopólio) is on the right on a terrace overlooking the road just past the church. There is plenty of room to camp on the grassy spur just left below the road.
>
> A bus runs to Mouzáki around midday on Tuesday and Thursday. It stops on the main road and does not come up to the village. Check with the *magazeé*.

THE AKHELÓÖS RIVER DIVERSION SCHEME

From the edge of Petrotó you can look down into the start of the finest stretch of gorge in the entire course of the Akhelóös river. The landscape has been totally disfigured by engineering work, part of a scheme to dam and harness the waters of the Akhelóös for hydroelectric production and irrigation in the plain of Thessaly. Work dragged on at enormous expense for nearly 20 years, in violation of the international Ramsar Convention on wetland conservation and of a Natura 2000 protection order for the wildlife and plants of this region. The EU withdrew funding and Greece's own supreme court more than once ruled the scheme illegal.

It appears finally to have been abandoned, but the work already completed includes a real eyesore of a dam upstream at Mesokhóra, a hydroelectric plant at Glístra, various tunnels and lines of pylons. The inspiration for the scheme was entirely political: to secure the votes of the farmers and prosperous towns of the Thessalian plain. An unbelievably expensive white elephant and a horrible eyesore!

STAGE 14

Petrotó (700m) to
Kalí Kómi (600m)

Start point	Petrotó
Distance	10km
Difficulty	1
Walking time	3hr
Height gain	100m
Height loss	200m
Waymarks	None

If you want to avoid the tarmac tramp to Kalí Kómi, call the Hotel Alkiviádis (English spoken) and they will come and fetch you.

It is roughly a 3hr tramp to Kalí Kómi, on the tarmac all the way. But there is no traffic; the road is narrow and getting narrower as bits of the outer edge fall into the ravine every year. You pass abandoned smallholdings way below you; a few still survive, largely self-sufficient, making what money they do mostly from sheep or goats. As you approach Kalí Kómi, you will see a number of primitive old wooden stable buildings under the trees, still in use. From the last col – by the mobile phone mast – you look

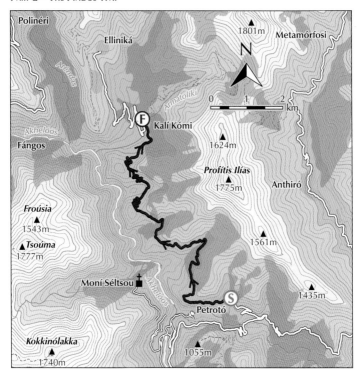

down into a surprisingly lush and very enclosed little valley, with the surviving houses of **Kalí Kómi** (**3hr**) widely dispersed among the trees.

For the *magazeé*, go down into the village. Continue straight along the road till you reach the church above the road R. Go up the steps and the *magazeé* is on a terrace overlooking the valley R at the top. It comes alive in the evening, when everyone gathers for company and a gossip. It belongs to Vasílis Kotsónis, a friend. Show him this guidebook and he will be only too pleased to help you.

> The main attraction of **Kalí Kómi** for the weary walker is the Hotel Alkiviádis, with rooms and restaurant (tel 24450-31511, mob 697-1617644, mob 698-0868455, mob 698-0718584, www.hotell-alkiviadis.no/eng). To get there, continue past the church, down the hill to the Armatolíki stream and a little way up the other side. It is a well-built, well-appointed modern stone building on the right, run by professional hotelier Jeanette Skylas, who is Welsh, and

Kalí Kómi: ewe with a broken leg

her Greek husband Thomas; in summer they are often helped out by Jeanette's Greek brother-in-law and Norwegian sister-in-law.

There is no friendlier or pleasanter place to stay anywhere along the Píndos Way, especially for non-Greek speakers weary of struggling with the language. There are no shops or other accommodation in Kalí Kómi. If you do not speak Greek, Jeanette is your best source of information and advice for miles around.

SIDE TRIPS FROM KALÍ KÓMI

Should you decide to take a bit of a break at the Hotel Alkiviádis, there are a couple of beautiful short walks you could do.

1) Turn left out of the hotel and go downhill to the bridge over the Armatolíki stream (5min). A path follows the right bank as far as a partially restored stone watermill (20min). Thereafter the valley narrows to an overarching rock canyon, obliging you to cross back and forth through the water before disgorging you into the ravine of the Akhelóös itself (50min) at a really beautiful spot with pools deep enough for swimming.

A short distance downstream on the same bank of the Akhelóös, there is an even narrower canyon, Váïna, by which you could return to Kalí Kómi. The first stretch is no more than three or four shoulder widths across. Where it begins to widen out and you can get up the bank, it is a bit of a scramble up the valley side to the left through overgrown fields to get back to the Kalí Kómi road just before the last col. It takes about 3hr to complete the circuit.

2) A further possibility is to make your way down the right (true left) bank of the Akhelóös itself for 600–700 metres – you may need to wade – to where the Aréndas, the next tributary stream, comes in from the right below a very obvious wooded and rocky eminence, said to have once been the site of the monastery of Ayía Karakounisíou. For a shorter – and drier – route, leave the bank of the Akelóös at the foot of this eminence and clamber up its flank to a small saddle just back from its highest point, whence you head down to the bank of the Aréndas and turn right upstream.

After a short distance you come to a beautiful arched bridge, built (as far as I have been able to ascertain) in 1241, which would make it the oldest in the country. In the old days, it carried the main 'road' from the independent medieval principality of Árta across the Píndos to the important town of Tríkala on the plain of Thessaly. (The bridge is 50min from the confluence of the Armatolíki with the Akelóös.)

STAGE 15
Kalí Kómi (600m) to Moskhófito (850m)

Start point	Kalí Kómi
Distance	19km
Difficulty	2
Walking time	4hr 30min
Height gain	650m
Height loss	450m
Waymarks	None

There are two ways of getting from Kalí Kómi to Mesokhóra: one way (described in Stages 15 and 16) is by a mixture of tarmac and track as far as the Stavrós shrine; the other (described in Stages 15A and 16A) is the more interesting and challenging route, following the Akelóös river to Mirófilo and going over the lower slopes of Mt Khadzí.

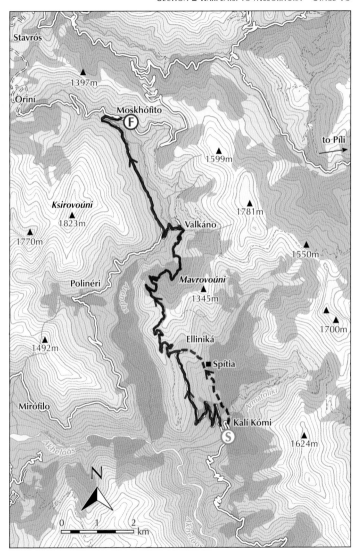

First stop is **Elliniká**, the village that lies just under the ridge about 5km up the hill N of Kalí Kómi and 300m higher (**1hr 30min**).

Elliniká by the old path

Coming from Kalí Kómi village towards the Hotel Alkiviádis, cross the river and take the track R (signed Armatolíki; 5min) by a red-roofed house on the first L bend in the road. Keep straight ahead, ignoring a L turn to a house, till you come to a chapel L (10min). Bear L, ignoring a track down to a house on the R. Past a tin shrine and a 'field' on the R, the track descends through trees to cross the stream coming down from Elliniká. There is a conspicuous water pipe L of the path with red paint marks. Immediately after crossing the stream, turn L up the bank, pass a plane tree and begin to climb, zigzagging steeply up the nose of a spur through the scrub, to reach some old 'fields' at the top (**50min**).

Keep up the L edge of the first 'field', following the rim of the now deep stream gully to your L. Clamber over a collapsed terrace wall and bear diagonally R and slightly uphill through the second 'field'. There is a copse of trees on a mound to your L. Keeping just below it, bear L round it along the upper edge of another grassy 'field' and you will come to a ruined stone house and a clear path (1hr).

Bearing R, the path brings you in 5min (**1hr 5min**) to two shuttered but recently restored cottages with red tin roofs (water on the terrace of the first). A track to Elliniká begins just behind them. For the moment keep straight up the old path L of the track and directly behind the cottages. In 5min (**1hr 10min**), past a fenced enclosure with new trees, you come to an inhabited cottage and sheepfold, marked **Spítia** on the map. Leave the house to your R and join the track just above it. The path ahead is blocked by fences. Follow the track to the first L bend, then to the second, R, bend (**1hr 20min**). Just past it is a large juniper tree, conspicuous among the surrounding smaller shrubs.

Directly opposite a clear earthy path climbs the L bank of the track into more *poornáree* scrub. Bear briefly R, then L and a couple of minutes later turn sharply R up a wide stony path beside a fence which brings you to a modern chapel at the corner of the village cemetery (**1hr 30min**). Pass the chapel and head diagonally L across a grassy 'field' with electricity poles. Bear R along the fence of an orchard with the deep stream gully to your L. At 1hr 45min you reach a tarmac lane in **Elliniká** by the village *plateéya*, *magazeé* and church.

From Elliniká, continue up the road for about 2km to the junction at the foot of the Mavrovoúni peak where you take the L turn up to the col (**2hr**). From here on, the road is no more than a dirt track. A kind of natural amphitheatre opens ahead, leading down L into the Aréndas river valley below the village of Polinéri. The big peak opposite is Mt Khadzí (2038m).

The track continues, contouring round the head of this amphitheatre to another col exactly opposite, where the long winding descent to **Valkáno** begins, through beautiful forest all the way (**3hr 30min**). There is a *magazeé* on the right as you enter Valkáno village.

The tarmac starts again here. Cross the river by the bridge below the village (fountain) and turn R at the junction with the Polinéri–Moskhófito road. Follow this all the way to **Moskhófito** (big spring under trees on L just before village; **4hr 30min**). You can get a meal at the magazeé, but there are no rooms. There is plenty of room to camp close by.

STAGE 15A
Kalí Kómi (600m) to Mirófilo (750m)

Start point	Kalí Kómi
Distance	9km
Difficulty	3
Walking time	4hr
Height gain	300m
Height loss	120m
Waymarks	None

The more interesting and more demanding way to reach Mesokhóra is to go via the Akhelóös riverbed and the village of Mirófilo. It involves very little road-walking but it is dependent on the water level in the river.

Turn left out of the Hotel Alkiviádis and go downhill to the bridge over the Armatolíki stream (**5min**). A path follows the R bank as far as a partially restored stone watermill (**20min**). Thereafter the valley narrows to an overarching rock canyon, obliging you to cross back and forth through the water before disgorging you into the ravine of the Akhelóös itself (**50min**). This is a really beautiful spot, with pools deep enough for swimming.

Follow the Akhelóös riverbed upstream for about 5km to a point just below the monastery of Áyios Yióryios. I have only done half this river section but my experience confirms that of the friend who marked the route for the relevant Anávasi map. You have to cross the river several times, but that presents no problem between June and October when the water is no more than a couple of feet deep if you cross at the upstream edge of the sections of rapids – except perhaps after a prolonged storm. The pools are often deep enough to swim, which in summer is a real bonus. The shingle banks are wide and not too hard on the feet; for much of the way you can see well ahead.

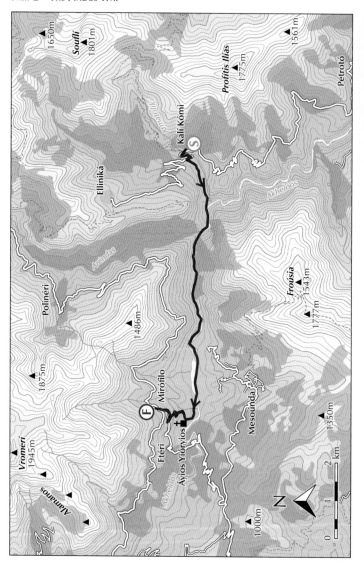

Áyios Yióryios monastery

Once past the Fángos side gully on the south bank, which is about half-way, the ravine widens considerably. For the last 30min you will find yourself walking on the south (true R) bank among lots of small plane trees. Just about where these come to an end and the river bank steepens again (about 3hr from first reaching the Akhelóös; **4hr** in total), cross to the plane-lined north bank, aiming for the location E00269576 / N04359545, where a not very clear path, albeit marked with streamers in the trees, leads in a north-westerly direction under the plane trees, over a stony dry streambed and through scrub to come out on a wide grassy track (**4hr 15min**).

Turn R uphill for 150m, then L beneath a tree-lined bank. The track ends at a well-fenced field with a shed in the corner. Just before you reach it, a path climbs back R up the tree-lined bank and follows the boundary wall of **Áyios Yióryios** up past its fortified entrance to a road (**4hr 30min**).

ÁYIOS YIÓRYIOS MONASTERY

The monastery of Áyios Yióryios (St George) dates from the 14th-century. Its fortress-like exterior testifies to the violence of the times it was built in. Much survives, including two chapels with beautiful frescoes, some of them signed by monk-artists from the monastery of Ayía Paraskeví in Samarína, two weeks' march further north on the Pindos Way. It is being lovingly restored with funds from a London-based Cypriot benefactor. To visit you have to get the keys from the *magazeé* on the *plateéya* in Mirófilo.

It is another 30min uphill on the tarmac to **Mirófilo village** (**5hr**). Turn R from the monastery and R again at the main road. There is a small guesthouse near the *plateéya*. George Raptis, the mayor, has been a friend for 40 years. If you need any help ask for him – and show him this book!

STAGE 16
Moskhófito (850m) to Mesokhóra (850m)

Start point	Moskhófito
Distance	9km
Difficulty	2
Walking time	3hr 15min
Height gain	400m
Height loss	400m
Waymarks	None

Cross the stream in Moskhófito and take the road doubling back L (W) after 500m, signposted Oriní. Cross the river at Platanákia and again at **Oriní** (**1hr 15min**) where the tarmac ends. Climbing out of Oriní, you reach the top of the ridge among tall firs at around 1250m (**2hr**).

The ground levels out and you emerge into meadows and abandoned fields, passing a water trough L. The track heads NW on the east-facing slope of a spur running down from Mt Khadzí (2038m). Ahead R you see the track winding up from the Mesokhóra road to the new-looking, mainly summertime, houses of Spítia. In about 30min (**2hr 30min**) you come to the crossroads by the shrine of **Stavrós**, with a series of telephone masts on the knoll in front of you.

There is a blank signpost, clearly meant to indicate the direction of the path to Mesokhóra, and a large orange paint sign a few steps down L. This marks the head of the waymarked path descending the flank of the spur on which the masts stand, but is surprisingly difficult to follow because of encroaching juniper bushes. Our route is much simpler, taking the easternmost or upper of the two paths marked on the Anávasi map.

Follow the track that leads up towards the masts. At the top of the incline, where it begins to bend sharply R round the back of the mast enclosure, go straight ahead, descending the grassy crest of the spur pretty much clear of the firs and keeping always close to its L (or W) edge. Do not drop down either side more than a few paces. In about 20min, still right on the crest of the spur, you come to a junction with a path going R down to a small chapel, whose pink roof you can see behind some trees, then

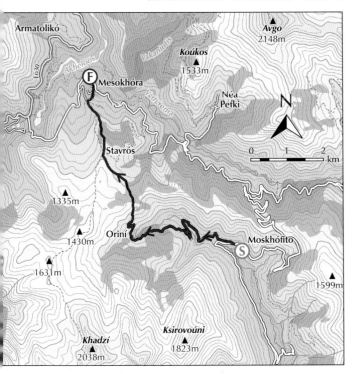

almost at once to a junction with the lower path that you did not take at Stavrós, which slants in L.

Continue NW, still on the line of the spur, and in 10min hit a track leading downhill into **Mesokhóra**. Bear R for the centre of the village and the *magazeé* (**3hr 15min**).

In **Mesokhóra**, the Hotel Akhelóös (mob 697-7803074; open all year) is just down to the right from the *magazeé* in the centre of the village. There is a daily bus to Píli and Tríkala in summer (Monday and Friday at other times of the year).

STAGE 16A
Mirófilo (750m) to Mesokhóra (850m)

Start point	Mirófilo
Distance	17km
Difficulty	3
Walking time	7hr 15min
Height gain	1000m
Height loss	1050m
Waymarks	Frequent in second half

Leaving Mirófilo, follow the road W from the *plateéya* and bear up R at the fork shortly after. Continue for about 1km to a plane-shaded stream gully where a concrete ramp forks uphill (E00268494 / N04360881; 778m). Turn R up here, passing first one and then a second house/farm. The concrete ends and the track begins to zigzag gradually up the mountainside. Pass a flat grassy area under plane trees (good for a campsite, but no water) with a rotting orange Lada car (E00268377 / N04361234; 913m). 45min later, heading W now, you pass a large water tank (E00267742 / N04361796; 1095m) on the R before rounding a corner into the gully at the head of which lie the Alamánc sheepfolds (**1hr 35min**).

Descent from Vromerí and Khadzí to Mesokhóra

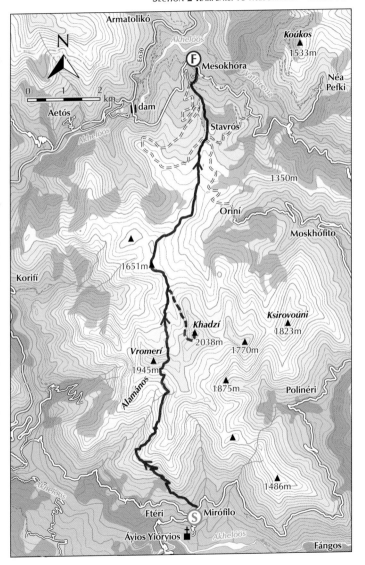

The track follows the R flank of the gully for 35min (**2hr10min**) and peters out. Continue up the rocky flank of a side gully, round the head of it (seepage/spring) and on to a small grassy saddle (E00268338 / N04363459; 1453m; **2hr20min**) with a view ahead of the Alamáno huts. You are above the treeline here. There is a beautiful little ruined settlement of huts on the knoll above you to the R, called Kompliá (beautiful campsite; you can get water from the seepage mentioned above).

From the saddle the path continues on the R flank of the main valley for 15min or so before beginning to drop down into an intervening gully and climbing up to the Alamáno huts (**3hr**). From here you zigzag up open slopes in a NE direction to hit the ridge just E of the 1945m high point, known as **Vromerí** (**3hr 45min**).

At your feet, a deep valley opens up, bounded on the N side by a sharp rocky ridge with the path to Mesokhóra heading clearly N. Drop down into the valley, heading for the intermediate ridge at E00268849 / N04365757 (1674m), reached in 30–40min (**4hr 25min**). Some 5min later you come to a signed fork in the path (E00268843 / N04365908; 1668m). Straight ahead leads to Mesokhóra.

Back to the right, the other branch of the fork leads up, into and round the scree cirque that leads to the obvious col below the sharp 2038m peak of **Khadzí** towering to the right (about 1hr to the top; red paint; retrace steps to the signed fork).

To continue to Mesokhóra, keep along the spine of a grassy ridge, with a gully R separating you from the western scree slope of Khadzí. Another 15min bring you to a first small col, a further 5min to a second, opposite the end of the main Khadzí ridge to your R (E00268860 / N04366650; 1598m; **4hr 45min**). There is a red diamond sign on the bump L. Continue N, traversing across the grassy east-facing slopes in front of you; be careful not to lose too much height. There are yellow-and-black paint blazes as well as signposts.

After 50min (**5hr 35min**), at a col leading to the NW side of the ridge, turn R down the ridge to a lone tree (3min) just above a lower col where a shepherds' track passes. Bear 30° up the grassy ridge ahead to the top of the knoll (red diamond; E00269220 / N04368075; 1464m) and continue along the spine of the ridge. At **5hr 55min** you reach a prominent stone cairn (E00269654 / N04369016; 1416m) with a fallen 'To Khadzí' signpost. Continue down the now broad ridge known as Malórakhi just slightly W of N for another 20min until you come down to a track at E00269789 / N04370014 (1230m). Here, turn R and continue down to the crossroads by the shrine at **Stavrós** (**6hr 30min**), with a series of telephone masts on the knoll in front of you.

Ignore the waymarked path descending the flank of the spur on which the masts stand, and instead follow the track that leads up towards the masts. This is the easternmost or upper of the two paths marked on the Anávasi map. At the top of the incline, where it begins to bend sharply R round the back of the mast enclosure, go straight ahead, descending the grassy crest of the spur pretty much clear of the firs and keeping always close to its L (or W) edge. Do not drop down either side more than a few

Komblíá: abandoned sheepfold

paces. In about 20min, still right on the crest of the spur, you come to a junction with a path going R down to a small chapel, whose pink roof you can see behind some trees, then almost at once to a junction with the lower path that you did not take at Stavrós, which slants in L.

Continue NW, still on the line of the spur, and in 10min hit a track leading downhill into **Mesokhóra**. Bear R for the centre of the village and the *magazeé* (**7hr 15min**). See end of Stage 16 for Mesokhóra accommodation and bus details.

SECTION 3 MESOKHÓRA TO MÉTSOVO

Krithária sheepfold on the Peristéri massif (Stage 20A)

This section covers the country north and west of Mesokhóra and the valley of the Akhelóös (known locally as the Aspropótamos), whose headwaters lie just beyond the village of Khalíki. It is the most southerly extension of Vlach territory in the Píndos.

The Vlachs are a pastoral people, semi-nomadic until the 20th century. The largest surviving community have their home in the northern reaches of these mountains. Today they are citizens of the Greek state and their culture daily becomes more and more indistinguishable from the Greek, but their really distinctive feature has always been their language, which is Latin, not Greek, and closely related to Romanian.

Their villages number about two dozen and are scattered from Pakhtoúri just west of Mesokhóra to Aetomilítsa/ Dénsko on the slopes of Mt Grámos on the Albanian frontier. In the old days, the possession of flocks made the Vlachs relatively rich. Their control of the wool trade extended their commercial influence throughout much of the Balkans and they founded banks and trading houses as far away as Vienna and Odessa. Because of their strategic position – in particular astride the Katára pass above Métsovo, the principal east–west trade route across the Píndos – they enjoyed favourable tax status under Ottoman Turkish rule, and the town of Métsovo became a sort of de facto Vlach capital. The substantial houses in villages such as Kalarítes and Siráko still bear witness to this former glory.

In spite of obvious decline, the flocks still return in summer, and in the *magazeé* you can still hear the elderly speaking in their unfamiliar tongue.

This is also the beginning of bear country, although they can be found further south. The Greek bear is the European brown bear. There is no reason to be afraid of them, not even when camping. The shepherds see them as they are out on the mountains day and night all through the summer. And some bears get a taste for sheep meat – a relatively easy meal – so they do try to get into the flocks at night. Generally they are very careful not to encounter humans and will only attack if they feel cornered. It is not unusual to see footprints, droppings (especially in autumn when they gorge on the scarlet cornel berries which give them diarrhoea), substantial rocks that have been turned over, and long grass flattened as if someone had drawn a sledge over it. You will be lucky to get an actual sighting. I have only seen them twice in 40 years. The same goes for wolves: I saw my first in 2017. Each time I was in a vehicle and that, I think, is significant. If you are on foot they hear you coming long before you get a sighting. In a vehicle, moving quickly, you surprise them.

LOCATION

Mesokhóra lies on the river Akhelóös, 50km west of Píli, the gateway to the region strictly known as the southern Píndos. It is a totally different world from the flat landscape and numerous towns of the Thessalian plain that stretches east from Píli.

MAPS

- Anávasi Topo 50 (1:50,000) 3.2/4.2 *South Píndos: Tzoumérka, Peristéri, Kóziakas, Avgó*

BASES

In **Mesokhóra**, the Hotel Akhelóös (mob 697-7803074) is just down to the right from the *magazeé* in the centre of the village. It is open all year.

Gardhíki has a *magazeé* in the square. For a hotel bed you need to continue 20min south down the road to **Athamanía**, to the Hotel Veloúsi (tel 2434-096500).

Kalarítes is not only one of the most beautiful mountain villages but it has perhaps the most characterful *magazeé* in the whole of the Píndos range, run by Napoléon Zágklis and his wife Lambriní (tel 2659-061518, mob 697-2265961, zagklisnap@gmail.com, www.xeno nasnapoleon.com). Located just above the village square, it provides good food and sometimes music too, comfortable and attractive rooms nearby, and is open all year. Two or three other *magazeé* operate in season.

Khalíki has several *magazeé* in the square and a welcoming guesthouse, La Casaria, on the northern edge of the village. Open all year and providing good food too, it is run by Andromache Tsoukála and her husband Yiórgos Argyriádis (tel 2432-087410, mob 693-7103906).

Métsovo offers all amenities: shops, banks, restaurants, hotels. We recommend the Hotel Egnatia on the main street 200 metres uphill from the main square (tel 2656-041900, www.hotel egnatia.gr).

Ascent to Hodja's ridge. Ascend the rocky spur in the bottom of the central V and bear diagonally L to meet the dirt track in the centre of the photo (Stage 21)

ACCESS

For Mesokhóra, several buses run daily from Athens (Odhós Liosíon terminus) to Tríkala and from Tríkala to Píli. In summer, there is one daily bus onwards to Mesokhóra, although there is always a good chance of a lift from Píli.

For Métsovo, there are several buses daily from Tríkala, and two from Yánina, which is accessible by daily flights from Athens.

STAGE 17
Mesokhóra (850m) to
Gardhíki (1100m) or Athamanía (1000m)

Start point	Mesokhóra
Distance	16.2km to Gardhíki (15.1km to Athamanía)
Difficulty	2
Walking time	4hr 50min to Gardhíki (4hr 10min to Athamanía)
Height gain	350m to Gardhíki (250m to Athamanía)
Height loss	100m
Waymarks	None

The day's route follows the beautiful valley of the Akhelóös (or Aspropótamos), staying close to the riverbank on easily navigable jeep track all the way. There is little variation in altitude. The only possible problem might be the level of the river as the hike involves fording it once at the old settlement of Fortósi. If it is too high, either from snow melt early in the season or after a storm, you can easily reach the track on the west bank by taking an alternative route through the village of Armatolikó, adding about 5km to the journey.

Alternative route via Armatolikó

If you have to take the alternative route, follow the road W out of Mesokhóra towards the horrible dam that was part of the abandoned Akhelóös river diversion project. There is a short section of tunnel on the approach (not really dangerous because traffic is very occasional). If, however, you prefer to avoid it, it is for the moment still possible for someone on foot to follow the old road: turn R before the tunnel, about 2km from Mesokhóra, and cross the river (a pathetic trickle here because of the obstruction of the dam) – with care – by the rapidly disintegrating old Bailey bridge.

After the bridge, turn R up into **Armatolikó**, where you take the lower road R, passing above the first church. Thereafter keep on the main track to **Ayía Triádha**, where you join up with the riverside route. Don't go off into any of the tiny hamlets along the way.

To follow the riverbank route, take the R fork by the *magazeé* in the middle of Mesokhóra and follow it downhill past the Hotel Akhelóös to the Vathírema river, close to its confluence with the Akhelóös. As you approach the bottom of the steep hill, past a traffic mirror on a pole, don't take the sharp L turn; instead, keep straight down through trees to the riverbank (**15min**), where there is a ford and a low concrete bridge. Cross over and follow the track L.

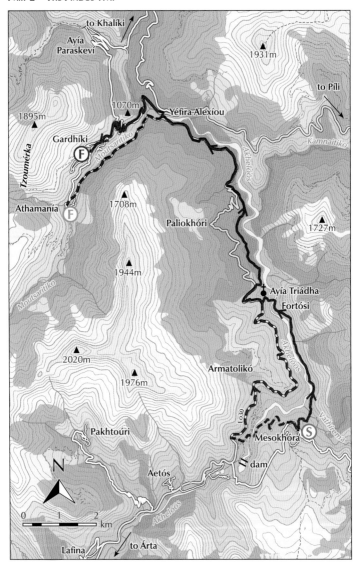

Vathírema bridge at Mesokhóra

Past the confluence with the Akhelóös, the track sticks pretty much to the water's edge all the way to **Fortósi (1hr)**, a tiny scatter of cottages overlooking a patch of fertile alluvial fields. Cross the river from the N corner of the Fortósi fields. Make your way up the flank of the spur opposite by an earthy track that zigzags up past a chapel and red-roofed house to join the main track from Armatolikó to Gardhíki (**1hr 25min**). Turn R. Round the L bend in front of you a gully cuts back into the valley side. Continue along the track to the point where you emerge from this re-entrant, and after the L bend take the first turn steeply down R, passing the chapel of **Ayía Triádha (1hr 40min)**. Do not miss this turn; do not be tempted to continue straight on by the concrete track climbing up L a little further ahead. The concrete track leads to the almost deserted hamlet of Paliokhóri and is much longer.

The Ayía Triádha track – rough and stony – soon bends L and follows the W bank of the Akhelóös N. In about 45min (**2hr 25min**) the surface becomes a bit smoother and you pass the junction (L) with the road coming down from Paliokhóri. Another 45min (**3hr 10min**) brings you to the modern **Yéfira Alexíou bridge** (*yéfeera alekseéyoo*) that joins up with the main road from Píli and the Thessalian plain.

For Gardhíki, cross the bridge and bear L. There is now no avoiding the 5km trudge, with 250m of height gain, up the hairpins to the village of **Gardhíki (4hr 50min)**.

You can get a meal in **Gardhíki** but for the moment there is no formal accommodation. There are plenty of places to camp round about.

If you are planning on spending the night in a bed, head for **Athamanía/ Moutsiára** and the Hotel Veloúsi, in which case do not cross the Alexíou bridge but keep straight on and bear left along a tributary stream on a new riverside track for 4km (about 1hr from the bridge; 4hr 10min from Mesokhóra).

STAGE 18

Gardhíki (1100m) or Athamanía (1000m) to Matsoúki (1100m)

Start point	Gardhíki or Athamanía
Distance	20.5km from Gardhíki (21.1km from Athamanía)
Difficulty	3
Walking time	7hr 30min from Gardhíki (8hr from Athamanía)
Height gain	1150m from Gardhíki (1250m from Athamanía)
Height loss	1150m
Waymarks	None

This is a long hard day, not because of any technical difficulty or danger, but simply because of the distance and the ascent. There are a couple of places where you need to pay particular attention to navigation: one is finding the bridge just a few minutes west of Ayía Paraskeví/Tzioúrtzia, the other is crossing the col between the Gréku spring and Krithária. For most of the day you are in open country and can see clearly where you are going. The route crosses the watershed of the Akhelóös and enters that of the Arakhthós, which drains the outer, western flanks of the Píndos from Métsovo to Árta.

From Athamanía, it is a 30min walk up the hill to Gardhíki, from where our cumulative walking times begin.

From Gardhíki, follow the road NE out of the village for about 800m. Where the tarmac begins to descend towards the Akhelóös valley (**15–20min**), turn L on the road that cuts across the shoulder of the prominent bluff in front of you. Pass an elaborate wayside shrine and descend N at a gentle gradient to the village of **Ayía Paraskeví**, lying in the narrow valley of a tributary stream. Ayía Paraskeví is still more commonly known by its old name of Tzioúrtzia, which is pronounced a bit like Georgia. Make your way L down through the village towards the mouth of the rocky defile in the valley bottom by the church of Áyios Yióryios (**1hr 5min**). A path leads into the defile and immediately crosses a bridge to the true L bank of the stream.

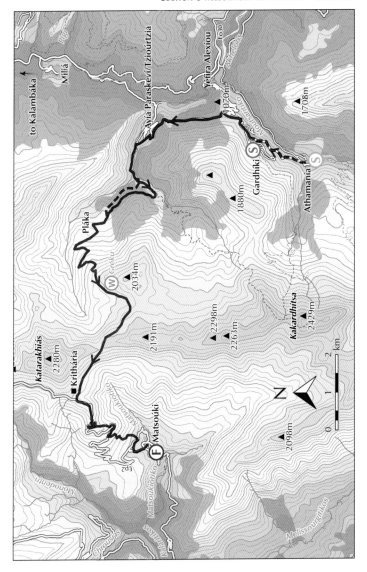

177

Turn uphill L. The valley bottom is filled with plane trees. The path climbs parallel to the river past some walnut trees and remains of old terraces (**1hr 15min**), while a steep fir-clad slope rises on the opposite bank. Past the terraces, with a red arrow painted on a rock, keep down to the L until you come to a goat pen. Here, ignore the red arrows pointing you onwards and up to the R; instead, cut down L to the river to find a bridge (E00263576 / N04383518). Cross over and turn L, winding up a steep path to join the end of a rough forest track that climbs steadily SW up the R flank (true L) of another stream gully.

We missed the sharp R turn in the path at E00263257 / N04383243 and continued SW to join the main shepherds' track by the stone chapel of Áyii Apostóli (**1hr 52min**) on the edge of some grassy fields with a spring and cattle trough nearby (E00262933 / N04382821; 1150m; great campsite). If you have taken this route, fork R on the track immediately above the chapel and follow it N through the firs back towards the now deep valley of the Tzioúrtzia stream, known as Kalí Piyí. In about 30min you exit from the trees. The path you did not take comes in from the R at E00262579 / N04383920; you would have saved perhaps 25min by taking it.

Ahead of you now is a big expanse of grass with a tin-roofed shed on the crest of the spur opposite; you could see it already from the village of Tzioúrtzia. Steep grassy slopes grazed by sheep and cattle enclose the valley in front of you. You reach the shed in about 30min (E00261789 / N04385017; 1359m; **2hr 50min**). There is a spring right on the crest of the ridge behind the shed. This area is called **Pláka**. Behind the shed, the Kalí Piyí valley swings sharply W.

The gradually deteriorating track continues up the slopes above the shed in long zigzags. It is generally easier to follow the track than make your way across the steep slope, cutting off the loops. As it gains height, the track heads into the upper part of the Kalí Piyí valley, high on its L flank. At **4hr** you reach the copious **Gréku spring** L of the track at an altitude of 1739m, with a dedicatory plaque (E00260326 / N04384557).

From the spring, continue up the track (heading S here) and, as you climb, you will see two huts above you to the SW. About 12min from the spring, the track turns sharply R and crosses a small streambed. Immediately after, a very poor track bears off L (S). Continue straight on the better track for a few minutes and arrive at a fork. The L fork leads to the two huts, which are now behind you. The clearer R fork continues to a building which is still out of sight, lying in a hollow due W of the Gréku spring.

Leave the track here (E00259995 / N04383928) and climb gently NW on grassy slopes towards a ridge. As you reach it, the solitary building in the hollow is now visible below you to your R. In front of you is a large rock-strewn bowl. You will see two distinctive rock bands across the bowl and above you – the L one being lower than the R one. You need to pass above both bands.

Traverse to your L around the bowl, climbing gently to reach the L side of the lower rock band. Here there are faint traces of an old path. Follow these over the 'top' of the rock band, passing a prominent white boulder to your R.

At the top of the band are a couple of flat grassy areas. Cross these and follow the obvious zigzags of an old path up to an obvious notch at the top of the 'taller' rock band above and to your R. At the notch (**4hr 50min**) there is another flat grassy area, which you cross.

Follow the fairly clear remains of the old path and head in a generally WNW direction, passing several more flat grassy areas to reach a false col. Here, the true col, with a stone windbreak, comes into view. Continue along the path in a NNW direction to reach it (E00258708 / N04384554; 2020m; **5hr 5min**), just S of the 2280m Katarakhiás peak. From the col, you look directly down on the village of Matsoúki, 1000m below in the valley bottom.

From the col, the line of the old mule route is clear, traversing N along the W slope of Katarakhiás to a shepherds' hut with a water trough about 1km distant at a locality called **Krithária** on the Anávasi map. Towards the end you slither and slide rather steeply down to the hut (**6hr 15min**), where you join the shepherds' track and turn R. After a few minutes you come to a more important dirt road and turn L to begin the long zigzagging descent to Matsoúki (7–8km if you stick to the road). You are traversing at a gentle gradient the steep E and S flanks of a spur whose peak is marked on the Anávasi map as 1811m.

To join the Kalarítes to Khalíki ridge route

For a more adventurous route, you could turn R on the dirt road to reach the Báros col in 1hr, turn L down the tarmac road for about 3km and just past the Nikoúltsa spring join up with the ridge route from Kalarítes to Khalíki (described in Stage 20A).

As you round the nose of the spur after about 1km, you can cut S down the nose to the L end of the next big loop underneath you. Turn R for about 300m and cut

View of Matsoúki and the river
Arakhthós from Krithária

down S again (E00256409 / N04383560) to the L end of the next loop (E00256531 / N04384320). There is no real path but it is not difficult and you save yourself a good couple of kilometres. When you reach the road at the bottom, turn L and enter the village of **Matsoúki (7hr 30min)**.

> **Matsoúki** is another Vlach shepherding village, with some 18,000 sheep on the village pastures in summer. There are three or four cafés and a taverna by the *plateéya* and church. There are no formal rooms to stay in, but, if you ask, someone will provide at least a space for you to spread out your sleeping bag.

STAGE 19
Matsoúki (1100m) to Kalarítes (1150m)

Start point	Matsoúki
Distance	8km
Difficulty	2
Walking time	2hr 45min
Height gain	450m
Height loss	300m
Waymarks	Frequent

Leave Matsoúki village by the upper tarmac road. Below and ahead is the deep gorge formed by the Matsoukiótiko river that runs down off the slopes of Mt Kakardhítsa. On the first L bend, a paved and signposted path heads R (W) along a ledge below the crags to the monastery of Víliza (**Moní Vílizas**, *monée véeleezas*), clearly visible on a spur about 1km W (**35min**). The buildings occupy a natural grassy belvedere above the gorge. Spring water is available from a tap by the walnut tree in front of the main building.

Continue past the monastery, bearing NW, along the contour into oak woods. In a few minutes you come to a fork in the path, where you turn briefly downhill. There are thickening oak woods below you. Do not go down into the woods. Keep along the contour after the initial short descent, moving R round a grassy spur, and descend to a small pathside spring (E00254347 / N04383657; marked on the Anávasi map; **50min**).

The path continues descending gently to an open grassy spur with a blue tin shrine (E00254176 / N04383218; 900m) perched on a kind of natural belvedere. On the terrace below it, a collapsed stone hut juts out over a confluence of valleys, with the village of Kalarítes visible at around 1200m on the opposite slope to the W. Turn 90° R (N). The path is clear, running along a sort of grassy ledge through thick vegetation, descending slightly but remaining pretty much on the contour line around 850m

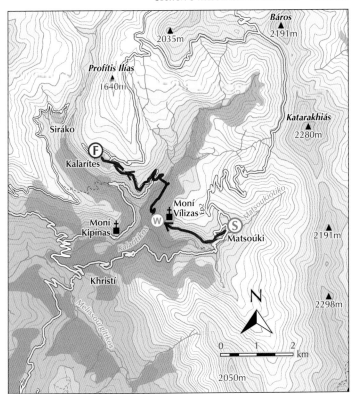

except for two brief sections of descent. At **1hr** the path makes a sharp L turn downhill, doubling back on itself for 3–4min before making a R hairpin and continuing N along the contour. Cross a dry gully (**1hr 10min**) beneath some big rocks. Some 15–20min later, the path makes a L hairpin, followed by a R hairpin and descends to a very overgrown bridge arching high across a river, boiling away in a deep shady defile beneath (**1hr 30min**).

Cross over and turn R. The path, recently cleared and signed, climbs up above the true R bank of the river (wonderful spot to bathe after a short scramble down to the water), then veers L uphill and away from the river. It winds steeply back and forth to reach the main road to Kalarítes by a large road sign (**2hr**). There is a spring 100m down the road L. Turn R at the signpost and follow the tarmac uphill for about 45min to the entrance to **Kalarítes** village (**2hr 45min**).

181

Kalarítes village

In **Kalarítes**, comfortable accommodation in two pretty stone houses is available with Napoléon Zágklis, who runs the beautiful old *magazeé* just above the main square (tel 2659-061518, mob 697-2265961); there is good food here, too. Napoléon and his wife speak reasonable English. They can help you with all kinds of things; for example, if you want to avoid some of the road-walking on the next stage, ask Napoléon to find you a lift with a shepherd.

KALARÍTES

Kalarítes is one of the loveliest and least-known villages in Greece. It stands on the rim of a deep, trench-like gorge. Like many of these mountain villages, it only acquired a road some 30 years ago. The zigzagging cobbled stairway, or *skála*, that used to be the only access from the valley below is still there.

Scarcely inhabited today but often well restored, the imposing stone and stone-roofed houses of Kalarítes testify to the former wealth of its gold- and silversmiths who monopolised the jewellery business in Ali Pasha's 18th-century Yánina. The original Bulgari jeweller began his career here. There is a small museum in the village, illustrating these smiths' work.

If you have time, try to visit neighbouring Siráko, an equally dramatic village, whose prosperity was based – among other things – on making capes for Napoleon Bonaparte's navy. It is an hour's walk away on the other side of the gorge via a steep and airy path.

STAGE 20
Kalarítes (1150m) to
Khalíki (1200m)

Start point	Kalarítes
Distance	23km
Difficulty	3
Walking time	7hr 30min–8hr
Height gain	850m
Height loss	800m
Waymarks	None

The route now crosses the Peristéri massif. For the first half, you have a choice: you can take the tarmac road to the Báros col, which runs along the eastern flank of the Profítis Ilías ridge just north of Kalarítes, or the dirt track to the west. The two routes converge in the upper valley of the Kalarítiko stream near the spot marked on the map as Mandrí, now used as a base for a large herd of cows. The distance is the same, but it is much more agreeable. The western route takes about 30min longer.

A third option (described in Stage 20A) is a beautiful and airy ridge walk, also reached via the Báros road.

The eastern route

The route starts from the fountain and car park at the upper N edge of the village and heads first E, then due N along the E flank of the Profítis Ilías ridge, for just over 6km (about **1hr 30min**). Here on a R hairpin (at about 1550m altitude), turn L off the tarmac where it turns sharply E and continue N on a shepherds' track over a low col, leaving a red-roofed shepherds' shed on your L almost immediately and crossing to the W side of the main ridge. The track heads N along bare grassy slopes, pretty much on a level after the initial descent. After about 30min, with the Mandrí cowshed very obvious on its stubby spur to your L, you pass a powerful **spring** and cattle trough (E00254321 / N04389987; 1485m; **2hr**). This is where the western route comes in to merge with the eastern route.

The western route

For the western route – leave the fountain and car park, bear L where the tarmac veers R and pass the chapel of Áyios Athanásios. The track, which serves the shepherds who graze their flocks in the area known as Kourkoúmbeta, climbs gently at first, then

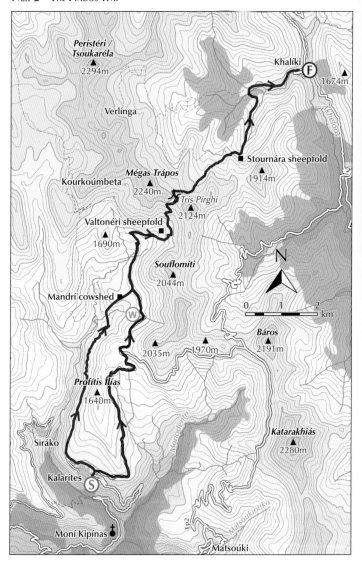

follows the 1300-metre contour for about 5km (**1hr 15min**), before descending into and crossing a deep stream gully. 30m short of the ford (E0025397 / N04389647; 1255m), on a grassy bank with scattered wild rose bushes, go up R and bear L for 5min, above the deepening stream gully below L. You come to a substantial stone-walled spring (E00253676 / N04389657; 1293m) in a little hollow among scattered bushes and open grassy patches. Ahead of you is a stony scrubby hill with some crags on its R slopes. The gully you have been following lies to its L; another subsidiary gully runs below those crags to the R. Aim diagonally L from the spring, in a northerly direction, towards your original gully, with a very obvious rounded hill with a hut on top blocking the view ahead. This is Mandrí: where you want to get to.

From the spring continue uphill bearing L-ish towards and across a dry stony stream gully aiming for the L slope of the hill dividing this gully from your original gully. Do not go R up this gully you have just crossed. As you climb towards the L slope of the hill ahead the path becomes quite clear. You are climbing up the R flank of your original gully. A subsidiary gully full of juniper scrub joins from the L. Your clear path descends to and crosses this side gully (E00253924 / N04389815; 1353m), before petering out in the scrub. The best thing is to follow this path towards the grassy slope at the head of the gully and begin to cut R up the grassy slope on your R wherever it seems easiest. The Mandrí hut is out of sight over the top of this slope at this point. It is only a ten-minute climb. On the top of the hill there is a ruined hut and just behind it a second inhabited one (about 1hr from where you left the Kourkoúmbeta track; **2hr 15min** total). Behind the hut a muddy track curls R to join the one described in the eastern route. The spring described in the eastern route is a few minutes back to your R. Turn L for Valtonéri.

The cumulative walking times from this point on assume an eastern route start. Remember to add 30min to each time if you took the west route.

The two routes are now one, and you are heading into the slopes that form the water-shed of the Kalarítiko stream. Ignore a first L turn on to a descending track and shortly after (**2hr 30min**) bear L (NW) across a gully. The track zigzags back R and joins another track running across the slope above you. Take the R branch (L leads to Kourkoúmbeta) and keep on to where it ends at the buildings of a **sheepfold** (**3hr**), nestling on a small plateau looking back out over the valley you have come up. This is Valtonéri, or moot-shiára as the Vlachs call it: the marshy place, where a number of stream gullies come together. The point on the ridge that you need to reach in order to cross over to Khalíki is the low point visible directly behind the sheepfold to the L.

About 100 metres E of the sheepfold, the grassy plateau is cut by an eroded dry gully. On the far side of it you can just make out the line of the old path following up the R flank of the gully. Cross the gully, climb up on to the stony path and head L uphill (E00255022 / N04391865). In about 15min, cross the gully to the L by an obvious crossing point and begin gradually gaining height in a northerly direction. Keep a sharp eye on the line of the path. It is not used any more, but it does become a little clearer – often in fact quite clear – as you get your eye in. At E00255198 / N04391577 (1747m), you reach a rocky promontory and a few minutes later a ruined stone sheep pen on a bit of flat grassy ground (E00255338 / N04391865), about 40min above the Valtonéri sheepfold (**3hr 45min**).

From here to the ridge, you need to gain another 200m in altitude, heading in the same northerly direction at the same kind of gradient for about 1km. (I can't give a precise time, for the mist came down and I had to turn back. That was late October; it won't happen to you in summer, when you can see the low point in the ridge up ahead of you.) The pass is a clear nick in the ridge just NW of the 2124m peak with its trig point. The line of the old mule road is still clear in the grass as you approach. It takes the best part of an hour, making a total of **4hr 30min–5hr** from Kalarítes.

From this point on the ridge (E00255590 / N04392864; 1862m), known as **Tris Pírghi** ('three towers', after the stone cairns that used to mark the spot), the old path zigzags L, then R, down to the shepherds' track traversing the slope directly below. The village of Khalíki lies at 40°, out of sight from here.

Cross the shepherds' track. The path drops down at 40° to meet the line of the stream in the wide, shallow gully below. The spring that gives rise to the stream – and does not dry up – lies 150 metres along the track R and about 50 metres below it (E00255730 / N04392862); possible campsite. Follow the path due N beside the probably dry streambed to a point where it passes through a narrow rocky defile

Stournára sheepfold

186

(E00255804 / N04393445; 1753m) and descends, bearing 40°, to join the track again. Keep L down the track. You can see a sheepfold ahead and below the track R. Continue along the track for nearly 20min, then bear steeply down R to the fold, which lies on a jutting shoulder above a deepening stream gully at a place called **Stournára** (E00256293 / N04394204; 1591m; **6hr**).

The Stournára sheepfold consists of a neat stone hut and milking pen. The onward path – part of the old mule road from Kalarítes to Khalíki – begins just below the hut on the E side (E00256370 / N04394188; 1546m) and descends northwards at first on the upper side of a wall of big rocks, losing height in a series of zigzags (general direction about 66°) as it drops down across a bracken-filled slope towards the stream gully R, eventually bearing R to a grassy open space dotted with big rocks (E00250495 / N04394226; 1484m; **6hr 15min**), with a waterfall hidden out of sight to the R among beeches.

Bear L down towards the stream. The path is often obscured by grass and bracken. In general, follow the L bank of the stream (30°–40°) as it flows down NE, never distancing yourself more than 50m away from it. You come to a stretch of old cobbled walled path running in under beech trees. Come out in the open a few moments later and round the upper edge of another beech copse. Cross a dry stony gully (E00256536 / N04394334; 1427m) and continue down through bracken and grass, following a line parallel to the main stream and never far from it. At E01256712 / N03494533 (1399m) you reach the edge of the fir forest (30min from Stournára; **6hr 30min**).

Once in the forest you descend quickly at a gentle gradient on a soft needle-strewn path running along a ledge of flattish ground high on the L flank of the stream gully. After about 15min the spur you have been descending begins to steepen quite precipitously and the line of the path becomes unclear. You can must make out the line of the old zigzags dropping L off the nose of the spur. Follow them down, bearing leftwards, as best you can to come out in open grassy ground by a good track (E00257036 / N04395181; 1228m; **7hr**).

Turn L on the track and in a few paces come to a ford. Cross over and follow the track to its junction with the main track from Peristéri. Turn R, following the true L bank of the river down to **Khalíki** (**7hr 30min**).

KHALÍKI

Khalíki is another seasonally inhabited Vlach shepherd village, on the banks of the Akhelóös river, close to its headwaters. Many of its sturdy traditional houses survive, along with two or three very attractive churches, in particular Ayía Paraskeví overlooking the western end of the *plateéya*.

At the northern end of the village just above the main road bridge, the *ksenónas* La Casaria (accommodation and food) is open all year round (tel 2432-087410, mob 693-7103906). It is definitely walker-friendly and its presence

makes Khalíki an attractive proposition as a base for a few days from which to explore the Peristéri massif, doing day walks, for example to Tris Pírghi, Verlínga, Tsoukaréla – Peristéri's highest peak – and the source of the Akhelóös.

There are also three or four *magazeé* on the square, which functions in summer as the centre of village social life.

The church of Ayía Paraskeví in Khalíki village

At the entrance to the village, one road forks uphill L and leads to the upper side of the *plateéya*; the lower road brings you in just below the *plateéya*.

STAGE 20A

Kalarítes (1150m) to Khalíki (1200m): the ridge route via Tris Pírghi, Mégas Trápos and Verlínga

Start point	Kalarítes
Distance	24km
Difficulty	3
Walking time	8hr 20min (+ 1hr 20min for Tsoukaréla summit)
Height gain	1260m
Height loss	1230m
Waymarks	Only on descent and inconsistent

From the fountain and car park at the upper N edge of Kalarítes, head first E then due N along the E flank of the Profítis Ilías ridge for just over 6km, to reach the track junction with the route to Kourkoúmbeta (**1hr 30min**). Continue up the main tarmac road towards the pass of Báros for about 30min, ignoring a track on your R leading to a sheepfold below the road.

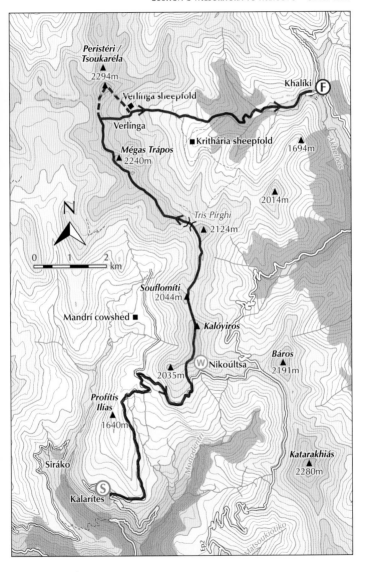

Although this is **bear country**, I have seen bears only twice in 40 years. My most recent sighting was in 2016 on the northern slopes of the Báros col, in the upper reaches of the forest.

A few minutes after the track R, a short spur of track leads up L towards another sheepfold. The Anávasi map marks the start of the ascent to the ridge from here. There is no obvious path, but it is straightforward to make your way up the S slope of point 2035m bearing NW, then N to hit the ridge about 300m E of the peak. Alternatively, start the climb from the Nikoúltsa spring, about 10min further up the road, since this is the last water until you come off the ridge. You reach the ridge at about **2hr 30min**. There is a sheer drop to the Valtonéri valley. Turn R and follow the ridge N along a series of faint goat trails on the R side of the ridge, avoiding the steep drops to your L.

As you descend from **Kalóyiros**, drop down steeply L of the ridge to a col with a good stone windbreak (**3hr 10min**), then continue on the ridge following the path/goat trails in a generally N direction, passing just R of point 2044m, **Souflomíti**. Continue to the notch S of point 2124m. A good path contours L on the SW slope of point 2124m to the **Tris Pírghi col** (**4hr**). From here, you could follow the route down to Stournára and Khalíki (see Stage 20).

To continue to Mégas Trápos, head NW along the ridge. Pass a subsidiary peak, and then another with two large prominent square stone cairns (**4hr 30min**). There are sheer drops to the R, but continue along the ridge, following trails just L of it to reach the summit of **Mégas Trápos** at point 2240m (**5hr 5min**). From here, continue up and

Looking south-east along Mégas Trápos ridge

down along the ridge, staying just L of it, for another 30min or so until you drop down on to a track (**5hr 35min**) just above the seasonal tarn at **Verlínga**. The track is blocked to prevent environmentally damaging 4 x 4 tourism.

Optional ascent of Tsoukaréla

From the track above Verlínga, just keep N along the gently undulating ridge in front of you and up the cairn-lined turf to reach the highest summit of the Peristéri massif, **Tsoukaréla** (2294m; 30min).

To rejoin the route to Khalíki, return the way you came to the base of the grassy summit ridge. Bear SE at 106° down to the Aspróvrisi spring at E00253462 / N04395702. Traverse 200m R, cross a second stream and turn down a dry gully L at E00253576 / N04395565 (2013m). You are just above the **Verlínga sheepfold**. Don't go down to it, but bear diagonally R towards an open grassy plateau, where a natural gully funnels you down to a rock with a red arrow at E00253973 / N04395356 (50min from Tsoukaréla summit). Here, you join the route from Verlínga.

To reach Khalíki (without ascending Tsoukaréla) from the track above the seasonal tarn at Verlínga, turn R (E) down the track, past the depression in which the tarn lies, and bear L (N) beneath the crags of Mégas Trápos, over a bump and down towards the huts of the **Verlínga sheepfold** just below a conspicuous rocky defile. Before reaching the huts, turn down R at 125° – a large rocky bump blocks the view ahead – to a red arrow on a rock at E00253973 / N04395356 (**6hr 5min**). This is where the route from Tsoukaréla comes in.

Descent from Verlínga towards Krithária sheepfold

At the foot of the bump, bear R and then round L, keeping the bump L (red arrows). The twisty rocky height of Mégas Trápos is in front of you. Go down through a chaos of boulders, where a few metres of the old cobbled road (*kaldereémee*) survive, to E00254292 / N04395330 at the foot of the boulder slope (**6hr 30min**). The way ahead is not clear: turn L at 330° up a grassy gully for a few minutes, then R and downhill across open grass to the track, visible below. Hit the track by a large boulder at E00254464 / N04395496 (1779m). It is marked with a red arrow pointing L towards the Mégas Trápos peak for those coming up.

Cross the track. The path continues on the other side, following below the track, bearing R and down into and along the bottom of the gully by the stream to a red arrow. Bear L across a flat grassy area contained within a wide bend in the track. Cross the track again where the stream crosses (two red arrows; E00254792 / N04395316; 1721m; **6hr 45min**). Below the track, the path continues, bearing slightly L. It almost joins up with the track again, then bears away R (remains of the old cobbled road visible) and down pretty much due E to the *stroónga* (sheepfold) at **Kritháría**, cutting off a considerable loop in the track. To avoid a possible congregation of dogs at the Kritháría sheepfold (water), stay on the track and keep straight ahead (E) at the fork about 200m N of it (**7hr 5min**). The old path follows parallel and lower down the slope. After 300m the track makes a sharp L hairpin (E00255628 / N04395485; 1623m). Leave it here and turn off R down the line of the projecting spur until you hit the main path again (**7hr 15min**), heading L.

A few minutes later you come to a noticeable juniper bush with red-and-white plastic strips hanging from it (E00255950 / N04395350; 1530m). Here, the path starts to zigzag down L towards the bottom of a deepish gully with fir trees growing either side. At the bottom of the gully (plastic strips and red arrow), cross to the L bank and descend E into the firs. In less than 10min, pass through a grassy clearing. Less than 15min later, you emerge into a patch of bracken and on to the main track again at E00256708 / N04395569 (1469m).

Turn L and downhill. A short way along, the path bears down L again through a rough corridor between the trees, while the track bears off R. Meet the track again (**7hr 45min**) at E00257060 / N04395467 (1301m) by two stone cairns. Turn L on the track. The next shortcut, signed by big red paint marks, is very overgrown. Keep on round the next sharp L bend till you come to the more open ground at Kraniés, with the remains of old terraces planted with cornel trees. Here, stone cairns mark the start of the old route (the line of the path is visible) down across the grass and through the trees to rejoin the track (which has swung off L) and follow the willow-lined river into the village of **Khalíki** (**8hr 20min**).

STAGE 21
*Khalíki (1200m) to
Métsovo (1050m) via Hódja's ridge (1634m)*

Start point	Khalíki
Distance	17km
Difficulty	3
Walking time	5hr 20min
Height gain	940m
Height loss	840m
Waymarks	None

Head N out of Khalíki on the Métsovo road. Just past the ramp leading up to La Casaria guesthouse, a track forks R off the tarmac and follows the W (true R) bank of the Akhelóös river. It passes a **cowshed** and ends at a **goat pen** in about 1km (**15min**).

Alternative route via the east bank
If you prefer to avoid the dogs which may be lurking at the cowsheds, cross the river by the bridge below La Casaria and turn L on to the path that follows the E bank. You pass a spring in a stone shelter by a footbridge across the river. Keep going until you are opposite the **goat pens**, then cross back over the river to join up with the route on the W bank (25min).

Just before the infant **Akhelóös** swings sharply right at the spot known as Paliomonástiro, a small tributary stream comes down behind the goat pens to join it. The springs and streams hereabouts are where this great Greek river rises.

Overshadowing the end of the track by the ramshackle buildings of the goat pens is a large willow E00259340 / N04397386; 1186m. Climb 30 metres L up the grassy slope above it and you will see the clear line of the old mule road. No one goes this way any more but it is followable, and far preferable to slogging up the tarmac. Turn R and follow it. Very soon you find yourself crossing a loose scree slope, created largely by rubble from the construction of the tarmac road above you. Below to your R is the tributary stream, whose far bank is formed by a steep rocky spur. Keep going for 150 metres or so, pretty much on a level.

In front of you is a smaller rocky spur, with a dense cluster of fir trees on its crest a little higher up. On its flank straight in front of you are the clear remains of an old stone embanked stairway for the mules. Your faint thread of path leads you

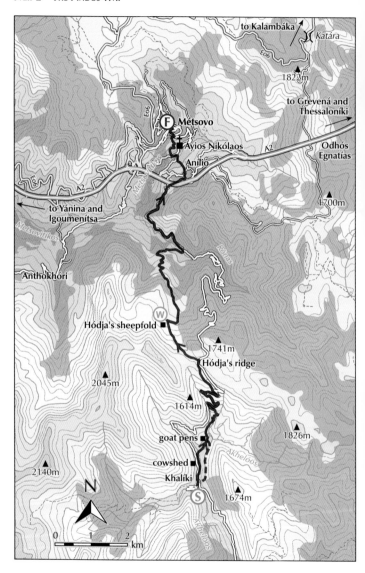

to it. Cross the little stream and zigzag up L to the top of the first stage of the spur. You cannot go straight up the spur line; the way is blocked by firs. Go horizontally R into more open ground on a faint but clear path for about 80–100 metres, then bear diagonally L uphill through the encroaching scrub. If you keep your eyes skinned, you can pick out the line of the overgrown path from the channels worn in the grassy ground by generations of mule traffic. Bear very close to N, a little way down R from the crest of the spur.

After about 20min (**1hr**), you meet a muddy farm track cutting horizontally across the slope. Cross the track and head more or less straight up the opposite bank, bearing slightly R to come out on the tarmac road. Turn R for 50m to a left-hand hairpin. Go round it. On your R there is a gently rounded open grassy space (E00259598 / N04398254; 1480m) with a rock in the middle (red paint mark). Go straight uphill past the rock and under the branches of a biggish thorn tree (E00259561 / N04398254; 1485m). The path has been out of use for many years and we have only had time to do a rough clearing and waymarking.

At E00259651 / N04398371 bear 90° R across a bracken-filled slope to pass below the edge of the fir wood that has grown up in the last 40 years to obscure this stretch of path. Clear signs of the old route are still visible, like the section of cobbles at E00259694 / N04398357 (1478m) in the bottom R corner of the fir trees, where you turn diagonally up L into the trees. At E00259752 / N04398360 curl up L round the edge of the firs with a gully opening to the R (east). Zigzag up R, L, R round the edge of the firs, then bear up L along the R edge of the firs above the gully, through a 'tunnel' of trees to reach the rubble embankment of the road by a white shrine (E00259706 / N04398442; 1502m) on the crown of a hairpin bend (**1hr 30min**).

Cross the road and go up a slanting path on to the spur opposite, which the road has cut. Follow it up all the way, parallel to the road, which remains to its R, until you reach the top of the pass known as **Hodja's ridge** (E00259284 / N04399485; 1634m; **2hr**).

Hodja's ridge (*rákhee tozó Khódza*) is presumably named after some long vanished Turkish landholder. Far to the north-west, towards the frontier with Albania, you can make out the bulk of Mt Gamíla.

At the crest of the pass where the road bends sharply R, leave the tarmac and head down the grass- and bracken-filled gully opening below you on a bearing of about 320°. Beech woods grow on the flanks of the gully. As you emerge from the gully into open meadow now scattered with juniper bushes, bear a few degrees closer to N towards the very visible sheepfold you can see beside a rough track about 10min ahead of you (**2hr 30min**). This is **Hódja's sheepfold** – *to mandreé too Khódza* (water).

Turn R and follow the track. There is a second sheepfold close by on the R with a junction just below it. Bear L here. Bearing right would take you back to the main Khalíki–Métsovo road in the beautiful beech woods to your right. Continue more or

Leave Hodja's ridge here and head down the gully in the centre of the photo

less on a level for 10min or so among open fir woods. After a second junction, where you keep R, the descent steepens until at a third junction you bear sharply R and down to cross the river Rónas by a small concrete bridge. This is followed by a sharp climb up to the narrow tarmac road that joins Khalíki and Anílio, the twin town of Métsovo (**3hr 30min**). Turn L on the road and follow it all the way into **Anílio**, passing under the modern highway.

> The modern highway, the **Odhós Egnatías**, is named after the ancient Roman road that linked Italy with Byzantium. The modern version connects the Adriatic with Thessaloníki and the north of Greece.

Pass the Hotel La Munte (Vlach for 'on the mountain'; **4hr 20min**) and turn L by the café with a large plane tree and an URSA trail sign in the wall. Go down the cobbled path that descends into the ravine separating Anílio from its twin, Métsovo. Cross the river, turn L and very quickly R to pass (visit) the **Áyios Nikólaos monastery**. Continue uphill to the path that climbs R and steeply up through the first houses of **Métsovo** to the *plateéya* (**5hr 20min**), which is home to several eating places and a copious fountain. There are several hotels. We recommend the Hotel Egnatia (tel 2656-041900, www.hotelegnatia.gr), which is 5min from the *plateéya* up the steep main street past the fountain.

Métsovo's main square

MÉTSOVO

The Vlach town of Métsovo is something of a metropolis in mountain terms, the unofficial capital of Greek Vlachdom. It is one of the few towns in Greece that has made a conscious effort to preserve its traditional architecture, costumes and customs. The result – sadly, although perhaps inevitably – is that it has become a rather over-commercialised tourist attraction. This means, however, that there are several hotels and eating places, banks, shops and transport connections, making it a useful hub for mountain activities.

The town has long been a prosperous centre of the Vlach wool and mule-teering business, and the weaving trade still flourishes; take a look at the Tositsa Foundation folk art museum, which also gives an idea of what a rich Vlach house looked like up until the 20th century. There is a small ski resort on the mountain-side above the town.

SECTION 4
MÉTSOVO TO THE ALBANIAN BORDER

Emerging on the tops above Ayía Paraskeví (Walk 28) (photo: Jane Laurie)

Section 4 represents the most northerly part of the Píndos Way, covering the heavily forested mountainous country between Yánina, the country's third largest city, and the Albanian frontier, which from the end of World War II to 1990 marked the southernmost reach of the Iron Curtain. It is cut by two enormous ravines – Víkos and Aöós – and dominated by three of Greece's highest mountains: Gamíla (2497m), Smólikas (2637m) and Grámos (2520m), the latter right on the frontier. Much of it is Vlach territory.

time immemorial the principal crossing over the Píndos mountains, connecting the Adriatic port of Igoumenítsa with the lakeside town of Yánina, capital of the province of Épiros (*éepeeros* in Greek), and the more prosperous cities of the Thessalian plain. It is pretty much the centre of the Píndos range. The old road has recently been superseded by a modern version of the Roman Via Egnatia, which connected Rome with Byzantium/Istanbul. Today it bypasses Métsovo and cuts under the Katára pass in a tunnel, heading north-east for Thessaloníki, Greece's second city, in just a couple of hours.

LOCATION

Métsovo lies at the foot of the Zygós (now Katára) pass, which has been since

MAPS

- Anávasi Topo 50 (1:50,000) Macedonia 6.4 *Valia Kalda*
- Anávasi Topo 50 (1:50,000) Epirus 3.3 *Gramos, Smolikas, Voio, Vasilitsa*

BASES

Métsovo offers all amenities: shops, banks, restaurants, hotels. We recommend the Hotel Egnatia on the main street 200 metres uphill from the main square (tel 2656-041900, www.hotel egnatia.gr).

Vovoúsa has rooms (Sofía Stangoyianni, tel 26560-22846; on the right just after the high-arched bridge) and there is sometimes a taverna as well. **Dhístrato** offers rooms and a taverna (ask George Pafilis in the *magazeé* on the square).

In **Samarína** you will find rooms, hotels, tavernas and shops. Try Lákis Avéllas at the big *magazeé*/restaurant on the far right corner of the square as you enter it coming from Dhístrato (tel

24620-95278, mob 697-7466474), or La Noi on the downhill edge of the village with its great view and cool bar, a magnet for the young (tel 24620-956600, www.lanoi.gr).

Ayía Paraskeví has rooms and a taverna, while **Kefalokhóri** has the very nice Hotel Fasoúlis and restaurant on its grassy village square (tel 26550-81481). Rooms and a taverna are also on offer in **Aetomilítsa/Dénsko**.

ACCESS

There are two buses a day between Métsovo and Yánina (one a day on Saturday and Sunday), with several onward to Athens; daily flights operate from Athens to Yánina.

Several buses run daily between Métsovo and Athens, changing at Tríkala (Odhós Liosíon terminus in Athens). From Kónitsa to Yánina, there are five or six buses a day on Monday to Thursday, one bus on Friday, and three on Saturday and Sunday.

On the tops above Ayía Paraskeví (Walk 28) (photo: Jane Laurie)

STAGE 22
Métsovo (1050m) to Vália Kálda (1250m)

Start point	Métsovo
Distance	28km (including initial tarmac); 15km (from north shore of the Aöós lake)
Difficulty	3
Walking time	5hr 30min (from north shore of the Aöós lake)
Height gain	1157m
Height loss	907m
Waymarks	Inconsistent: P1 signs on trees as far as Flénga; P6, red paint and E6 thereafter

Just above Métsovo, where the old road climbs up over the Katára pass, is an extensive plateau called Politsiés, to whose well-watered summer pastures transhumant Vlach shepherds have for centuries brought their flocks. It is here that the Aöós, one of the main rivers draining the northern Píndos, in this case through the mountains of Albania to the Adriatic, has its springs. These have been dammed to form an artificial lake that now largely covers these pastures. It is bounded to the north-east by the 2000m ridge of Mavrovoúni, Flénga and Aftiá, with a refuge at about 1800m overlooking the lake. This is where the continuation of the Píndos Way runs.

The start of the route now unfortunately involves 13km of tarmac. It is possible to take some shortcuts, but it is not advisable because of the number of sheepdogs on the loose from June to October. A compromise solution is to take a taxi out of Métsovo to the start of the refuge track at E00254400 / N04412900 on the north shore of the lake or, if you are staying at the Hotel Egnatia, arrange a lift with them.

It makes sense to divide the journey from Métsovo to Vovoúsa, the next village to the north, into two parts. There are at least three good potential camping places. The first, the Mavrovoúni refuge (1hr 30min), comes perhaps a bit too soon, unless you want to get up there in the afternoon, leaving yourself the possibility of doing the whole of the remaining distance the next day. The most spectacular spot is the hollow by the Flénga lakes (4hr). We have chosen the almost equally lovely (and sheltered) needle-strewn ground under the pines when you first get down to the Arkoudhórema river (5hr 30min) in the Vália Kálda (Vlach for 'warm valley').

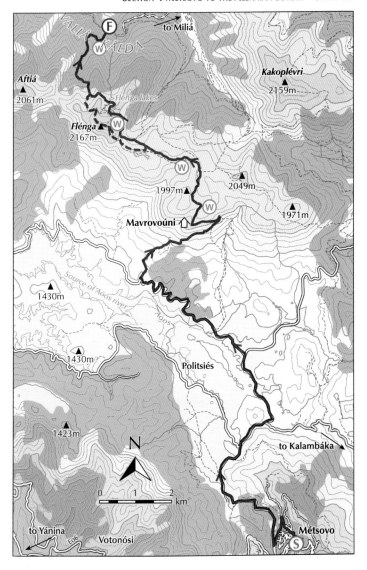

Assuming a car journey from Métsovo and a start up the refuge track from the **Aöós lake shore**: the hike begins with a steady slog in a NE direction for **1hr 15min** to a fork by a (probably dry) spring, where the track for the refuge doubles back L (NW). It is another 15min to the **Mavrovoúni refuge (1hr 30min)**.

> The **Mavrovoúni refuge** is normally locked but it has a well-protected porch for shelter and makes a good campsite. The views over the lake and away to the south Píndos are superb. The nearest sure supply of water is the spring on the far side of *páde la láklu*, the Vlach name for the green meadow that lies 15min higher up the track behind the refuge (there is also a cowman's hut at the green meadow).

Continue up the track behind the refuge to reach *páde la láklu*, the green meadow (**1hr 45min**). From this meadow follow the track NW, then N, through a rather desolate landscape scattered with felled and rotting trees to its end at E00256187 / N04415742 (1956m; gentle gradients). About 100 metres ahead, there is a P1 and a red diamond on a tree. Bearing 290°, then 280°, descend a shallow grassy gully round the head of a deeper gully to a spring at E00255730 / N04416139 (**2hr 45min**). Continue uphill and L at 280° and over a small saddle into another broad grassy gully at 308°.

At **3hr** you reach the head of this gully at E00254681 / N04416510. Ahead, grassy ground with scattered trees slopes down into the start of a substantial valley

Ascending Flénga peak

descending NNE. To reach the Flénga lakes, keep straight ahead more or less on the contour for about 10min. You can see a yellow P1 sign in a clump of young pines some way L above the faint path. The rounded stony Flénga peak is now straight ahead. Once past the clump of young pines, climb steeply L up on to the narrow neck of land (E00255248 / N04416413) that serves as a bridge to the rising SE ridge of Flénga, and turn 90° R. You can now see the artificial Aöós lake again below L. If you wish to continue over Flénga, follow the line of the ridge and descend on the far side, just past the Flénga lakes.

At the point where the Flénga ridge begins to rise (**3hr 20min**), turn steeply down R to join a clear but unsigned rocky path (E00253942 / N04416786; 1962m), traversing through box scrub N and NW round the flank of the peak to a rocky shoulder at E00254037 / N04417053 at the edge of a red boulder scree. Go down R for 30–40 metres, L across the boggy ground in the hollow below and up the opposite side, bearing L to a dead pine by a seepage. Passing a spring at E00253881 / N04417414 (1979m), climb the slope ahead to the rim of the grassy cwm (**4hr**) in which lie the two small jewel-like **Flénga lakes**: a beautiful campsite.

From the crest of the ridge enclosing the W side of the lakes, keep W for 200 metres, then bear down N into the trees and the gully opening below. To find the head of the marked path, look for a sheepfold under the ridge E00253230 / N04417896). The path is quite clear with red marks on the fir trees.

The path descends N, then NW across the head of a gully on to the narrowing spine of a spur that descends N in mixed forest of beech and black pine between two streams. P6 signs, small cairns, occasional red paint and plastic strips mark the way. After 50min (**4hr 50min**), cross to the true R bank of the R stream. Be very careful here, for the path – at least in spring – can be invisible, obscured by young beech growth, fallen leaves and boulders, and there are no markings.

After crossing the stream, continue for 30 to 40 paces before bearing gradually L at about 30°. Don't go too high above the stream (into an area full of big boulders) and don't lose height either. Keep more or less on the contour, climbing very slightly. In 5min, you come through the dense beech growth on to a slope with more mature, widely spaced beech trees mixed with black pine, and suddenly the path becomes clear, 'lined' by fallen trunks. It levels off along the contour above a steep grassy slope covered with pines. After 10min, pass a grassy dingle R, with a P6 on a tree L (E00253093 / N04419202; 1522m). There follows a gentle descent through open pines on the steep grassy L flank of a spur to reach and turn a corner at E00253055 / N04419474 (**5hr 7min**).

The path veers E and down to emerge on the open grassy nose of a spur (P6), overlooking the Arkoudhórema (Bear river) in the valley bottom and a stand of big burnt pine trees. Continue descending E, traversing across a slope and over a small shoulder, bearing S then NE. A few moments later you come to a pathside spring in a clump of beeches, emerge into pines, bearing 50°, and zigzag steeply down to a second spring. Bearing 30–40° you drop down into **Vália Kálda** to a wooden signpost at the junction with the E6 path (**5hr 30min**). The onward route to Vovoúsa (Stage 23) turns L and follows the E6 along the true L bank of the Arkoudhórema. With water from the two springs passed on the descent, you can camp near the river anywhere here.

To return to Métsovo
If for some reason you wish to leave the route and return to Métsovo, turn R (E). The E6 leads in a couple of minutes to a wooden bridge, then on to a path that turns into a forest track which follows the riverbank to its confluence with a stream flowing in from the L. Cross by another wooden bridge a few moments later and emerge in a wide and beautiful meadow by a junction of rough tracks (about 40min). One leads to the village of Kraniá (guesthouse), the other to Miliá, both about 20km away by forest track.

STAGE 23
Vália Kálda (1250m) to Vovoúsa (1000m)

Start point	Vália Kálda
Distance	10km
Difficulty	3
Walking time	3hr 45min via Aöós west bank (3hr 20min via E6 and Aöós east bank)
Height gain	100m
Height loss	400m
Waymarks	E6

Following the E6 signs (either yellow squares or yellow-and-black paint blazes) downstream, cross one tributary stream descending from the S, then a second (E00252607 / N04420455; **25min**). After a few minutes of level going beneath the pines, climb up and over a short sharp rise before continuing again on a flattish stretch on a clear path to reach the riverbank (**50min**). Cross the river and turn downstream on the opposite (true R) bank for 50 metres, where, by a large yellow-and-black arrow, you climb up L. After about 10min (**1hr 10min**), pass through a grassy clearing some way above the riverbank, and begin a steady climb to the top of a pine-clad spur.

The path turns immediately downhill to reach a stream a few minutes later with a waterfall R. Cross over and climb steeply up L to the edge of a landslip (**1hr 20min**), then up R round its top edge and, gradually losing height, traverse down to a large signpost on a tree on the crown of the spur above **Smixómata** (confluence of the Arkoudhórema and Aöós rivers; **1hr 40min**). The signpost indicates Vovoúsa (R), Katafíyio (L) and Vália Kálda in the direction from which you have come. From here, you have a choice of two routes to Vovoúsa.

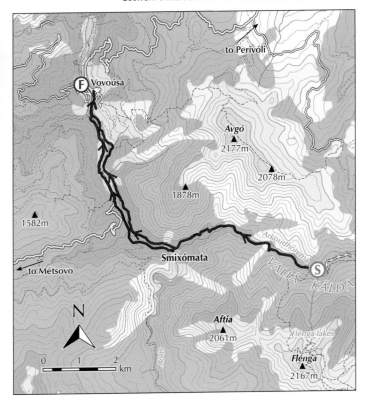

Vovoúsa via the Aöós west bank

The easier route goes via the Aöós W bank. Turn L at the **Smixómata** signpost and continue down to the bank of the united streams, together called the Aöós. Turn L down the bank to the water's edge. About 50 metres upstream there is a yellow Katafíyio sign on your side, plus another on the opposite (true L) bank. Cross the river (almost certainly a boots-off exercise) and take the path up R, which brings you in a few minutes to a clearing in the trees and the start of a forest track (**2hr 10min**). Follow the forest track beside the river, ignoring a L fork after 15min, until you reach the main tarmac road (**2hr 47min**). Turn R. The Katafíyio stands in a riverside meadow some 500 metres along on the R. It is a hotel, with uncertain opening times, and not a refuge (in spite of its name, meaning 'refuge' or 'shelter').From here it is about 3.5km into **Vovoúsa** (**3hr 45min**).

Vália Kálda: the E6 path to Vovoúsa

Vovoúsa via the E6 and Aöós east bank
This is the more interesting route and is the way the E6 goes; keep a sharp lookout for E6 signs.

Turn R at the **Smixómata** signpost. In about 10min (**1hr 50min**) you come to the edge of a big scree slope. Cross over and a few moments later traverse a steep open slope. The path descends to the river (E00249606 / N04420503; **2hr 5min**), where you turn R and follow the water's edge for 5min beneath scree slopes. Climb back into the woods, bearing gradually more N than W through open pines. The path is often obscured by box and heather. Cross a little stream by a patch of open water and 10min later you will be opposite the Katafíyio hotel on the far bank (**2hr 40min**; see margin note above).

About 10min later, cross a stream with an E6 sign on a pine tree close to the main river. In another 5min, cross a flat meadow and re-enter the forest (**3hr**). Shortly after, go straight across another stretch of meadow, cross a stream and start to bear L downhill towards the bank of the Aöós, through a tunnel of greenery and into a riverside clover meadow with old cherry and fruit trees (**3hr 12min**). Cross the meadow in a straight line to meet a grassy track which passes a riverside sawmill, then some sheds, and brings you out on the tarmac by the road bridge. Keep straight along the road and into **Vovoúsa** (**3hr 20min**).

Vovoúsa is a tiny place and very remote, in effect the end of the road. There is a Píndos National Park information centre at the further end of the village (tel 26560-22003, pevovousas@germanosnet.gr, www.pindosnationalpark.gr/en), but it is seldom open.

Vovoúsa

STAGE 24
Vovoúsa (1000m) to Dhístrato (950m)

Start point	Vovoúsa
Distance	16km
Difficulty	3
Walking time	5hr 30min
Height gain	550m
Height loss	700m
Waymarks	Red-and-yellow squares, red paint: inconsistent

The main route of the Píndos Way continues northwards following the E6 footpath to Dhístrato and then on to Samarína (as described in Stages 24 and 25). It is, however, possible to branch west from Vovoúsa to Mt Gamíla and the Zagóri region, which until now has been just about the only bit of Greece's mountains known to foreign walkers. We have described various routes you could do there (see Part 3), from a circuit to a straight traverse, which would allow you to link back to the main Píndos Way if you so wished. If this idea appeals to you, go to Stage 24A for a description of the link.

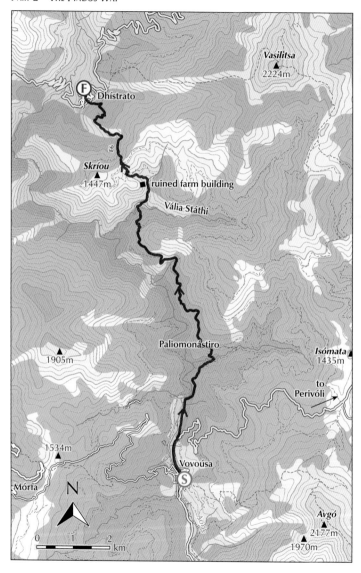

Leave the village by the tarmac road that leads N up the R flank of the Aöós river valley towards Perivóli. About 10min from the Vovoúsa bridge, leave the road and fork L downhill on a rough forest track (yellow-and-black paint marker on tree). In September 2017, the entire E6 path from here to Dhístrato and on to Samarína was cleared and re-signed with red-and-yellow paint flashes, so navigation should be straightforward. Continue along this track through riverside meadows and into a forest of black pine. The track begins to climb. At **30min** you pass a red-and-yellow sign on the L. The forest stretches as far as you can see; I have seen fresh bear prints on the track here.

The track begins to bear E away from the Aöós, high on the flank of a tributary valley. At **45min** keep down L on a logging track. Opposite on the far side of this valley is the locality known as Paliomonástiro, a grassy conical hill with a short white column and the remains of a wooden cross on top. Legend has it there was once a monastery here. At **1hr 5min**, on a R hairpin, a track cuts down L. It is the first L fork you have come to and is easily missed. In 5min it brings you to the river; turn downstream for 20 metres and cross on to a track heading up the opposite bank.

After a steepish climb through open pine woods, you reach a more important forest track (E00248991 / N04428025; **1hr 20min**). Turn L on the track. Very soon you come to some E6 signs and 10min later you reach **Paliomonástiro (1hr 35min)**. There is an expanse of meadow either side of the track, and the hillock with the white column is just to your L. The track climbs steadily for a while, then descends. You are heading N and just W of N up the E flank of the Aöós valley.

At **2hr 10min** ignore the track that turns downhill L. The going is steadily uphill. After 10min you pass a spring R. Ignore the L fork a few minutes later by an E6 and red-and-yellow signs and keep on uphill. Just past the point where the track begins finally to lose height again, an E6 and red-and-yellow sign point L down some wooden steps on to the old path (E00246753 / N04431136; 1198m; **2hr 45min**).

The path winds down steeply through tall pines towards the mouth

Bear prints at Paliomonástiro

of a red, rocky defile where a tributary stream of the Aöós flows down from the NE. In 20min you reach the bottom of the slope by some sycamore trees and emerge from the woods on to a path that traverses R round a rocky spur till it reaches the bank of the stream in a tunnel of willows and greenery (**3hr 15min**). Cross the stream and go straight up the grassy slope opposite, bearing L uphill along the R flank of a second stream gully to quite substantial never-finished and now **ruined farm building** (**3hr 30min**).

From the ruined building, aim up the grassy slope bearing slightly R and into the tall pine trees at E00247033 / N04432290 (red square; 1080m). Keeping to the L flank of the spur, with a deepening gully below L (E6 sign at E00247009 / N04432360), you come to a confluence of two small streams (**3hr 40min**). Cross (E00246998 / N04432498; 1089m) and follow the L stream. The path climbs among open pines. At E00246990 / N04432521 bear up L by a red-and-yellow square on a pine on the R. At E00246650 / N04432647 (1167m), a red arrow on a tree points L, and a little further up a big red arrow points you back R. Through a little grassy clearing (E00246475 / N04432644), guided by an E6 sign, bear up slightly L and emerge from the trees on a sharp R bend in a rough grass-grown track climbing up from your R (E00246431 / N04432645; 1198m; **4hr 10min**).

Continue uphill and just round the next L bend, clamber up the steep, grassy bank (no sign) towards the more mature pines above and bear L straight uphill towards the ridge above. Just below the ridge, you come out on a superior track (E00246342 / N04432956; 1343m; **4hr 45min**). Turn L here, passing a red-topped white wayside shrine at the foot of a pine about 50 metres along. A few moments later, on the R in a narrow nick in the ridge, you can see where the old path passed over (red-and-yellow square). It is marked by a now broken metal shrine (E00246342 / N04432956; 1343m; **4hr 50min**). On a clear day there is a fine view ahead of Mt Smólikas.

From the ridge, a good path (the E6 still) leads diagonally R down to rejoin the continuation of the track you left on the ridge (E00246168 / N04433252). Turn R past a spring and cattle trough. Take the subsidiary track that heads uphill to the R. About 30 metres up here, you should find the continuation of the E6 turning off L and heading NW along the flank of the spur parallel to and just above the track. If you cannot find the continuation of the E6, just follow the track.

Rounding the nose of the spur, you rejoin the track, pass above a pink-roofed chapel and shortly after turn down L at the first junction. You come to a big white cross and a neatly cobbled lane that leads down among the first houses and into **Dhístrato** (**5hr 30min**).

On the *plateéya* of **Dhístrato**, the *magazeé*-cum-taverna, the Briáza (the village's Vlach name), is run by Yiórgos Pafílis (tel 26550-24919, mob 697-20540960). Rooms are available near the *magazeé* with Yánnis Máipas (mob 697-4669250).

If you need help, ask Yiórgos. To leave the mountains at this point, there is a bus to Kónitsa (banks, hotels, main transport routes) on Friday and Monday in summer. A lift is always possible.

STAGE 24A

Link: Vovoúsa to
Skamnéli for the Zagóri and Mt Gamíla

Start point	Vovoúsa
Distance	30km
Difficulty	2
Walking time	8hr +
Height gain	1142m
Height loss	1048m
Waymarks	None

If you decide to include a loop through the spectacular and distinctive villages and landscapes of the Zagóri in your Píndos Way itinerary or indeed to end it in Kónitsa rather than going on to the Albanian border – an additional week's walking altogether – this is the way to make the link.

The route is mostly on well-maintained forestry tracks. There is a section at the beginning marked by Anávasi as footpath which is really disused forest track reclaimed by nature and reduced to slightly overgrown footpath dimensions – it nonetheless makes a worthwhile shortcut. The going is pleasant and easy and mostly in the shade, and there are fine views of the Zagóri and onward route from the Mórfa ridge. There is not a lot of water on the first half and the few streams are quite likely to be fouled by cattle. Further west, however, the Tsoúkas and Alí Pasá springs are pretty reliable.

Leave Vovoúsa by the high-arched bridge you passed as you entered the village. The route begins on the W bank of the river and climbs into the forest. Basically, apart from the footpath section at the beginning, you follow the route marked on the Anávasi map.

The footpath section is well waymarked, but does not follow the exact route shown on the Anávasi map. The starting point (E00245885 / N04424546) is on the L about 2km from the village, exactly where the Anávasi map shows it, just before the main track heads N. It heads briefly S, before looping up WNW. It then crosses another track, continuing WNW. If you miss the starting point, take the L turn a little further along the track and you will join the route again at this point.

After crossing the track, the footpath briefly follows the route shown on the map before diverging from it WNW again (E00244925 / N04424858). The last section runs W again parallel to the Farmáki forestry track, which it then joins (E00244492 / N04424872).

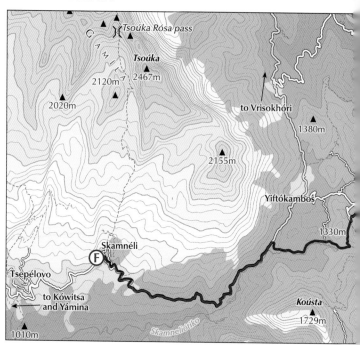

Tsoúka Rósa pass

Tsoúka
2467m

2120m

2020m

to Vrisokhóri

1380m

2155m

Yiftókamboś

1330m

Skamnéli
(F)

Tsepélovo

to Kówitsa
and Yámina

Koústa
1729m

1010m

Skamneliótiko

Salamander

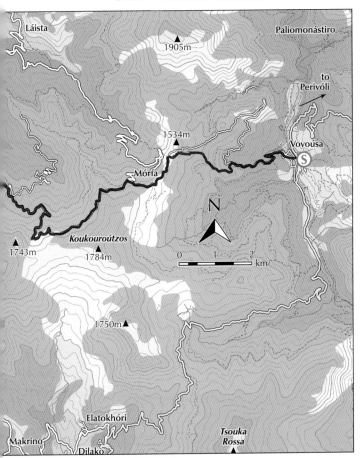

The rest of the route is straightforward. The intersections are occasionally confusing, but the main thing is to keep going roughly W (E00244066 / N04424497; E00243589 / N04424008; E00242889 / N04424118; E00240529 / N04422824; E00239569 / N04424098; E00237655 / N04423491; E00237352 / N04422601). Your track eventually joins the main asphalt road 7km E of **Skamnéli**. The walk to the village runs through forest with plenty of shade.

DHÍSTRATO (950M) TO AYÍA PARASKEVÍ/KERÁSOVO (950M)

Stages 25, 25A, 26, 26A and 27 of the Píndos Way involve getting to the village of Ayía Paraskeví – Kerásovo by the still commonly used old name – and that means crossing the bulk of Mt Smólikas, at 2637m the highest peak in the Píndos and the second highest in Greece. There are two ways of doing this, both too long to do in one go. The first (Stages 25, 26 and 27) is to tackle it via the village of Samarína on its eastern flank, climbing back west towards and over the summit to the mountain lakelet of Dhrakólimni and thence descending north to Kerásovo: a hike that requires three days.

The other possibility (Stages 25A, 26A and 27) is to stay on the south side of the mountain – the Dhístrato side – and make your way to the village of Palioséli by the tarmac road that runs west down the Aöós gorge. It is 24km and could be done by car, which would leave you time to get either to the Smólikas refuge or to Dhrakólimni for the first night, thus cutting the whole trip to two days. If you were to walk to Palioséli, that would of course make this option three days too.

Both routes are beautiful. In the main, Smólikas is rounded, grassy and forested, craggy only on its north faces. The forest is mostly black pine, interspersed with beech on the colder north-facing slopes and giving way at the higher levels to the rubbery-barked *róbolo* or Balkan pine. Because of its geology – serpentine rock rather than the almost universal limestone – it supports an unusual range of wildflowers.

The Samarína route is the more rugged and demanding, and Samarína itself is one of the liveliest and most flourishing mountain villages in Greece and one of the last real centres of Vlach pastoral life. It would be a pity to miss it.

The Palioséli route is easier and if you get Yiórgos Pafílis in the Dhístrato *magazeé* to find you a lift, you gain a day. Even if you choose to walk it (5–6hr), you have the gorgeous scenery of the Aöós gorge to enjoy, including the spectacular alpine crags of Mt Gamíla enclosing the southern flank. There is hardly any traffic and the road sticks pretty much to the contour.

COMPARISON OF ROUTES

Distance	35km via Samarína; 39.5km via Palioséli
Height gain	2397m via Samarína; 1480m via Palioséli
Height loss	2430m via Samarína; 1620m via Palioséli
Difficulty	3
Walking time	15hr 10min via Samarína; 11hr 15min–12hr 15min via Palioséli
Waymarks	Fairly clear and regular

STAGE 25
Dhístrato (950m) to Samarína (1500m)

Start point	Dhístrato
Distance	15km
Difficulty	3
Walking time	5hr 40min
Height gain	850m
Height loss	400m
Waymarks	Red-and-yellow squares, E6

Samarína lies about 10km due north of Dhístrato as the crow flies. The route follows the E6 along the thickly forested eastern flank of the deep and precipitous ravine separating Mt Vasilítsa, with its popular but modest ski station, from Mt Smólikas. From it, you get an all too clear view of the terrible fire damage done to Smólikas' beautiful pine forests in 2000. Luckily no one was hurt in the blaze, but shepherd friends who graze their flocks on those slopes reported that the fire advanced at terrifying speed, setting off a veritable firework display of exploding munitions left in the ground since the end of the Civil War in 1949. Happily, nearly 20 years on, the trees are gradually growing back.

Note that this stretch of path (like the section from Vovoúsa to Dhístrato in Stage 24) was cleared and re-signed in September 2017.

Leave Dhístrato by the tarmac road to Mt Vasilítsa ski station and Grevená. You round the head of a deep gully below the village and after 20min pass a shrine L by the beginning of a rough track. Keep on along the road. Past a trout farm, you begin a long uphill slog, with pine forest either side. To your L is a big gully, which forces you to gain a considerable amount of height before you can get round the top of it.

Keep your eyes skinned around the **1hr** mark. There is a power line R, and to the L a single supporting pole anchored to the ground by a cable. Just past the supporting pole a rough logging track climbs into the pines L of the road. There should be an E6 or red-and-yellow sign (E00246439 / N04436655; 1200m). The road takes a sharp R bend a little further up; do not go that far.

In 5min, the logging track leads into a bit of a clearing, where the way becomes unclear. Turn hard R following the trace of a grassy track at about 20° between the pines. Gradually it bears L, climbing among young pines across the gritty, earthy flank of a spur (several red-and-yellow signposts) until it brings you up on to the crest of the spur (**1hr 30min**) where you turn hard R, doubling back up along the crest of the spur.

215

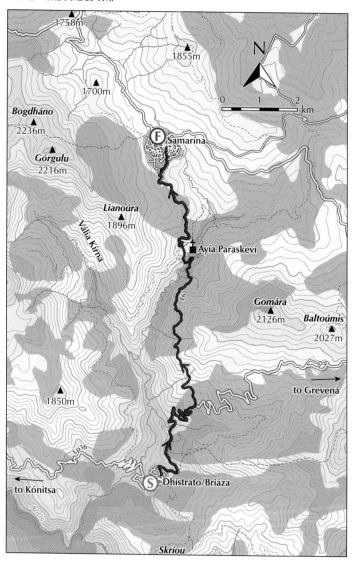

From here on, the path is fairly clear and signed all the way. At **1hr 38min** bear off the ridgeline to the L to round the head of the big gully to your L (E6 and red-and-yellow signs). Be a little careful traversing earth banks here.

At **1hr 48min** cross a stream and 10min later, on the top of a spur, go up R. About 50 metres later, traverse an open stony slope to come out on another spur at around 1550m (**2hr 5min**) above a conspicuous tall dead pine tree. Continue traversing to reach a spring by a fallen pine (E00245988 / N04438139; 1484m; **2hr 15min**) and then on, losing height now, to a wooden bridge over a stream (**2hr 32min**). Climb L and up to the top of a bald spur (**2hr 45min**). Here, you get your first glimpse of Samarína's monastery, Ayía Paraskeví, standing on the edge of an expanse of meadow to the north amid surrounding forest.

About 20min later you begin a steep descent over grass, box and scree with short zigzags and frequent signposts, then round another spur and descend again through open pines to reach a small stream by a very rotten wooden bridge (**4hr 10min**). Turn 90° L immediately; do not go up to a big split pine in a rather obvious clearing. Keep straight ahead through young pines, pretty much on the contour, through a wet wallow used by wild boar, with a gully below L. In 5min, turn 90° R by a big pine where a spur juts out towards the river below. Shortly after, bear R round a conspicuous rocky outcrop and then L down a series of log steps. At around **4hr 20min** you are getting close to the river, bearing R above the base of a vanished bridge. You can see waymarks on the further bank.

Go down to the water's edge and cross over. Go a little way upstream and turn L, without crossing the dry streambed in front of you, and up another log stair. At about

Róbolo, or Balkan pine

4hr 40min you come out on a forest track by a largely unreadable map. Turn L uphill and at the first L bend leave the track and turn R up a grassy slope past a sheepfold (beware the dogs, if it is in use) to the low stone church of Áyios Sotíras and, beyond it, the **monastery of Ayía Paraskeví** (**4hr 50min**).

> The **church of Áyios Sotíras** possesses wonderful 18th-century frescoes, although it is unlikely to be open. At the apse end is a copious spring.
>
> To take a look at the **monastery of Ayía Paraskeví**, turn right at the church, cross a stream and follow the track to the end – only 100 metres or so: the buildings are clearly visible. Ayía Paraskeví, or Saint Friday, has given her name to countless villages and churches throughout Greece. The Samarína monastery of Ayía Paraskeví is not be confused with the village where this traverse of Mt Smólikas ends.

To continue, turn L at the church up a couple of zigzags on to the forest road (L takes you back to Dhístrato in 20km) and turn R, climbing gently, first through pine woods, then beech, until you reach **Samarína** (**5hr 40min**).

SAMARÍNA

Situated at an altitude of 1500m, Samarína is the highest village in Greece. Its name is almost a household word, thanks to a famous song celebrating the part played by men of the village who formed the rearguard in an attempt by the Greeks to break out of the Turkish siege of Mesolónghi in 1826. Wars and the ravages of time have destroyed practically all the old buildings, the most notable survivor being the church of the Panayía on the green below the *plateéya*, with wonderful frescoes, a superbly carved iconostasis and a very old pine tree that has been growing out of the roof of the apse for far longer than anyone can remember.

The busiest time of year is around the festival of the Virgin Mary on 15 August, when Samarína fills with thousands of visitors and the *magazeé* all hire gypsy bands to entertain them in a wild cacophony of music and merrymaking. It is fun, but everything is booked and you do not really get a sense of Samarína the flourishing shepherding village.

Samarína used to be deserted over the winter months, but the improvement of the road means that the hotels now stay open and winter tourism is beginning. For accommodation, ask Lákis Avéllas at the café/taverna (bottom right corner of the square opposite the cigarette kiosk; open all year; tel 24620-95278, mob 697-7466474).

STAGE 25A
Dhístrato (950m) to Palioséli (1080m)

Start point	Dhístrato
Distance	24km
Difficulty	1
Walking time	5–6hr
Height gain	400m
Height loss	420m
Waymarks	None

Either find a vehicle or do a straight plod along the Kónitsa road. Cross the valley below Dhístrato, take a L on the tarmac on the far side and keep going through the tiny and surprisingly lush villages of **Ármata** and **Pádhes** until you reach **Palioséli**. Be careful not to take the dirt road R; it leads to Samarína.

E6 path to Samarína. First glimpse of Samarína monastery in the meadow below.

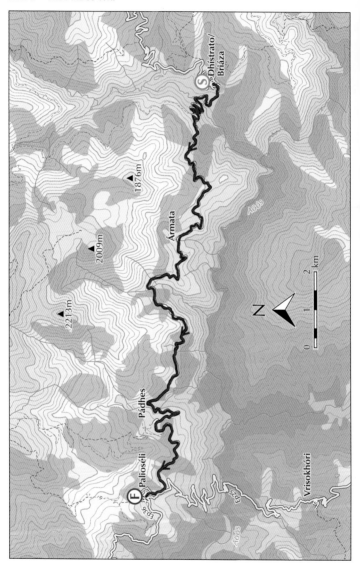

STAGE 26
Samarína (1500m) to
Dhrakólimni (2150m) via Mt Smólikas summit (2637m)

Start point	Samarína
Distance	12.5km
Difficulty	3
Walking time	6hr 30min
Height gain	1547m
Height loss	830m
Waymarks	Intermittent paint

From the *plateéya* in Samarína, take the concrete road that leads uphill L behind the cigarette kiosk. Follow it up past the baker's (L), ignoring the R turn by the handsome stone fountain. At the top of the steepest bit, the road bends R past the church of Mikrí Panayía (the Little Virgin), then L up and clear of the village (**15min**).

The marked path starts just N of the football pitch. Leaving the football pitch on your L, cross bare ground for 300 metres and enter the trees atop the first little spur. At first, the path heads slightly R, then at **35min** bends back L. After a more open grassy area (**50min**), you come to the **Soupotíra spring** (**1hr 7min**). Here, the black pine begins to give way to the Balkan pine (*róbolo* in Vlach) that you only find in northern Greece. About 25min later cross a stream gully (**1hr 32min**), heading upwards and rightwards. The trees begin to thin out. Above L rises the bare rocky peak of Górgulu.

A few moments later, with the Bogdháno spring visible in the gully just below the path, cross a stream. The path switches back L, the ground beginning to level out towards the col. At **1hr 42min** you cross the turf of the col between the peaks of **Górgulu** L (S) and **Bogdháno** R (N). You get your first view of Mósia, Smólikas' second peak (2600m), rising ahead above the deep wooded ravine of Vália Kírna. The path bears R (**2hr**), losing height at first beneath the Bogdháno peak, then gradually L and SW (**2hr 7min**) along the top of the curving ridge that borders the deep bowl of the Vália Kírna ravine.

From the ridge, you can clearly see the bulk of **Mt Grámos** (2520m) closing the horizon to the north-west and forming the border with Albania, the end of the Píndos Way. The white spot visible on the shoulder of Grámos (at 32° west of north) is the Civil War Memorial, commemorating the final defeat on 29 August 1949 of the last stand of the Communist partisans who had fought for three years to overthrow the Greek government.

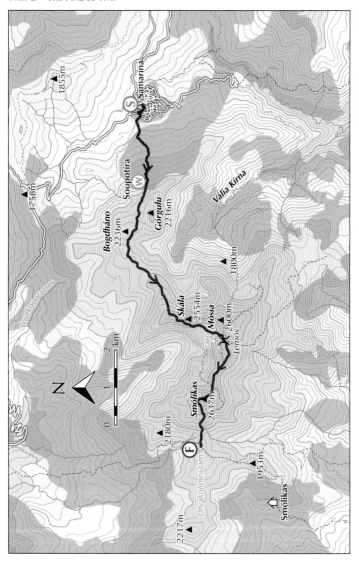

The going is pretty level here, the ground bare and covered with fragmented pieces of red rock. The path keeps well R of the rim of the Vália Kírna. Aim straight ahead (SW) for the first peak, marked as point 2554 on the Anávasi map. The path begins to climb in a more westerly direction, gradually at first, then quite steeply up a rocky gully, emerging at **3hr** on a featureless, flattish, red rocky plateau. Cross it diagonally R, bearing SW again but keeping away from the drop L. There may be a line of cairns. At the end you reach the lip of a huge cirque (**3hr 15min**), where the ravine of the Vathílako stream that flows NW down to Ayía Paraskeví/Kerásovo begins. Mósia is to your L; the summit of Smólikas is opposite. The path descends steeply L down what is known as the **Skála** (Stair), marked as such on the map. A few minutes down, there is a small spring under a rock.

Make a stony descent into the cirque, then an equally stony ascent to the small **tarn** (**4hr**) that was visible from the top of the Skála. Patches of unmelted snow lie here late into the year; big crags form the E wall of the cirque. From the tarn, continue climbing almost S out of the cirque through the obvious gap in the S wall (**4hr 10min**). This is **Lemós** (the Neck). Mt Gamíla comes into view south across the ravine of the Aöós river. A little way ahead, bear R and keep along W just below the ridge line; do not lose too much height to your L. In about 30min (**5hr 10min**), you come to a narrow 'bridge' in the ridge line where you cross over and begin to ascend the conical summit of **Smólikas** – another 30min of gritty climb (**5hr 40min**). The all-round views are magnificent.

Smólikas: Dhrakólimni tarn

Descent down the W flank on a clear zigzagging path to **Dhrakólimni tarn** takes 45min (**6hr 30min**). You can camp anywhere round about, with a wonderful starry night overhead if, as is likely to be the case, the weather is clear.

STAGE 26A
Palioséli (1080m) to
Dhrakólimni (2150m) via Smólikas refuge (1680m)

Start point	Palioséli
Distance	8km
Difficulty	2
Walking time	3hr 15min
Height gain	1000m
Height loss	0m
Waymarks	O3, red paint, hut symbol; fairly regular

The path, all the way to Ayía Paraskeví/Kerásovo, is part of the O3. It is an easy and steady plod, grassy and in open forest most of the way.

In the middle of Palioséli, a large plane tree shades a fountain and the main church, with a paved *plateéya*, the commune office and a taverna beside it. Opposite is a *magazeé* called Bárba Míkhas. Opposite that, L of the road, a concrete lane climbs past a chapel and divides almost at once (red-on-yellow waymark and green hut symbol). Take the L fork. You come very soon to a concrete bridge over a stream. Keep R on the R bank (true L) of the stream. At the last house, just before a wooden bridge, an arrow points R – 'Προς Καταφυγιο' (*pros katafeéyo*: 'To the refuge'). Go up here, passing on the R a restored and red-painted *dristélla* – a chute for fulling newly made rugs and blankets with water. Keep close to the stream. You come out on a dirt track. Turn L for 30 metres, then sharp R up a walled 'ramp' to a red-roofed fountain and shrine, bearing the date 1868 (**10min**).

The deepening stream gully is now on your R. Two minutes later, past an oak tree bearing red waymarks and green waymarks, the path traverses L away from the stream, turns back R and climbs to a *freyátyo*, a junction box in the village water supply. A few moments later it emerges on to abandoned fields, with a hut L. Up the R side of the fields it brings you out on the dirt road to the refuge (E00234082 / N04437519; **25min**).

Turn R up the road. In about 20min (**45min**), by a red waymark and a green hut sign (E00234209 / N04438618), scramble up the stony bank to the R.

Palioséli village

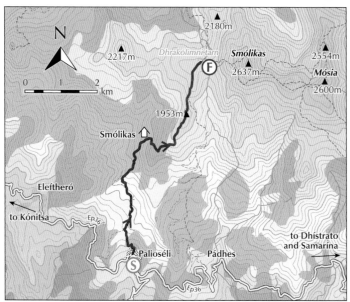

Just below the road to the left is the **Turk's spring** (*ee vreésee too toórkoo*), named to commemorate an attempt by a Turk to shoot an icon of the Virgin Mary; the story goes that his gun exploded and the Virgin remained unhurt.

The path runs parallel to the road across a grassy slope through open trees towards a ridge. At the top of the first slope, bear R, then sharply L up to a small col (E00234046 / N04438896; **57min**). Turn 90° R up the ridge into the forest (frequent waymarks). The path bears L off the ridge to traverse along a steep slope through the trees. At **1hr 5min**, cross an open grassy clearing along its lower edge to a much bigger clearing with a sheepfold, where a track leads L to the dirt road. Go straight up the wooded slope behind the sheepfold to the old wooden refuge of Náni (E00234406 / N04439674; 1710m; **1hr 20min**). There is a copious spring here and, just beyond, a wide grassy clearing (good campsite) beside the dirt road. The path continues uphill through the pines behind the hut at 70° and brings you in 5min to the attractively sited **Smólikas refuge**, where the dirt road ends. The refuge is not continuously manned; you need to ring ahead (mob 694-2939939, mob 698-8015656, katafygiosmolika@hotmail.com).

From the refuge, head NE down on to the path, which is marked by ancient red discs and paint splodges. Turn R and come to a big spring (last sure source of water). Turn R and begin to climb, winding steadily up a spur through beautiful open grassy pine woods. In about 20min (**1hr 40min**) you reach a grassy hollow where a red arrow on a tree indicates the way, straight up through the middle of the hollow to a small saddle where you look out over the Aöós valley. A curling red arrow on a rock indicates that the path doubles back L, climbing through trees to a little rocky shoulder (**1hr 50min**).

Traverse R beneath a rocky knoll to an open grassy col, where you bear L (a sign at the foot of a pine tree). In another 10min you reach an open shoulder with reddish stony ground. Here, you get your first view of the conical summit of Smólikas. Heading N at 24°, in line with the peak, you reach another wide grassy shoulder (**2hr 25min**). Cross it, heading N, and in a couple of minutes meet the path coming up from the R from the village of Pádhes (red square on a yellow ground; E00236168 / N04440326). There is a sheepfold below R and one of the rare O3 signs. You are heading N on the L flank of the deep main gully draining S from the peak.

At **2hr 42min** there is a spring 5 metres below the path on the R, which in late summer may be no more than a seepage. After a long stretch of gentle gradients you are approaching a saddle (E00235922 / N04441023; 2050m) where a yellow signpost indicates Pádhes 2hr, Dhrakólimni 15min, summit 2hr. Turn R up the ridge and begin to climb. You emerge above the treeline and continue L, then R to reach the **Dhrakólimni tarn** at **3hr 15min**.

Surrounded by gentle grassy banks, the **Dhrakólimni tarn** makes a lovely campsite, as does the grassy cwm just below it to the north (when the sheep are not in residence), should you require a more sheltered spot. The views north-west to Mt Grámos and south to the alpine crags of Mt Gamíla are spectacular (although not as fine as from the summit of Smólikas itself).

If you want to climb **Smólikas**, the path for the summit begins from the south-east corner of the tarn, dodges behind a stony hillock, then zigzags steeply up for 30–40min before the gradient eases on a long grassy slope. A long line of posts marks the route over well-cropped turf. The route veers well out to the left, before returning right and up to the summit (1hr 15min from the tarn). Stick to the path; the gradient is much easier. On a clear day you can see Mt Olympus, way to the east. Retrace your steps to the tarn.

STAGE 27
Dhrakólimni (2150m) to
Ayía Paraskeví/Kerásovo (950m)

Start point	Dhrakólimni
Distance	7.5km
Difficulty	3
Walking time	3hr
Height gain	0m
Height loss	1200m
Waymarks	O3

From the NE corner of the tarn, drop down into the grassy cwm below, where there is a sheepfold. Cross the grass to the NE corner to pick up the O3, the path that the shepherds use to come and go on horseback. The shepherds do not like the path and keep agitating for a road. For now, however – and luckily for walkers – their appeals are falling on deaf ears.

From the rim of the cwm (about **25min** from the tarn), the path loops down into trees on the R flank of a deep gully with a river in the bottom. After about 20min (**45min**) the gradient eases and the path crosses a wide but well-stabilised stretch of scree. About 10min later (**55min**), it bears R away from the river gully at 326° and starts to descend more steeply. At **1hr 10min**, descend along the L edge of a grassy clearing. In 10min you pass a bigger clearing on the L of the path with a wooden hut. Shortly after, the village of Kerásovo (officially now Ayía Paraskeví) comes into view for the first time at 340°. The path heads NE at 40°, then switches to a long reach at 280°.

Pass a third grassy clearing to the L, with piles of old stones, followed by a fourth, also on the L, in a hollow by an O3 sign. A few moments later you come to a spring. Heading in a northerly direction, pass a clearing with the remains of old terraces. Cross a narrow bridge of ground between two gullies and, at **2hr 5min**, you come down to the corner of open fields with a stream in willow trees L and a second stream in

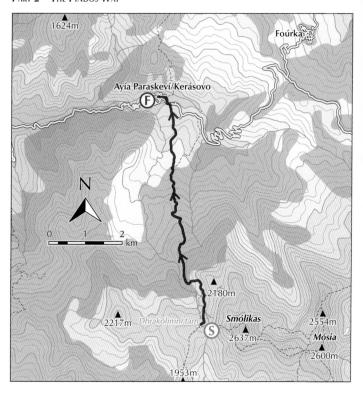

willows R. The route from here down into the village lies across long abandoned fields. There are paint marks, but not always obvious; keep your eyes skinned, especially in open grass.

Turn R across the grass for 80m to the further stream (spring just on the other side), bear L for 100m and you come to a big boulder L of the path, marked with red paint dots. About 10 metres further on, a red arrow on the ground points L. Turn L, following the red dots. Straight ahead is the path to the chapel of Profítis Ilías. Your direction is 344°; the willow-filled stream course is on your L and you are walking along the top of an old terrace wall. About 5min later, at the edge of a group of trees, turn R at 30° and continue to a junction of paths in the middle of a field (**2hr 15min**). Turn 90° L. Walk uphill for 2min, then the path levels off and starts to descend quite steeply at 336°. It is quite broad, with a gully below to the R. At **2hr 30min**, at a small saddle (E00235732 / N04447390; 1116m), turn 90° R.

Going up to the sheepfold

The path descends first through a tunnel of hazel with a barbed wire fence R and an old orchard below, then bears L down a narrow spur, with the village houses visible below. A water channel crosses the path at right angles. Step over and carry straight on downhill on a narrow sunken path, between old stone walls and overgrown gardens, till you hit the road by a telegraph pole marked with a red arrow and a hollow red diamond (**2hr 50min**). Turn R into **Kerásovo**. It is a 10min walk to the square (fountain) and *magazeé* (**3hr**). The main *magazeé* on the square does food and rooms.

STAGE 28

Ayía Paraskeví/Kerásovo (950m) to Kefalokhóri (700m)

Start point	Ayía Paraskeví/Kerásovo
Distance	20.5km
Difficulty	3
Walking time	6hr 45min
Height gain	740m
Height loss	990m
Waymarks	Orange and red paint, EOS Ioannínon discs and occasional O3

Head E from the square, back in the direction from which you arrived from Dhrakólimni. Very soon, turn L into a concrete lane marked by a K3 sign and follow

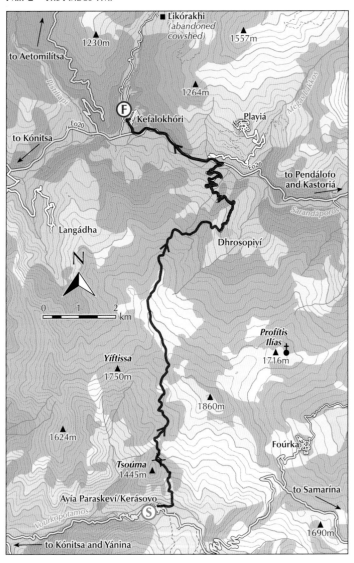

it R and out of the village on a clear track with the river below L. Past the last houses and just after a sharp L bend, keep a lookout for a signed L turn down past a walled spring to a bridge across the river. Cross it and bear L up along the dirt bank in front of you. The ground ahead is open and stony with a few scattered broom and small juniper bushes. Keep L up along the bank of a tributary stream gully.

A couple of hundred metres ahead, the pines become denser. A yellow square seems to be enticing you into the wood. Do not enter, but turn down L through broom bushes into the streambed where there is no clear path on the gritty bank; cross over among boulders (paint splodges) by a collapsed wall/weir. Haul yourself out on to the L (true R) bank with the aid of some roots and climb steeply R up the slope parallel to the stream. The path is stony and fairly clear. There are waymarks but you need to keep a sharp lookout; the orange paint marks are the most reliable. The ground beside the path is relatively open and grassy. You should never be more than 30–50 metres L of the stream gully. Be careful around 50min: the path bears L past a large oak tree and into an open grassy patch, in the middle of which you need to bear sharply back R (cairn in 2017; E00235684 / N04448643; 1089m).

You come to the remains of terrace walling (E00235672 / N04448740; 1106m) and the path winds in among scattered trees and bushes. Be careful not to stray left-ward. At about **1hr 15min** (E00235658 / N04448996; 1175m) bear R and cross the stream, heading up diagonally R into open ground. There are magnificent views back south to Mt Smólikas.

Bear N for a few minutes, then NW over grassy ground among open pines to reach the **col** just N of the 1445m **Tsoúma peak** at **2hr**, by a little painted shrine right on

Shrine on the Tsoúma col

the ridge. From here, a generally clear and soft path heads N just under the ridge on the W side through open pine forest. There is a rather messy seepage and an ancient cattle trough after about 10min, where you could scoop up some water. Keep a good lookout in the clearings; it is easy to lose the path in the grass. On a grassy open spur at E00235413 / N04450101 (1447m; **2hr 20min**), a collapsed signpost warns of land-mines (from the Civil War), but you need not be too concerned as I have not heard of any accidents in 40 years.

> You can see traces of **trenches**, for instance just on the reverse edge of the spur; for it was along these ridges close to the Albanian frontier – the Iron Curtain at the time – that the Communist partisans made their last stand against the US-backed Greek government forces.

The path continues N under the ridge, climbing gradually to the 1700m contour for another 40min until it joins the end of a shepherds' track (E00235589 / N04451814; **3hr**) connecting to the villages of Foúrka and Dhrosopiyí. On the second sharp R bend (E00235600 / N04452700; **3hr 25min**), where the track doubles back E, head off NW on the path once more, on the open tops here, for a further 20min until you cross another track at E00235404 / N04453911 (**3hr 50min**) and bear off NE to join the main track (E00235578 / N04454117) down to Dhrosopiyí.

The way is all downhill on a clear earth track through the pines, descending the W flank of a steep spur. There is no point in trying to find the odd fragments of the O3.

The magazeé at Dhrosopiyí

Approaching the end, the track doubles back to the E side of the spur to meet the tarmac road just short of **Dhrosopiyí** village. Turn R and come to a parking area. A narrow lane leads up to a small *plateéya* by the church, with a *magazeé* (**5hr 30min**) – it might be open; it might not.

You can easily find a place to camp outside Dhrosopiyí, but not necessarily anywhere to eat. It is best to carry on to Kefalokhóri, about 7.5km on the tarmac, from the point of view of both board and lodging and being a better starting point for the next day's journey.

The first 4km is downhill to the Sarandáporos river, where you turn L and follow the riverside main road for 3.5km to **Kefalokhóri**, a new village about 400 metres R of the main road (**6hr 45min** in total).

On the village square of **Kefalokhóri**, rather unexpectedly, is the very welcoming Hotel Fasoúlis (tel 26550-81481).

On Monday and Friday, the Dhrosopiyí bus from Kónitsa calls here; from Kónitsa, there are buses every two hours to Yánina. On Wednesday there is a bus north to Eftakhóri and Kastoriá. There is also a taxi (mob 697-2331695); a ride to Grevená and the main road to Thessaloníki or Yánina and the port of Igoumenítsa costs around €40.

GRÁMOS

You are moving into the heart of the Grámos massif from here on: sparsely populated, thickly wooded and slightly spooky. The name Grámos had immense emotive power for the older generation of Greeks. It was here that the forces of the Communist Democratic Army, who had been trying for three years to overthrow the Greek government, made their last stand in 1949. For the political Left, it stands for heroic resistance against the forces of evil in the form of Anglo-American imperialism and capitalism; for the Right, it symbolised the scheming wickedness of godless Bolshevism and Greece's hated Communist neighbours.

For many years, lying as it did on the Iron Curtain frontier, Grámos was a military zone. The populations of many border villages fled – and not always willingly – to the Soviet-dominated eastern European states to save their skins after the Civil War, from which, suspected of dangerous revolutionary tendencies, they were not allowed to return, in the case of actual combatants, for up to 30 years. The villages never recovered and several have actually been abandoned. From the 1990 collapse of Communism, it has been a conveniently remote and 'leaky bit' of the border for the many Albanians who want a clandestine route to the relative riches and freedom of Greece.

STAGE 29
Kefalokhóri (700m) to
Aetomilítsa/Dénsko (1400m)

Start point	Kefalokhóri
Distance	12km
Difficulty	3
Walking time	4hr 55min
Height gain	700m
Height loss	0m
Waymarks	Red paint and streamers for about half the route

From the village, cross the bridge to the true R (or W) bank of the river and head N for about 4km on a stony farm track, climbing steadily past various cowsheds, towards the now abandoned village of Likórakhi. Around the 1hr mark, you cross to the true L bank by a ruined mill and 10min later come to a R hairpin where the track doubles back uphill away from the river (**1hr 10min**). There is a **cowshed** right on the corner (E00235702 / N04461719; 907m), above the confluence of two streams. From here on, the way is perfectly findable but no longer very clear.

Start of the path by the cowsheds below the ruined village of Likórakhi

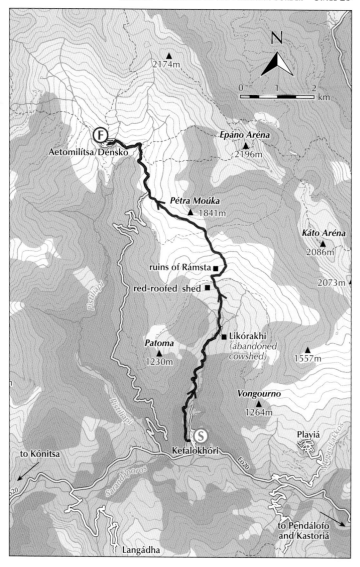

235

It is said that there were once two or three **villages** on the slopes above you to the left. There is visible evidence in piles of stones, crumbling terrace walls, several still recognisable ruins and a lot of unkempt fruit trees.

Prominent on the horizon above is a conical peak called Pétra Moúka, its grey stone face rising very noticeably clear of the dark green of the forest. Just below it, you can make out a patch of lighter green ground, the site of the now long-vanished village of Rámsta. The route you follow is obviously the once well-used path that served the village and continued on to Aetomilítsa. If you stand in the apex of the bend by the cowshed looking at Pétra Moúka, you will see the square ruined wall of a house on the ridge of the spur flanking the tributary stream in front of you, directly in line with Pétra Moúka. This is the first landmark to aim for.

To reach this point, turn down L to the stream. Cross over the wooden bridge below the further of the cowshed buildings. Clamber L across the boulders and cross the second stream. A path begins in the edge of the trees in front of you, at first bearing diagonally L up on to the spur in front of you. Once on the spine of the spur, turn sharp R and follow the spur line up past the ruined house you saw from the cowshed. The general direction is 320°. Keep to what was obviously the old path, most of the way right on the rim of the deep gully to your L. Don't go down either side. You pass at least three ruined houses on the spur line and the obvious remains of fields.

After around 55min (**2hr 5min**), you find yourself in a bit of a clearing with walnut and plum trees and a tin hut built inside some ruined walls R (E00235355 / N04462909, 1205m). Beyond it the old path bears off slightly L, still keeping close to the edge of the gully L, which it soon crosses, emerging into another 'field,' leaving a collapsed tin hut on the L. Shortly after, bearing L up some steeper grassy ground, you come to a water trough beneath an old pear tree (E00235154 / N04462889; 1210m; **2hr 10min**). Directly behind it is an unmistakable **red-roofed shed** just below a little-used track that traverses across the slope on the contour line.

Make your way past the tap end of the cattle trough on to the track and turn R. A stream crosses the track on a R bend after 5min (**2hr 15min**). Just past it (E00235311 / N04463115; 1245m), take the cow path L up the bank of the track on to grassier, more open ground. In a few moments you come to a second water trough (E00235375 / N04463194; 1276m; **2hr 20min**), behind which the ground begins to rise more steeply, the near skyline lined with big pine trees. Go diagonally R uphill at about 20°, aiming just R of the mature pines on the skyline. Young pines are rapidly encroaching here. Over the rim of the steep bit, begin bearing L through the bracken. You are on a sort of small plateau or hollow here (E00235420 / N04463417; 1335m; **2hr 35min**), covered with heaps of stones and old fruit trees (E00235699 / N04461720), the site of the vanished village of **Rámsta**. At the back of it, the ground rises steeply again, covered with pine trees.

Keep bearing L at 310° into the NW corner of the plateau/hollow, where a path, well trodden by cows, tunnels in under big beech trees (E00235226 / N04463514; 1354m; about 20–25min from the last water trough; **2hr 45min**), crosses a probably dry stream,

Climbing the spur to the red-roofed cowshed

and 40–50 metres later bears R up a steepish pine-covered slope. As it is mainly trodden by cows, there are various branches; just keep fairly close to the dry gully on your R and the path will bring you out at the top of the slope by what used to be a 'field' with a couple of plum trees (E00235028 / N04463696; 1463m; **3hr 8min**). Bear L for a few metres, then R, along a clear wide path that looks as if it may have been bulldozed at some point in the past. It leads along the L side of this 'field,' across a stream (drinkable; E00234919 / N04463770; 1438m) and on through young pines to the edge of a clearing directly below the **Pétra Moúka** crag. Here, turn R, bearing 300°, then L round a low bump and hard L (90°) down into and across a pine-flanked stream gully (**3hr 30min**).

Cross over, bearing R into the edge of a wide meadow. Turn sharply uphill to the R, aiming for the low point in the skyline at 300°, passing a big isolated pine tree at the start of the worn gully-like path leading to this saddle (E00234268 / N04464131; 1500m; **3hr 40min**). Here, you have two options, both of which will bring you to the Aetomilítsa road in about 30min.

Via the shepherds' track

The simplest option is to turn 90° R from the saddle, follow the spur up to the shepherds' track just above (**3hr 45min**) and turn L to meet the Aetomilítsa road (**4hr 10min**).

Via the old path

Alternatively, continue along the old path, which contours gradually R and N to a patch of meadow with an old and distinctive cattle trough made of linked, dug-out pine trunks (E00234009 / N04464727; 1515m; **3hr 45min**). The first option, via the shepherds' track, runs about 40 metres above the old path.

The old path continues across open grassy slopes among well-spaced pines until it joins the shepherd's track (E00233692 / N04464939; 1508m; **3hr 50min**). Follow it down to the Aetomilítsa road (E00233749 / N04465348; 1470m; **4hr 10min**), signposted 'Arénes, Lianotópi, Grámo'.

237

On reaching the road, both routes turn R and keep on to **Aetomilítsa** (**4hr 55min**). The road leads straight into the village square, where you will find the *magazeé* (rooms). You can camp in the churchyard (fountain nearby). A road forks L down to the church 200 metres before the square.

Aetomilítsa (Dénsko by the old name) lies on the edge of a wide cwm where a tributary of the Sarandáporos rises. It too is a Vlach summer village that comes alive when the flocks return in May.

In the battle for Grámos in 1949, the Communist commander-in-chief, General Márkos, had his headquarters in the village. There are still some people living in the village who were in their teens or older in 1949, who spent more than 30 years in exile in various parts of the old Soviet Union.

STAGE 30

Aetomilítsa/Dénsko (1400m) to
Mt Grámos summit (2520m) and return

Start point	Aetomilítsa/Dénsko
Distance	11km by either route
Difficulty	3
Walking time	5hr to summit (8–9hr total there and back)
Height gain	1000mm
Height loss	100m
Waymarks	Good for much of the way
Warning	The Albanian frontier runs along the top of the ridge just west of peak 2520 or Tsoúka Pétsik, the summit of Grámos. Straying across it may not have consequences as dire as they would have been before the collapse of Communism. Nonetheless, be careful not to wander into Albanian territory.

Aetomilítsa (Dénsko by the old name) is enclosed to the north by a wide largely treeless horseshoe ridge, which curves from Kiáfa peak in the east to Gkésos peak (2163m) in the west. You have a choice of two routes: one route comes up via the Civil War Memorial and the other heads due north from the village to the col west of Kiáfa peak, then west along the ridge enclosing the horseshoe to Skírtsi peak, where you meet the old military road. Neither route is difficult to navigate; the Memorial route is a little less exposed than the Kiáfa route.

It is then a couple of hours straight along the ridge to the 2520m summit, a scree cone overlooking the Albanian frontier, the erstwhile Iron Curtain, running along the crest of the north–south ridge: a total of 5hr (or just over) by either route and the end of the Pindos Way.

Via the Civil War Memorial

A popular route comes up from Aetomilítsa via Gkésos and the Civil War Memorial (or Grámos Memorial). The line of the path is marked on the Anávasi map and is not difficult to navigate.

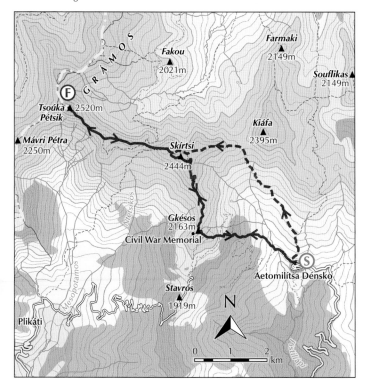

Grámos: Gkistóva tarn with Tsoúka Pétsik, the summit, in the background (right)

Coming up this way, it takes about 1hr 30min to reach the **Civil War Memorial**, 1hr to **Skírtsi**, plus 2–2hr 30min to the **Tsoúka Pétsik** summit of Grámos – in total about 5hr, as for the Kiáfa route.

The Kiáfa route

This route is well marked with a combination of red triangles and red squares on white backgrounds mounted on poles as well as paint marks on rocks. To find it, leave the highest point of Aetomilítsa village and bear R, looking around for the poles which are about waist height. Once you find them, it is straightforward.

After about **30min** you pass a concrete structure which protects water pipes. There is a prominent red triangle painted on a rock just up from it. At this point, the path splits. Take the L path, which drops slightly. Pass R of a prominent landslip at about **1hr 20min**. Continue on the path to reach the col just W of **Kiáfa** at **2hr** (around 2150m).

Turn L at the col and follow the obvious path, which remains generally L of the ridge. There are no waymarkings until you reach the old military road (**2hr 45min**). Turn R and follow it round the back of the **Skírtsi** peak and on to the ridge, first W, then NW. From here, the path is marked once again with red triangles on poles and red paint marks to the **Tsoúka Pétsik** summit of Grámos (**5hr**).

To return to Aetomilítsa from Grámos summit, retrace your steps towards **Skírtsi** (2444m) and join the military road heading S to **Gkésos** (2163m) and the **Civil War Memorial**.

There is a track from the Grámos Memorial back to Aetomilítsa (about 10km). It intertwines with the walking route which winds down into open forest, heading pretty much due E for the village. The waymarks – red triangles on white, mounted on poles – are not always easy to spot, but the terrain is very straightforward and it is easy enough to continue down the slope in an easterly direction. When you see the Áspro Potámi river in the valley bottom below you, bear slightly R (SE) on to the track, then L to cross the bridge and climb back up into **Aetomilítsa** (about 3hr 30min from Grámos summit; **8–9hr** in total there and back).

PART 3
ZAGÓRI AND MT GAMÍLA

Astráka refuge (Stages 4, 5 and 5A)

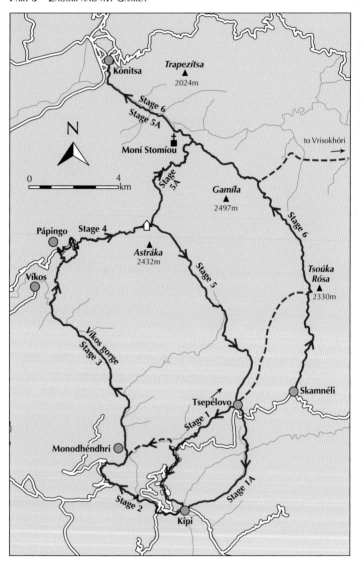

Of all the mountainous areas of mainland Greece, the Zagóri probably offers the best combination of natural wilderness and eco-sensitive development. At its heart is the massif of Mt Tímfi/Gamíla, whose uplands conceal limestone pavements, deep swallow holes, alpine pastures and a lovely tarn, Dhrakólimni (meaning 'dragon lake'). Bordering Gamíla to the west is the dramatic limestone gorge of Víkos, whose 1000m cliffs make it one of the most impressive in Europe. To the east lies the deep forest-clad valley of the Aöös, dividing it from neighbouring Smólikas, the second-highest peak in the country.

Most unusually for Greece, the region's handsome stone-built villages have been carefully protected and even the paths are maintained and waymarked to near-Western standards. An unexpected highlight is the graceful arched stone bridges, which have survived from the region's 18th- and 19th-century heyday, when the 46 villages of the Zagóri (*zagorokhórya*) enjoyed a privileged tax and trading status within the framework of the Ottoman Empire. Happily for the walker, many of the old cobbled mule paths that facilitated this commercial activity survive to this day.

LOCATION

The Zagóri region lies in the north-western province of Épiros, 1hr drive north of the regional capital, Yánina, and within sight of the Albanian frontier.

MAPS

- Anávasi Topo 50 (1:50,000) Epirus 3.1 *Zagori*

BASES

Yánina is a big university city and offers all amenities. **Kónitsa** has hotels, shops and banks.

Pápingo gets busy in season, so it would be wise to book ahead. In **Megálo Pápingo** you will find the Khristodhoúlou Ksenónas guesthouse (tel 26530-41335, mob 693-2847752), Saxónis Houses (tel 26530-41890 and 26530-41615, mob 693-7151624, www.saxonis-papigo.gr) and several tavernas. **Mikró Pápingo** has the Días guesthouse and taverna (tel 26530-41257 and 26530-41892, www.diaspapigo.gr/en). On the col above Pápingo is the **Astráka refuge** (tel 26510-46818, mob 697-3223100, www.astrakarefuge.com/en, open May–October).

Hotels and tavernas are on offer in **Monodhéndri**, while **Tsepélovo** has tavernas and the Gouris guesthouse (tel 26530-81214, mob 695-7541437).

In **Kípi** you will find a hotel and a taverna, and in **Skamnéli** a taverna and the Hotel Píndos.

ACCESS

There are daily flights (three a day in summer, two at other times) from Athens to Yánina, and frequent buses from Athens (Kifisoú terminus) to Yánina.

Three or four buses run daily from Yánina to Kónitsa, one minibus daily to Monodhéndri and one per week (on Tuesday) to Pápingo.

HOW TO USE THE ZAGÓRI ROUTES

The routes described here make a beautiful and rewarding walking destination by themselves. If your intention is

Víkos gorge from Víkos village

is the forest track described in Part 2 Stage 24A from Vovoúsa to Skamnéli.

If you are planning to incorporate the Zagóri into your Píndos Way trek, the most varied experience would be to follow our Stages 1, 2, 3, 4 and 5A which would take in the villages, the Víkos gorge, the high mountain experience and the Aöós gorge, and you would end up in the little town of Kónitsa which has one or two comfortable hotels together with banks and shops: a good place for a rest day and the chance to stock up before completing the last northward section of the Píndos Way. It might also be a convenient place to stop, as there are daily buses to Yánina and back to the real world!

If you simply want to cut straight across the length of the Gamíla massif by a spectacular mountain route,

to walk just in this area, then the best places to start are Monodhéndhri or Pápingo. Using our stages, you can easily construct a five- to seven-day circuit for yourself.

But we also had in mind using these Zagóri routes as an alternative end to the Píndos Way, or as a sort of extended looping excursion into a rather distinctive and different landscape which you could incorporate into your mainstream Píndos Way itinerary. In either case, the link from the main Píndos Way itinerary

then you should follow the route from Skamnéli to Kónitsa described in Stage 6 below.

The only drawback about ending in Kónitsa if you intend to rejoin the Píndos Way at Palioséli (see Part 2 Stage 26A) is that you are faced with about 25km of asphalt road, mostly on the contour and through spectacular scenery along the north flank of the Aöós gorge, but hot work in the sun. Our advice is to take a taxi from Kónitsa.

244

STAGE 1

Tsepélovo (1100m) to
Kípi (800m) via Kapésovo (1100m) and
Koukoúli (900m)

Start point	Tsepélovo
Distance	11km
Difficulty	3
Walking time	3hr 10min
Height gain	240m
Height loss	580m
Waymarks	Signposts and paint

If you are coming from Skamnéli via the Stage 24A link from the main Píndos Way at Vovoúsa, you have 4.5km of asphalt to walk to reach Tsepélovo, unless you can get a lift.

From the main square and plane tree of Tsepélovo, follow the wide, cobbled path which passes R of the church, descends to cross a bridge (spring R) and then climbs L. At a R curve (**5min**), turn L along a small path (faint red dot on rock L) descending gently between brambles.

At the streambed, continue upstream for a few minutes to a dense clump of walnut trees. Here, turn sharp L up the far bank, keeping uphill. There are several faint goat trails, but aim for the high crag top L of the steep mini-ravine W of Tsepélovo. You should soon cross the bottom of a boulder spill, where the large border stones of the old path are just visible. Ignore the goat trails, which tend R, and stay with the red-dotted route, which carries straight on, passing above a large hawthorn tree and climbing steeply through pine saplings to rejoin the original path.

Bearing L, the path improves and zigzags up, at times cut into the rock, past an old stone shrine (**30min**), before deteriorating again as it traverses to meet the gully floor beneath the high crag. Approaching the gully, ignore the red dots ahead and turn sharp R along traces of the old path, which resumes L and improves again. After a section along the gully bottom, you come out on a jeep track, with the crude **chapel of Áyios Yióryios** 250 metres L.

Follow the track straight (W) up to a grassy saddle (**1hr**) with wide, fern-covered terraces and a dewpond. From the saddle, continue straight ahead and slightly down L into and across a gully, where the path bears SW across a flattish spur pretty much on the

245

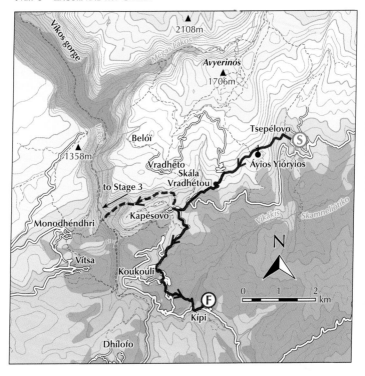

contour to join the Vradhéto–Kapésovo road just below a series of hairpins (**1hr 20min**). Turn L and follow the road downhill to reach the main Kapésovo–Tsepélovo road.

On your right, the spectacular **Skála Vradhétou**, with its 39 switchbacks descending a total of 1100 beautifully cobbled steps, descends into the intervening Mezariá ravine: the most impressive and most photographed section of ancient mule road in the country. Until 1973, it was Vradhéto's sole link with the outside world.

It is possible to climb the *skála* to Vradhéto village and walk thence to the **Belóï viewpoint** where there are fabulous views over the Víkos gorge, with just a low wall separating you from the 800m drop. (The viewpoint is 4.5km from Vradhéto; around 3hr there and back.)

At the main Kapésovo–Tsepélovo road, turn R into **Kapésovo** village (**1hr 40min**).

Alternative route from Kapésovo direct to Víkos gorge

This route provides a quick link of just over one hour to the upper Víkos gorge (700m), saving a couple of days on the complete route via Kípi and Monodhéndhri.

Follow the main cobbled lane down through the centre of Kapésovo (sign to 'VICOS'), past the huge plane tree. About 100 metres below the plane tree, fork R down an unsigned cobbled lane. At the bottom of the village, you pass the covered springs (dry) and the first red-on-white waymark. These and the occasional 'VIKOS' sign guide you down the small, sometimes steep path to the gorge bed. Follow the gorge bed downstream for 10–15 min (O3 waymarks) to join the route from Monodhéndhri (see Stage 3) at the 45min point.

To continue to Kípi, turn L at the main road and immediately R up a rough jeep track, passing below two rectangular churches. About 10min later, drop steeply down to rejoin the road and turn L. Follow it for about 1km and, just before a R bend (**2hr 10min**), turn L on to a dirt road (no signpost). This leads all the way down to **Koukoúli** in 2.5km, but there are two worthwhile shortcuts. The first comes after 5min, dropping L off the road, across open ground and past a water reservoir, to rejoin the dirt road in 7–8min. The second is also on the L, but much shorter, passing a hut.

The dirt road joins an asphalt road at the SE edge of Koukoúli (**2hr 40min**), near a café in the shade of a giant plane tree. It is worth exploring this tranquil, car-free village, with its proud stone mansions and the region's finest botanical collection at the Lazarídhis Exhibition. After visiting the village, follow the asphalt road S for 5min to reach a bench beneath a fir tree on the R. Opposite this, a small path climbs the L bank of the road (flimsy wooden sign 'Steps of Koukoúli to Kontodhímos/Lazarídhis bridge') and crosses a clearing into the woods. It then threads through the oaks in an easterly direction, either on the level or gently descending, for 10min.

At a broad band of shattered shale underfoot (**2hr 55min**), bear R, then L (waymarks resume). The path becomes a paved *skála* (stair), passing a camouflaged shrine under a rock face on the L and descending more steeply to the riverbed. Here, the path heads R (downstream) and across a single-arched bridge. The bridge was built in 1753 by Tólis Kontodhímos, interpreter at the French Embassy in Constantinople. On the far bank, a narrow path leads R to the modern road bridge 200 metres W of **Kípi** (**3hr 10min**). Follow the road L into the village centre.

STAGE 1A

Tsepélovo (1100m) to
Kípi (800m) via Khadzíou bridge (800m)

Start point	Tsepélovo
Distance	7.5km
Difficulty	1
Walking time	2hr 40min
Height gain	250m
Height loss	550m
Waymarks	None

This is a much easier – but also less interesting – route than the one via Kapésovo, but convenient for those carrying heavy packs or wanting a short day.

Follow the main road out of Tsepélovo towards Kapésovo and Yánina. After 500 metres, pass the school boarding house L (next to a grove of tall evergreens). The road bends R. Keep L/straight along a dirt road, with the basketball pitch R. The dirt road descends steadily through sparse oak woods, becoming impassable for cars, to reach the valley floor (830m) after **40min**, where a drivable dirt road joins from the L. Ahead is the graceful **Khadzíou bridge** (built in 1804) over the Skamneliótiko river.

Before crossing the bridge, it is worth heading downstream – a tiny path threads down the R bank – to see the impressive but dilapidated stone span now known as **Palioyéfiro** ('the old bridge').This links the sheer rock faces at the point where they converge dramatically, forcing the river into a 4m-deep channel.

Retrace your steps to the **Khadzíou bridge** (**1hr**), cross over and follow the jeep track S up the side valley. After 800 metres, it crosses the stream (flowing in spring), zigzags once and continues steadily SW, climbing all the while. After a further 30min you reach the top (1030m; **1hr 45min**) and a T-junction with a larger dirt track. Turn R and follow the road along the summit line. Enjoy the intermittent views to the left over the densely wooded, interlocking spurs of the Víkos valley head.

Keeping W, the track climbs to 1100m before starting its descent towards Kípi. At one point the track forks and rejoins; other than that, ignore minor turn-offs and, after 2km, pass below a large stone shrine R. At the junction of tracks just below, keep R. Alternatively, dive straight on down a small shortcut path which rejoins after 5min or

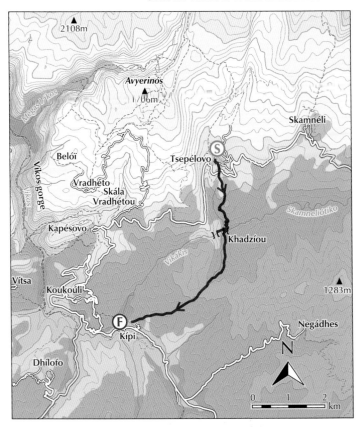

so. By a stand of firs, branch R down a narrow path past a smart walled house at the top of **Kípi** and follow your nose into the village centre (**2hr 40min**).

STAGE 2
Kípi (800m) to
Monodhéndhri (1050m) via Vítsa (900m)

Start point	Kípi
Distance	8km
Difficulty	1
Walking time	3hr
Height gain	300m
Height loss	50m
Waymarks	O3 (red diamond on white square) as far as Mítsios bridge

Follow the main road W out of the village, across the Vikákis stream (R is the Kontodhímos bridge and walking route from Koukoúli). About 0.5km from the village, fork L down a dirt track descending to the triple-arched stone bridge of Plakídha or Kaloyerikó.

Do not cross the bridge. Water level in the river permitting, continue downstream along the R bank through willow saplings (O3 red-on-white diamonds). After 100 metres you are forced into the boulder-filled riverbed, with dramatic rock stacks overhead. Follow this carefully downstream for 1km to the single-arched Kókoros bridge and adjacent road bridge (**45min**). Only in winter, and after very heavy rains, will this involve river-crossings or wading, in which case follow the road from Kípi, keeping L, to the Kókoros bridge.

Again, inviting though it is, there is no need to cross, but continue along the R bank, passing walnut trees (red waymark) and then a series of riverside ledges and a cave shelter. Under tall oaks (**1hr**), fork L to continue along the valley floor, through abandoned fields, and then along a stony path. At **1hr 15min** a paved path from the Koukoúli road joins from your R and shortly after this you reach – and cross – the last bridge of the day, the well-preserved Mítsios span (built in 1748).

Downstream lies the full length of the main **Víkos gorge**, but since the first 2km are pathless and boulder-strewn, we strongly recommend approaching from Monodhéndhri (Stage 3).

Head back up the L bank for 100 metres before starting the zigzagging climb known as the Skála Vítsas. The path is well built, the gradient steady and the waysides bursting with wildflowers in May and June. After a good 30min climb (**2hr**), you reach the first houses of **Vítsa** and, at the church of the Virgin Mary, keep R to emerge on the

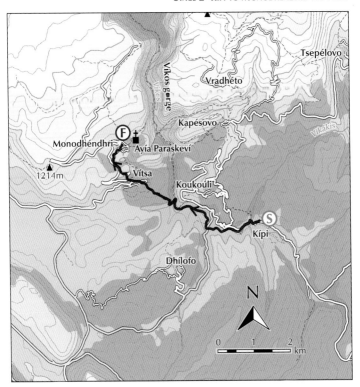

plateéya of Káto Vítsa, with its vast, spreading plane tree. Continue 100 metres W to the main road and follow this straight/R for 100 metres. On your L a cobbled lane leads up to the *kióski*, the covered belvedere alongside Áyii Pántes (All Saints) church, which makes a good picnic spot. Opposite this is the 17th-century church of Áyios Nikólaos, with its broad yard and porticoes.

To continue to Áno (upper) Vítsa and Monodhéndhri, take the upper of two cobbled lanes, passing above the church of Áyios Nikólaos. You emerge on the asphalt road serving Áno Vítsa and follow this up to the junction with the main Monodhéndhri road (**2hr 35min**). Opposite is the rather unlikely site of a Geometric (9th–4th century BC) settlement, with the remains of a dozen houses and two grave-yards nearby.

Follow the road towards **Monodhéndhri** and fork R (lower road). About 0.7km after this, you can bear L up a cobbled path, a shortcut into the village centre (**3hr**).

251

Rock formations above Monodhéndhri

To visit the disused but spectacular **monastery of Ayía Paraskeví** (a 15min walk away), continue to the huge plane tree, with Kikítsa's taverna ahead and the beautifully frescoed church of Áyios Minás on the right. Turn left (north), signed to 'Víkos gorge' and 'Ayía Paraskeví monastery'. The broad, paved lane leads after 1km to the 15th-century gate.

There is a heart-in-mouth viewpoint over the gorge, with even more giddying views if you climb the steps to the left and follow the old trail – basically a ledge in the sheer cliffside, with a wooden bridge and a walled gate at strategic points – to the hermits' caves.

STAGE 3
Monodhéndhri (1050m) to
Pápingo (950m) via Víkos gorge (500m)

Start point	Monodhéndhri
Distance	14.5km
Difficulty	3
Walking time	6hr 10min
Height gain	500m
Height loss	600m
Waymarks	O3 (red diamonds on white square) except for first hour

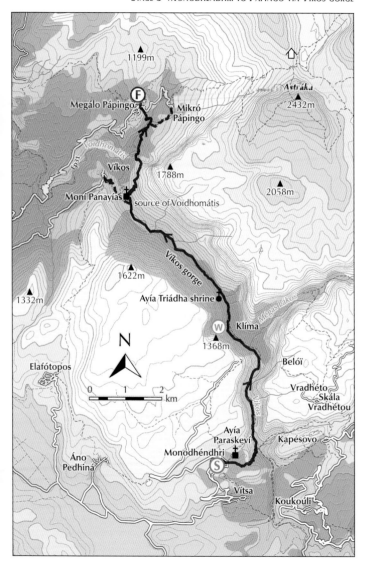

The Víkos gorge is the jewel in the crown of Zagóri hiking, over 12km long (and this only the middle section) and dwarfed by cliffs rising 500–1000m above the riverbed. From the magnificent turquoise springs of the Voïdhomátis river, the route climbs to Pápingo, for easy onward access to the Astráka refuge and Mt Gamíla. But it is quite possible – easier and shorter, in fact – to climb out to Víkos village, which has a simple pension and road access to Arísti.

Take plenty of water and watch out for snakes, which are attracted to the pools of the riverbed.

From the central plane tree (Kikítsa's taverna), head E up a cobbled lane (not the lane heading N to 'Víkos Kanyon'). Two signs give slightly optimistic times to Pápingo (6hr) and, in Greek only, to Kípi (2hr) and Víkos village (4hr 30min). Past the public toilets on your R and then the large church of Áyios Athanásios, whose grounds would make a reasonable campsite, the lane becomes gravelly.

Pass between an open-air theatre and its unused outbuildings (all EU-funded). The rough-paved path zigzags down through hornbeam and other deciduous trees, speckled with autumn crocus, hellebores and cyclamen in late September and October. Pass a shrine R (**15min**). Views ahead to the cliffs of the Mezariá side-canyon herald a steeper, more relentless descent, but the cobbles are firm and the path shady. Approaching the gorge bed (**45min**), ignore small paths forking R (for Kípi) and continue straight on, passing a low rock face on your L. You are now in the depths of the canyon, 300 metres vertically below **Ayía Paraskeví monastery**.

From here, the path, well blazed with O3 red-on-white diamonds, follows the L bank of the gorge, at times next to the riverbed, at times climbing over rocky shoulders, all the way to the Voïdhomátis springs 10km downstream.

After a beautiful stretch 50–80m above the gorge floor, descend iron steps to the dry bed, keep along the L bank (O3 waymarks) and climb again past the worst of the scree slopes. This ascent climaxes at a narrow saddle beside a rocky outcrop (**1hr 35min**). The descent which follows is steep and slippery. You pass an overhang and a rocky ledge with tree-trunk bridges before climbing through gentler woods. Do not be tempted into the bed itself, a jumble of enormous boulders interspersed with scummy, seasonal pools. The path demands some care, but is maintained every spring and should be easily passable.

At **2hr**, the sound of running water and a metal sign – 'EOS Papigkou' – announce the turn-off R to the junction of the Mégas Lákos and Víkos watercourses, where a clean stream flows year-round. Known as Klíma, this is the only drinkable water until the Voïdhomátis springs. The main path continues NW, past flat, shady ground at the base of a moss-covered boulder spill. After the stone **shrine of Ayía Triádha** on the R (unreliable spring; **3hr**), the going improves, with semi-open meadows affording views up to the soaring pinnacles R. Later, a knuckle-line of rock gendarmes climbs the L slope. At **3hr 45min** you earn your first views up to Víkos village, appearing as a single

Panayía monastery church

house atop the lowest knoll of the L ridge, where this descends into woodland. Shortly after this, a tree-mounted O3 plaque points R, alongside the riverbed, for the easily missed trail to Pápingo.

For Víkos village

To climb out to Víkos village (rooms and meal), stay on the main path. Intermittently paved, it climbs gradually L between twin hawthorn saplings (more paths down to the river here in case you missed the earlier fork); then past a smaller R fork which leads in 10min down to the now defunct little **monastery of Panayía**; then, more steeply, up to the asphalt road at the southern end of **Víkos** (**5hr** from Monodhéndhri).

From Víkos, there is road access to Arísti or you can retrace your steps to rejoin the trail to Pápingo.

For Pápingo, follow the O3 route along the riverside to some huge, grey, rounded rock buttresses on the R bank (**4hr 10min**); you will see O3 waymarks pointing up the R slope.

Here, at **Voïdhomátis springs**, the subterranean aquifers of the Voïdhomátis river well up into an icy, clear and surprisingly forceful stream. Dye tests have revealed that the water takes over a week to filter through the 1200 vertical metres separating the springs from the Épous (or Épos) and Provatína sinkholes above.

From the rounded rock buttresses, follow the O3 path up the steep R (NE) slope. In the afternoon sun, the relentless zigzagging ascent through sparse Jerusalem sage shrubs is a killer, so take it gently. A massive granite finger (**4hr 45min**) makes a good rest spot, with views over the lower, impassable section of the gorge. Beneath huge orange cliffs – the first of the towers of Astráka – the path crosses a scree slope. After a short descent, you pass beneath a pretty overhang R, before resuming the climb towards Pápingo. On your L comes a dramatic drop to the ravine separating Mikró from Megálo Pápingo.

Shortly after this, by a wooden sign in Greek (**5hr 40min**), the path forks: L (downhill) goes to Megálo Pápingo, R (uphill) to Mikró Pápingo. The former descends past the Stefóvrisi spring (trickle) to cross the ravine and climb to **Megálo Pápingo** in about 30min (**6hr 10min**), emerging across the road (S) from the large village church.

The path to **Mikró Pápingo** twists up through old fields at the foot of the towers (O3 waymarks), bears R at a stony shoulder and climbs even more steeply to a pair of walled springs at the southern limits of the village. Cobbled lanes lead you into the village centre (about 35min from the fork).

PÁPINGO

Pápingo is a lovely old village that has in recent years become something of a mountain tourist centre as Greeks have rediscovered the beauties of their countryside. It would be wise to book ahead for accommodation, although there are now several places to stay.

In Megálo Pápingo, our two particular recommendations are close to each other in the heart of the village. The first is the Khristodhoúlou Ksenónas guesthouse (tel 26530-41335, mob 693-2847752). It is run by the sons of Koúlis Khristodhoúlou, whose death in 2015 sadly removed from the scene one of the first people in Greece to take mountaineering and mountain tourism seriously. For 40 years, he was the person we all went to for information about the area; he took

Eroded rock finger on the path to Pápingo

care of the refuge and carried your food up by mule.

The second is the more luxurious and intimate Saxónis Houses (tel 26530-41890 and 26530-41615, mob 693-7151624), run by Vasílis Nasiákos and his wife. The accommodation is in lovely stone-built village houses on a beautiful courtyard. Vasílis himself is an experienced mountaineer and can fill you in on the best routes and the current state of them.

In Mikró Pápingo, there is the Hotel/Taverna Días (tel 26530-41257 and 26530-41892). It is a panoramic location and a handy, often sociable, base for exploring the uplands of Mt Gamíla.

STAGE 4

Pápingo (950m) to
Astráka refuge (1900m)

Start point	Pápingo
Distance	5km (+ 6km round trip to Dhrakólimni)
Difficulty	3
Walking time	3hr 30min (+ 2hr 30min round trip to Dhrakólimni)
Height gain	950m (+ 300m to Dhrakólimni)
Height loss	0m (+ 300m from Dhrakólimni to refuge)
Waymarks	O3 (red diamonds on white square), orange or red dots and arrows to refuge

From Megálo Pápingo, the day starts with a 30min hike up the road to its end under a plane tree in the **Mikró Pápingo** car park. From here, go straight ahead on the cobbled lane in front of you (S) and then L, passing Hotel Dias L. At the junction, keep L (signs to 'Refuge 3hr, Provatína cave 3hr, Dhrakólimni 4hr, Gamíla 5hr'). Leave the village and pass the covered spring of Avraghónios and shrine of Áyios Pandeléïmon R (possible camping spot under plane tree; **40min**). This is the first of four springs which irrigate your ascent and which sometimes shelter yellow-bellied toads. Shortly after, fork R at a sign to 'Katafíyio' (*katafeéyo*) and wind uphill through juniper, oak and hazel, following occasional red dots/orange arrows (and droppings from the pack animals which service the refuge).

At **1hr 15min**, after the next spring, Andálki (1220m; sign to 'Refuge 2hr 20min'), the path switchbacks up stony, eroded slopes and the trees thin out, making it hot work. An hour later, pass the unreliable spring of Tráfos (1550m; sign to 'Refuge 1hr 20min') and veer slightly away from the dry gully L, zigzagging uphill. Ignore the short-cuts used by those descending. About 15min above Tráfos (**2hr 30min**), there is a R fork to the Astráka peak and Provatína 'cave.'

> You could spend an extra night at the refuge and bag **Astráka** (2432m) on a 5hr circular route. It is a reasonably clear cross-country trail, accurately marked on the Anávasi map.
>
> At 405m, the **Provatína 'cave'** vies with various Mexican *cenotes* for the title of deepest straight-drop sinkhole in the world. Another contender is the Épous (or Épos) sinkhole, almost directly above the Voïdhomátis springs; this has been measured at 447m, but not in a straight drop.

Ignore this fork (it is possible to shortcut and miss it anyway) and continue NE towards the clearly visible refuge. In another 15min you reach the fourth and last

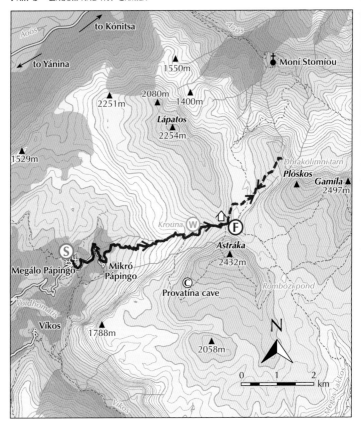

spring, **Kroúna** (1800m), and a final 25min slog sees you at the col, with the **Astráka refuge** just to your L (**3hr 30min**).

From the **Astráka refuge** you can see the path to Dhrakólimni winding lazily up the grassy slopes to the north-east. The ground drops away abruptly eastwards to a perfectly flat *loótsa* (seasonal lake), with shallow, muddy waters in spring and colourful algae in autumn. There are some shepherds' huts and *lákes* (meadows) visible to the left.

The warden of the refuge is Yiórgos Rokás, himself a qualified mountain guide. (Tel 26510-46818, mob 697-3223100; open May–October; €11 per

Kroúna spring en route from Pápingo to Astráka refuge

night for members of the British Mountaineering Council, Club Alpin Français and other climbing clubs; €13 for non-members; restaurant available.)

Optional ascent to Dhrakólimni tarn

From the Astráka refuge, continue down the abrupt E slope along a steep and rocky path. After 10min, ignore the R turn for Gamíla and Tsepélovo (G painted on the rock) and continue straight on (D for Dhrakólimni), descending to the N end of the seasonal lake. Find a small red-dotted path climbing E over a rocky hump (aim just R of a prominent rounded boulder on the skyline), then descending NE over grassland to some boggy turf (**35min**).

There are several drinkable springs here. From the easternmost one, follow the previously visible path, climbing steadily NE up the grassy spur with the sheer scarp of Plóskos R. Another 45min (**1hr 20min**) should see you through a V in the rim of **Dhrakólimni tarn** (2000m), where you would expect it to drain out; but its reed- and snow-fringed waters are plentiful, clear and surprisingly unglacial. Climb the cairned summit on the far side (2050m) for the views over the Aöós valley to Mt Smólikas (which has a namesake Dhrakólimni at a similar altitude). Return to the refuge the way you came (**2hr 30min**).

STAGE 5

Astráka refuge (1900m) to
Tsepélovo (1100m) or Kapésovo (1100m)

Start point	Astráka refuge
Distance	13km to Tsepélovo (15.5km to Kapésovo)
Difficulty	3
Walking time	5hr 30min to Tsepélovo (6hr 15min to Kapésovo)
Height gain	350m to Tsepélovo (400m to Kapésovo)
Height loss	1150m to Tsepélovo (1200m to Kapésovo)
Waymarks	O3 for first section; yellow-diamond-on-blue for last section and occasional red and blue dots throughout

Follow the stony path down (E) from the refuge and at the junction of paths (**10min**) turn R (G for Gamíla, painted on rock). This descends steeply to the S end of the seasonal lake, crosses the grassy flats and starts climbing among the boulders. You may hear the springs of the Romióvrisi gurgling underneath the boulders R. To your L is a curved rock wall where wallcreepers can sometimes be seen.

Keeping your eyes peeled for O3 waymarks, thread SE up through the boulders for 20min until the path levels out on the W side of a gentle, grassy dip. Along here, the O3 (Karterós pass) and red-dotted Gamíla trails branch L (SE); for Tsepélovo, stick on the R side of the dip, heading SSE (occasional blue dots). The path winds, like a notch in the limestone strata, up to an unexpectedly large dam at the N end of the **Rombózi pond** (**1hr 5min**). Here, on the saddle linking Astráka and Gamíla peaks, you are almost at the high point of your route (1970m). In late May and early June, thousands of crocuses poke their purple and yellow heads through holes in the melting snow.

You can head around the pond, but a clearer option is to strike L (E) up the slope to the top of the mound (2000m). Here, between two cairns, pick up a clear path descending S, past a spring (tapped in summer), to a thistly meadow with a ruined hut L (**1hr 30min**). This is Stáni Mirioúli, where the Astráka circuit path joins from W. Continue SE down a rocky hump with gullies developing on both sides. After 15min it flattens off and bears R, contouring, then descending gently past the 1800m mark. After another 15min you reach a lip with an easily missed sinkhole R. Known as the Nifótripa ('bride's hole'), it is apparently 113m deep.

Here, the path drops L into the dry gully separating you from the lunar, indented slopes of Gamíla, Karterós and Megála Lithária. On the way down, you pass another grassy balcony below some spiny plum saplings, before reaching the gully floor at **2hr 30min**. The path climbs the far bank and straightens out in a southerly direction. Pass some scree and boulder fields dropping away to the deepening ravine now on your

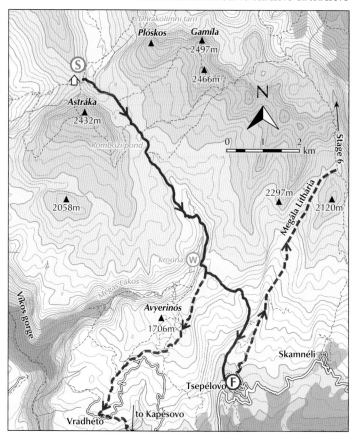

R. This is the head of the Mégas Lákos, which eventually joins the Víkos gorge at the Klíma springs.

Nearly **3hr** from the refuge you pass an overhanging rock L, at the foot of which a weak but year-round spring fills a tiny, fern-fringed pool. Known as **Kroúna**, this is the only reliable water (and shade) en route.

There follows a long, stony ascent L out of the ravine until, around 1750m, the path resumes R (S) and passes over a mini-saddle. At the first level ground below this (**3hr 35min**), there is an important and easily missed junction, where you have the option of heading to Vradhéto and Kapésovo instead of to Tsepélovo.

Mégas Lákos and the path to Tsepélovo

Variant to Vradhéto and Kapésovo

Continue straight on the main path, passing a dry or murky *loótsa* (pond) and a bump on the R where once a Turkish *kazárma* (prison fort) stood. Here, you can enjoy your first views over Tsepélovo and the wooded hills to the south. Do not descend towards Tsepélovo. Despite what other guidebooks tell you, this is a steep, rocky, pathless descent. Instead, follow the main path over some grassy humps to a shaly section, where you descend to a visible jeep track. This descends in an anticlockwise loop for just over 1km; then, where it straightens out, you can follow it down to the Kapésovo–Vradhéto road and turn R, or you can bear R onto the signed path which is shorter. Either way, you should reach **Vradhéto** within 1hr–1hr 30min of the junction (just over **5hr** from the refuge). From there, you descend to **Kapésovo** by Skála Vradhétou in about an hour (**6hr 15min**).

To descend to Tsepélovo from the 3hr 35min junction, turn L up a side gully, past your first yellow-on-blue waymarks. You soon amble through a grassy corridor bordered by limestone pavements. About 20min from the junction (**3hr 55min**), you leave the corridor and start the careful descent to Tsepélovo, which is waymarked with red dots and blue-on-yellow squares all the way.

After 10min (**4hr 5min**), a path joins from the L and you descend to a bowl filled with thistles, mullein and hellebores. Bearing L (E), continue down the stony and grassy slope, then curl R around the base of a meadow to a spur with square boulders R. Bearing L again, the path drops steeply down to the walled, dungy spring of Pétrino

(**4hr 30min**). From its lowest trough, drop SE into the dry gully, then branch R along a clearer, stone-built path. After zigzagging down past a lone walnut tree, it meets a jeep track on a spur known as Kángena (more walnut trees just below; **4hr 50min**).

Follow this track S for a minute, then turn R (SW) down a faint but waymarked path. This descends just L of the valley-line, past shrubs and saplings, to meet the same jeep track at a bend near some more walnut trees (red painted 'ΚΑΤΑΦΥΓΙΟ' on a rock for those coming the other way; **5hr 10min**). Follow the track straight/R (S), passing a dewpond R (Láko Boúti). After about 500 metres, the route drops R to shortcut a corner and rejoins the track. After a similar distance, with a wooden/wire fence L, keep L. About 100 metres later, by a concrete cabin, fork R down a small path which joins a cobbled lane by the first houses. This lane leads down past a walled spring and up, passing the church on your R, into the main square of **Isepélovo** (**5hr 30min**).

Tsepélovo to Megála Lithária to join Stage 6

Taking this route to join up with the Skamnéli–Kónitsa route in Stage 6 allows you to complete a pretty much full circuit of the Gamíla massif.

From the *plateéya* in Tsepélovo, with your back to the shops on the lower side, take the path which goes up to the R in front of you. It soon turns into a rough track bearing R round the scrub-covered spur above the village. In 20min you reach a fork in the track by a walnut tree. Turn L, round the back of the intervening hill, then keep straight up the gully in front of you. The L side of the gully is defined by a line of cliffs, the R by the Kourtétsi ridge which separates it from the Goúra valley above the village of Skamnéli.

At **30min** you pass a shepherds' hut and a grove of trees in the gully bottom, after which the gradient steepens. At **1hr 5min**, beneath a big cliff L, it levels off again. On your R are sloping pavements of fissured rock.

The path keeps R of a grassy hollow. At **1hr 20min** you are heading R towards a ridge and cliffs, and in 5min you come to a round pond for the sheep. Another few minutes (**1hr 30min**) and the gully narrows; you start to climb towards a high V-shaped pass, which you reach in 30min (**2hr**). Ahead of you are the great crags of the Goúra–Tsoúka ridge. Cross the hollow beneath the L cliffs, keeping over to the R (**2hr 15min**) and aiming for the Goúra–Tsoúka cliffs. The Kourtétsi ridge on your R ends here. Keep R of the stony hummocks covering the valley floor. This is the locality named **Megála Lithária**, after the huge boulders which dot the ground. The Stage 6 route up the Goúra valley from Skamnéli comes in here on your R (around **3hr 30min**; see Stage 6).

STAGE 5A
Astráka refuge (1900m) to
Kónitsa (650m) via Stomíou monastery (700m)

Start point	Astráka refuge
Distance	12km
Difficulty	3
Walking time	6hr 30min
Height gain	0m
Height loss	1250m
Waymarks	Signposts and paint

From the Astráka refuge, follow the path descending diagonally L down the stony slope E of the refuge and crossing the narrow neck of ground between the two marshy seasonal ponds on its way to Dhrakólimni. There is a sheepfold on the L as you cross between the **two ponds**. Take the path that branches L beside the sheepfold. Leaving the second pond on your R, follow this path N along the stream draining the two ponds, losing height only gradually for 25min or so until it begins to bear increasingly R (NE) and steeply down, still following the stream (E00224153 / N04432138). Although rocky and a bit of a scramble, it is well marked with cairns and not exposed or dangerous. The stream here is the last water until you reach the Stomíou monastery.

At the bottom of this steep section (E00224153 / N04432138), the path leaves the stream and turns NE along the foot of sheer cliffs. There is some scree, but no dangerous drops, and the path remains clear. After a while it opens out with scattered trees, alpine pastures and great views, then starts to descend again steeply (E00225509 / N04432915) through mixed forest to join the track leading to **Stomíou monastery** (**4hr 30min**).

From the spring outside the monastery perimeter fence, follow the main track W and downhill, crossing the powerful Ghrávos stream (**4hr 40min**) to the riverbank. At the water's edge, follow the cement wall on the L side before resuming along the track, initially uphill. You rejoin the river at **5hr 20min**. A (drinkable) side stream gurgles under the boulders, and the sandy bank makes this perhaps the best swimming spot.

Within 10min the track brings you to a weir and continues, now passable by car, down the plane-shaded L bank. Opposite, russet-barked arbutus trees poke out of the rock face at zany angles. Pass a sign listing the park by-laws, then a metal post where another path comes in. At **6hr**, just after the cable crossing for monastery goods, you reach the gracefully arching stone bridge of Kónitsa R, which you cross. Look upstream for tremendous views up to the pyramid of Gamíla I (2497m). Continue up the road. Just past a hotel/café, a lane forks R and climbs quite steeply up past the minaret of a ruined mosque to join the main road at a hairpin bend opposite the vast plane tree of the Hotel Dendro. Follow this road R to reach the centre of **Kónitsa** (**6hr 30min**).

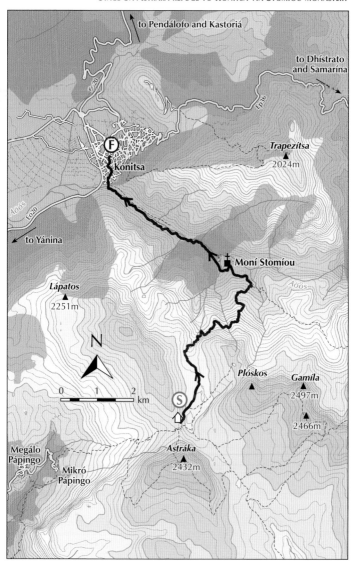

STAGE 6
Skamnéli (1150m) to
Kónitsa (650m)

Start point	Skamnéli
Distance	27km
Difficulty	3
Walking time	11hr 30min
Height gain	600m
Height loss	1950m
Waymarks	To Goúra, infrequent; to Stomíou, intermittent red paint and red-on-cream plaques, with a short section of O3 red-on-white squares in the middle

This is a tough but exhilarating route over the crest of Mt Gamíla via the 2320m Tsoúka Rósa pass and then down the wild, wooded flanks of the Aöós gorge to Kónitsa. It is best divided into two parts, the first night spent camping by the Goúra spring below the Tsoúka Rósa peak. You need a tent or bivvy bag even in summer, as the Goúra campsite is high (2000m). The second night you might be able to sleep in the dormitory of Stomíou monastery (monks permitting). There is very little water on these north-eastern slopes of Gamíla. The two campsites suggested here are the only reliable year-round springs on the whole route.

An alternative, shorter descent – achievable in a long day – takes you to the remote village of Vrisokhóri, whence it is possible to rejoin the Píndos Way at Palioséli (see Part 2 Stage 26A) for the traverse of Mt Smólikas on the far/north flank of the Aöós gorge.

The ascent to Goúra is not the most beautiful in the region, being largely treeless and laced with jeep tracks, but it is a relatively painless way of gaining 900m altitude, and you may be able to get a lift in a cowherd's pick-up. The old path has practically disappeared, so – apart from the first and last sections – the route described follows jeep tracks.

From the asphalt road (1150m), go up the main cobbled lane passing the huge plane tree and Hotel Píndos on your R. After 100 metres keep R, passing the school on your L. Follow the main lane L (twin telegraph poles L) and then R again. The path leaves the village, climbing through stony walnut and cornelian cherry groves. Follow the most trodden path and the occasional ground-painted red arrow, aiming for a tree-speckled hill NNE, bisected by the faint diagonal line of a dirt road. Above this are cattle meadows, known as Vourtápa (Vourtápes on the Anávasi map).

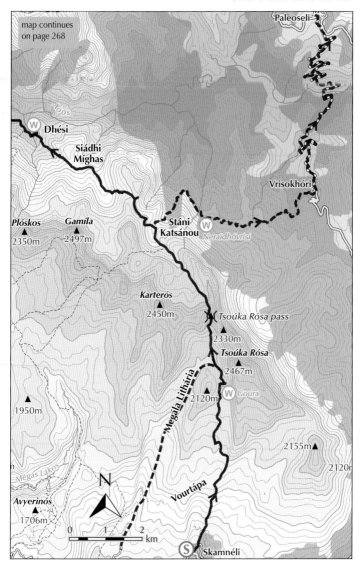

map continues on page 268

Paleoseli

Ⓦ Dhési

Siádhi Míghas

Vrisokhóri

Plóskos
▲ 2350m

Gamíla
▲ 2497m

Stáni Katsánou Ⓦ

Neraïdhóvrisi

Karterós
▲ 2450m

⭐ *Tsoúka Rósa pass*

▲ 2330m

Tsoúka Rósa
▲ 2467m

Megála Lithária

▲ 2120m Ⓦ *Goura*

2155m ▲

▲ 1950m

2120m

Mégas Lákos

Avyerinós
▲ 1706m

N

Vourtápa

0   1   2
km

Ⓢ 🏠 Skamnéli

267

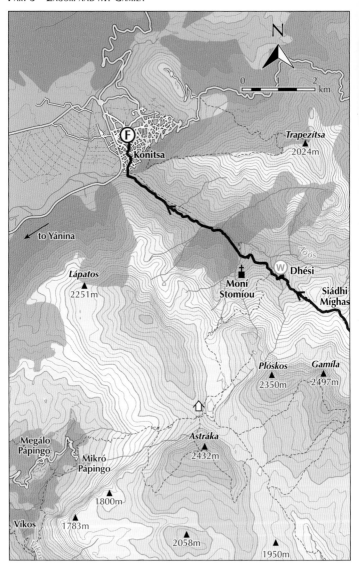

At a disused concrete water channel (**10min**) before the telephone wires, turn L (red arrow) and follow the channel uphill past a covered stone water reservoir. Ignore the L bend (water pipe) and continue straight up the dry gully (no waymark). This becomes a disused jeep track, bending R. At **20min** it joins a larger track and almost immediately they debouch on to a wider gravel road at a hairpin bend 80 metres above a rusty shrine.

This is the main 'road' up to Vourtápa; given the difficulty of finding the old path, we suggest that you follow it. Turn L (uphill). The track bears R, zigzagging steadily uphill away from the gully and crags of Gomarórakhi on the L. At **50min** pass on your R a shepherds' pen in the lee of a giant limestone pavement. After this, bear L across a rocky streambed and stay on the track for a couple more switchbacks. It flattens out by the circular dewpond and the first crude huts of **Vourtápa** (1550m; **1hr 30min**).

At the junction (straight on leads over and down to Tsepélovo), turn R along a smaller track leading NE into a jumbled cirque of rock castles and cliffs crumbling into scree, with verbascum-choked meadows R. This crosses the ridge S of Káto Tsoúka and joins a larger track (**1hr 55min**). Turn sharp L up the track back across the ridge, crossing the scree fields at the SW foot of Káto Tsoúka to pass beneath a cairn-topped triangular crag. You can see a tiny trail traversing the face of Káto Tsoúka – the only safe way up the main peak of Tsoúka. Finally, the track descends slightly to end by some huts and a walled spring (1850m; **2hr 15min**). The huts and the spring function only in summer when the cowherds overnight here.

Turn R (N) up a dung-spattered path, heading towards the W crags of Tsoúka and two silhouetted, nipple-like cairns on a closer hump. Underfoot you may see sections of the metal pipe feeding the spring, which follows the shortest (but not the easiest) route from Goúra spring. At a sea of jagged boulders (**2hr 27min**) the path veers R, away from the pipe, to a low ridge where it resumes N.

At a P-shaped boulder (**2hr 45min**), do not cross the grassy bowl ahead but bear R to another grassy dip. Lunar grey screes, scoured rock faces and twisted crags surround you. Pass below (R of) the twin cairns (pipe rejoins) and, a little higher, bear R into a grassy corridor. The Tsoúka Rósa pass (2320m) – an open V – where the route continues N, is clearly visible ahead. At the top of a string of puddles in a grassy meadow lies the covered ground-well of **Goúra** (2050m; **3hr**), below a knobbly, overhanging face E.

There is plenty of soft, flat ground for camping by the **Goúra spring**, although it may be snow-covered until May. Choughs wheel around the crags, and a muffled crash of stones spilling near the summit may signal an elusive Balkan chamois.

To continue to the Tsoúka Rósa pass and on towards Stomíou, keep up the slight valley ahead, aiming now just W of N, and over the gentle saddle linking the rocky summit of Vlási (also called Kourtétsi; easily climbed) to the W with the more for-bidding Tsoúka (a steep scramble) to the E. Descend the cow-trodden path into and across a boulder-ridden cwm, known as **Megála Lithária** (big boulders), passing a low stone corral L. The path dwindles, but make for the rocky summit L of the pass and look out for occasional red-on-cream metal waymarks lying on the ground. At a small, flattish pasture, bear R (NE), climbing more steeply towards the L-most needle of Tsoúka, before resuming L (NW) to a spill of big boulders (which gave the area its name, Megála Lithária). A fading red arrow directs you R, zigzagging up a messy slope, until a visible trail straightens out to reach **Tsoúka Rósa pass** (2320m; **4hr**).

> The **Tsoúka Rósa peak** (2330m) juts up ahead to the right, at the end of a knife-edge ridge (for experienced scramblers only). Clouds broiling up the 1000m drop to its right (north-east) usually obscure the flanks of the more distant Mt Smólikas, but further left (north-west) the sheer cliffs and forests of Mt Trapezítsa are often visible and sometimes, in between, Mt Grámos and the Albanian hinterland. A steep 5min up to the right is an exhilarating rocky summit overlooking the chasm above Vrisokhóri and Iliokhóri.

The descent starts R from the pass, then cuts back L across loose scree. Pass below (R of) a cairned bluff, keeping near the gully floor to a thistle-filled meadow (**4hr 30min**). On your L is a dramatic skyline of cliffs, gendarmes, couloirs and year-round snow patches – the dark side of Gamíla and Karterós peaks. From the far end of the meadow (old corral) continue NW, climbing slightly (red splodges) and aiming for a large cairn atop a mound. Pass just to the R of this (**4hr 45min**) and pick out, in the pathless rocky valley below, two red-on-cream squares. Beyond you can see the onward path climbing NW of Stáni Katsánou.

Make your way as best you can down past the two square waymarks, then drop to the valley floor where more waymarks (in this direction only) guide you across the loose rocks. Looking back, your cairned mound is the L-most of three. At **5hr 15min** drop R to some low stone corrals and a crude hut, then turn L to regain the main valley. The waymarks are now the red-diamond-on-white of the O3 trail, which joined imperceptibly after crossing Gamíla via the steep and tricky Karterós pass. These guide you down the R flank and then into the valley floor, where a small circular dewpond and a makeshift hut mark the milking pasture of Kátsanos or **Stáni Katsánou** (1670m; **5hr 45min**).

Alternative descent to Vrisokhóri (3hr 45min)

As you look N towards Mt Smólikas across the Aöós ravine, a steep gully drops away in front of you. From the far L lip of the grassy Stáni Katsánou bowl – by a plaque on a rock commemorating the death of a young Greek rambler named Voúla – a path drops steeply NE into the gully (red and orange arrows, mostly positioned for those coming up). After 45min (**6hr 30min**) it crosses the gully, winds through mixed forest, rounds a spur and continues descending SE to the spring of **Neraïdhóvrisi** (1275m; **7hr 30min**). This is the first reliable water since Goúra.

There follows 30min of climbing and descending through beech woods, before hitting a logging road. Follow this for about 30min (there are stretches of old trail L) until, after a RH bend (**8hr 30min**), the O3-signed trail continues L. It crosses an older dirt road and slips down shaly gully-sides before veering R to cross two bridges and climb to the chapel of Ayía Paraskeví, at the E end of **Vrisokhóri** (**9hr 30min**).

Link to Mt Smólikas

From Vrisokhóri, it is possible to cross the Aöós valley to **Palioséli** on the southern slopes of Smólikas by 12km of asphalt road, whose construction unfortunately put paid to the beautiful old path. It is a frustratingly twisty route, particularly on the far side. The only consolation is the possibility of a swim in the Aöós by the bridge. It is possible to see the line of the old path in places as it climbed up to Palioséli; it would be wonderful to have a proper path connection again between the Zagóri hikes and Smólikas.

From the far L of the bowl below Stáni Katsánou, a path climbs steeply back L (SW) over loose rocks, towards the peak of Liméria Kleftón ('the lairs of the brigands or *klephts*'). It looks suitably unassailable. In the shade of pines, the path bears R (N) to cross the spur below this peak (**6hr 10min**), offering final views back to Tsoúka Rósa and Karterós and down to the red roofs of Vrisokhóri. Descend to a boulder with a red-on-cream square – these have resumed – before bearing L and uphill again through beech woods to the next saddle (**6hr 30min**). Here, the views extend north-west down the Aöós river gorge to its flood plains below Kónitsa.

Pass to the R of a large half-burnt pine and find a path zigzagging nastily down the stony slope. After a few minutes, a gentler option forks L into low woods before heading R across the gully to rejoin the main path. Pass under and around some monster pine trunks, before turning L (unsigned) across a dry gully to an open patch (**6hr 55min**) with fabulous glimpses up to the saw-toothed peaks of Gamíla and Plóskos. Ignore an old arrow pointing R and aim L of Gamíla, following red-on-cream squares in a big clockwise loop into the head of the meadows of the **Siádhi Míghas** (Vlach for 'pasture of the flies'). A clear path leads NW through these meadows, past a dewpond and a house-sized boulder (**7hr 20min**). In the lee of this, you stumble upon a shepherds' lean-to and, often, his fierce untended dogs.

From here, a path leads down the dip into enchanting beech woods, then climbs slightly to round a spur. Ignoring small paths which join R, continue W and level, in mixed forest now, hemmed in by the rocky flanks of Trapezítsa R and Plóskos L. Bright yellow arrows join in the waymarking, scratched with directions by Albanian immigrants using this path as an illegal entry into central Greece. At the next spur (1300m; **8hr**), a path joins from the L (very faded sign) and the descent begins in earnest: a steep but always clear and shady path zigzagging down the R banks of the Kerasiás gully for nearly an hour. Drawn on by the sweet sound of a gushing stream, cross the main gully (880m; drinkable water all year; no possible campsites) just shy of **9hr**. A sign confirms that this is the *dhési* (pipe intake) for the monastery's water supply.

Consequently, the path widens and improves as it descends the L bank, past a sort of layby R (just wide enough for a tent), after which a gap in the pines allows your first glimpse of Stomíou monastery, a large, modern-looking walled compound perched on an outcrop above the Aöós. The final descent is loose and stony, dropping to a walled spring and larger track outside the perimeter fence (**9hr 30min**). The main gate of **Stomíou monastery** is straight ahead.

> **Stomíou monastery** was founded in the 1770s. Most of the original building was burnt by the Germans in 1944, so what you see today is largely modern. The view over the Aöós river from the far corner is breathtaking; the whole setting is almost Tibetan in its wild grandeur.

Descent towards Stomíou monastery in the Aöós gorge

To visit the monastery, you should wear clothes that cover your arms, shoulders and legs, not shorts or short skirts. Be warned that it closes shortly before sunset and may be locked up when you visit.

The larger track outside the perimeter fence leads to the right in 5min to another walled spring set amid tall pines, with ledges flattened out for pilgrim-campers who gather here in droves for the 8 September festival. Camping here is the best option if the monastery is closed or you prefer privacy.

From here it is only another 6km, of mainly gentle riverside descent, to reach Kónitsa. From the spring outside the monastery perimeter fence, follow the main track W and downhill, crossing the powerful Ghrávos stream (**9hr 40min**) to the riverbank. At the water's edge, follow the cement wall on the L side before resuming along the track, initially uphill. You rejoin the river at **10hr 20min**. A (drinkable) side stream gurgles under the boulders, and the sandy bank makes this perhaps the best swimming spot.

Within 10min, the track brings you to a weir and continues, now passable by car, down the plane-shaded L bank. Opposite, russet-barked arbutus trees poke out of the rock face at zany angles. Pass a sign listing the park by-laws, then a metal post where the old path rejoins. At **11hr**, just after the cable crossing for monastery goods, you reach the gracefully arching stone bridge of Kónitsa (R), which you cross. Look upstream for tremendous views up to the pyramid of Gamíla I (2497m).

Bridge on the Aöós river at Kónitsa

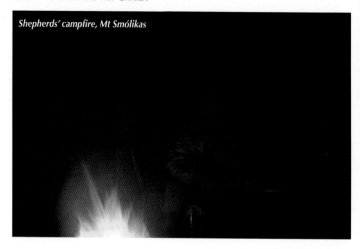

Shepherds' campfire, Mt Smólikas

Continue up the road. Just past a hotel/café, a lane forks R and climbs quite steeply up past the minaret of a ruined mosque to join the main road at a hairpin bend opposite the vast plane tree of the Hotel Dendro. Follow this road R to reach the centre of **Kónitsa (11hr 30min)**.

PART 4
MT OLYMPUS

Mt Olympus

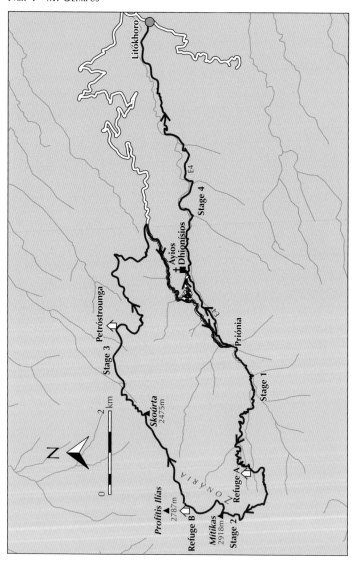

Rising almost straight out of the sea, Mt Olympus (*óleembos* in Greek) at 2918m is both the highest and the most beautiful mountain in Greece, and it boasts two of the country's only manned refuges. It is covered in dense forest of beech and of black and Balkan pine. Its wild-flower population is without parallel, even in Greece. Its main paths are well signed and well maintained. Although the mountain is steep and rugged, walking it in favourable weather conditions requires no special expertise. The last half-hour to the summit, however, does involve some modest scrambling, with a degree of exposure that some people may find disturbing.

The weather is deceptively fickle. It is easy to be seduced on a hot summer's day with the sea at your feet into thinking that nothing can possibly go wrong. Take no chances: It is not unknown for lightning, snow and hail to succeed each other in the space of minutes on a fine August day. Patches of frozen snow can block the path, especially in the Zonária area, until the middle of June.

The classic starting point for walkers is Priónia (named after the now vanished water-powered sawmills) where the road from Litókhoro ends, 18km up the north flank of the Enipéas ravine. There is a good chance of a lift in summer and there are always taxis on the square in Litókhoro. If you have your own vehicle, it is best to leave it at Priónia, where there is food in season and water.

Our route unfolds clockwise from Priónia. The advantage of this is that – even after travelling all day to reach Olympus – you still have time to do the 3hr hike to the Spílios Agapitós hut (Refuge A) before dark.

An anticlockwise circuit of Mt Olympus begins 14km along the road from Litókhoro to Priónia, at the spot known as Dhiakládhosi (*dheeyakládhosee*, or Dhiastávrosi on the Anávasi map), where there are two large signs on the right of the road displaying maps of the paths. It leads up to the right to the Yiósos Apostolídhis (Refuge B) hut in a 5–6hr hard climb. The anticlock-wise route has its supporters. First, having slept much nearer to the summit, you can get up the Loúki couloir before other walkers appear and cause rock falls. Secondly, it makes descent from Priónia to Litókhoro by the old footpath (the well-marked route of the E4) a much more logical end to your hike. This is a truly beautiful path along the Enipéas ravine back to Litókhoro. It takes a good 3hr going down. Coming up this way adds around five hours to the total hike to Refuge A.

You can of course simply go up and down by the same route.

LOCATION

Mt Olympus is on the north-east coast, on the shore of the Thermaic Gulf, 90km south of Thessaloníki.

MAP

• Anávasi Topo 25 (1:25,000) *Central Olympus*

BASE

Litókhoro has hotels, tavernas, shops, seaside campsites and a tourist office.

REFUGES

- Spílios Agapitós/Refuge A (2050m): manned mid May–end October; 110 beds; night €10, meal around €5. Efficiently run by the Zolótas family (fluent German/English) for more than 50 years. Booking essential in July and August (tel 23520-81329, tel 23520-81800, www.mountolympus.gr).
- Yiósos Apostolídhis/Refuge B (2730m): on the Plateau of the Muses (*pedhiádha ton moosón*), at the foot of the Throne of Zeus peak; manned mid June–end September; 80 beds; food. Belongs to Thessaloníki climbing club, SEO. Booking recommended (tel 23520-81329, tel 23520-81800, www.apostolidisrefuge.gr).

- Kákalos/Refuge C: also on the Plateau of the Muses; unmanned; keys from Refuge A.
- Petróstrounga is a new refuge at 1945m on the north side of the mountain by the old sheepfold of Petróstrounga, accessed by a 2hr 30min climb from Dhiakládhosi/Dhiastávrosi; May–end October; 80 beds (tel 23512-00766). For information contact the municipality of Litókhoro, which owns it (tel 23523-50100).

ACCESS

The quickest access is from Thessaloníki. Several buses run via Kateríni and direct trains operate every day to Litókhoro (railway station 9km from village). There are also frequent daily buses and trains from Athens.

STAGE 1

Priónia (1040m) to
Spílios Agapitós/Refuge A (2100m)

Start point	Priónia
Distance	6km
Difficulty	3
Walking time	2hr 30min
Height gain	1050m
Height loss	0m
Waymarks	Frequent

This account assumes you have arrived at Priónia by the road. It is a beautiful spot, enclosed by forest and dominated by towering crags. There is a small taverna-cum-snack bar. Do not be surprised to find a lot of people here in July and August and the car park full. Fill up with water; there is no more until Refuge A.

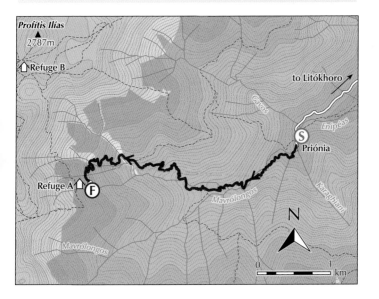

View up to Zonária from Refuge A

The path to Refuge A begins just uphill from the taverna. An EOS signpost indicates the way, giving the time to the refuge as 2hr 30min. Cross a stream with a small waterfall R, and start to climb steeply up through woods of beech and black pine. The path is well trodden and there is no danger of losing the way. As you gain height, there are superb views across the Mavrólongos ravine L and to the summits above your head. Keep following the path all the way to **Refuge A (2hr 30min)**.

Spílios Agapitós/ Refuge A lies close to the treeline at an altitude of 2100m, on the edge of an abrupt spur surrounded by huge, storm-beaten specimens of Balkan pine.

The refuge staff run a tight ship, so get into their good books on arrival by exchanging your boots for a pair of slippers (provided) and let them know in good time if you want a meal and bed or are just passing through. The refuge can get very busy in July and August. This is the place to ask for information about the mountain.

STAGE 2

Spílios Agapitós/Refuge A (2100m) to Mítikas (2918m)
and Yiósos Apostolídhis/Refuge B (2730m)

Start point	Spílios Agapitós/Refuge A
Distance	5km via Kakí Skála and Loúki
Difficulty	3
Walking time	3hr 30min via Kakí Skála (3hr 15min via Loúki)
Height gain	968m via Kakí Skála (1010m via Loúki)
Height loss	338m via Kakí Skála (278m via Loúki)
Waymarks	Frequent

It is best to make an early start – dawn or earlier – for the summit if you want a clear view. Cloud often gathers on the peaks in the middle of the day. Fill up with water; the next source is at the Yiósos Apostolídhis hut/Refuge B (when open).

The path continues behind Refuge A, climbing L-handed up a steep spur among the last of the trees. After **1hr** you come to a signpost. From here there are two possible routes to Mítikas, the summit: via the Kakí Skála (*kakeé skála*, meaning something like 'the Devil's Ridge') or the Loúki couloir.

If you do not like the sound of the exposure on either of these routes, the best thing is to follow the Zonária path to the signpost at the foot of Loúki and just keep straight on to Yiósos Apostolídhis/Refuge B, which you reach in a total time of about 2hr from Refuge A.

Kakí Skála ridge route (2hr 40min)

The Kakí Skála route goes more or less straight ahead up the R flank of the featureless stony valley ahead, with the peak of Áyios Andónios L. You reach the summit ridge after about 1hr (**2hr** from Refuge A), between the peaks of Skolió L and Skála R. You know when you've got there because there is a 500m sheer drop on the other side, into the chasm of Kazánia (the Cauldrons).

The **Kakí Skála** itself begins in a narrow cleft on the R just short of the ridge. Paint splashes mark the way. The route starts with a slightly descending traverse R to a narrow nick in the ridgeline revealing the drop to **Kazánia**, which is easily negotiated. In

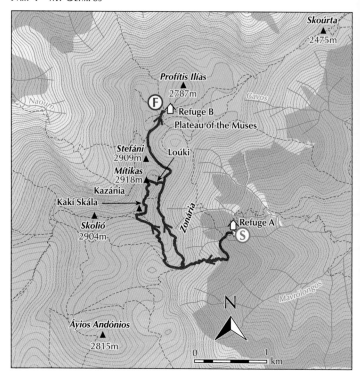

the main, the route keeps just below the ridge, so you are protected from the drop. The drop R is steep, but not sheer. Although it can be alarming for someone unused to heights, there is no real danger.

Continue traversing R, skirting the base of the Skála peak, then climb L up a steep-ish gully made a little awkward by loose rock on sloping footholds. Bear R at the top over steep but reassuringly solid rock, and through a narrow neck (paint waymarks). Step L round an awkward corner and there, scarcely 100 metres away, is **Mítikas**, a narrow boulder-strewn platform with a trig point, tin Greek flag and summit book (about 40min from the beginning of Kakí Skála; **2hr 40min** from Refuge A).

The Loúki couloir route (2hr 25min)

To reach the foot of the Loúki couloir, turn R at the signpost above Refuge A, up and over the rounded spur above, then all along the tilting striations of rock known as Zonária that lie directly beneath the tooth-like pinnacles guarding the summit area.

282

Zonária and Kakí Skála, the obvious nick in the skyline

The path here is cut by several gullies, which hold deep wedges of snow until mid to late June. Crossing them in those conditions requires care.

After about 40min (**1hr 40min** from Refuge A) – just before the highest point on the path – a signpost indicates the Yiósos Apostolídhis/Refuge B hut in 20min. The start of the **Loúki couloir** is just up L. It is a steep but straightforward scramble; a couple of moves at the top are airy, but not dangerous. I like this route, although there are some who strongly counsel against it, for it is exposed to rock falls when there are other people on it. The couloir leads you to **Mítikas** in about 45min (**2hr 25min** from Refuge A).

> From **Mítikas**, on a clear day, you can see Mt Smólikas and all the peaks of the Píndos range to the west, Parnasós in the south and Mt Áthos in the north-east. Just north of Mítikas is the Stefáni peak (2909m), known also as the Throne of Zeus. It is a precipitous hog's back closing off the north side of the Kazánia cirque. As you can see from Mítikas, it is not for hikers.

Whichever ascent route you picked, you have to now make your way from Mítikas to the signpost on the Zonária path below Loúki (see Loúki couloir route above) in order to go on to Refuge B. If you have ascended Mítikas via Kakí Skála and want to come down Loúki, the mouth of the couloir is just a few metres N of the summit and, although it may appear that any move in that direction will lead to instant immortality, you are in fact quite safe; the **Loúki couloir** brings you down to the signpost in around 30min.

The Zonária path to Refuge B and the Plateau of the Muses

Beyond the signpost, turn downhill L below the NE face of Stefáni. The Plateau of the Muses is on your R across an intervening corrie, bounded to the W by the Toúmba and Profítis Ilías peaks. **Refuge B** hut is between them, another 20min level-pegging round the base of the Stefáni peak on a path that is very vulnerable to avalanches in winter (**3hr 30min** via Kakí Skála, **3hr 15min** via Loúki).

From **Yiósos Apostolídhis/Refuge B**, the Toúmba and Profítis Ilías peaks can be climbed in 20min or so; the chief interest is the view. A small herd of chamois (*agreeyokátseeka*) still survives on Olympus and can often be seen in this area, especially towards evening.

STAGE 3

Yiósos Apostolídhis/Refuge B (2730m) to
Priónia (1040m)

Start point	Yiósos Apostolídhis/Refuge B
Distance	21km
Difficulty	2
Walking time	5hr 30min
Height gain	200m
Height loss	1630m
Waymarks	Signposts and paint

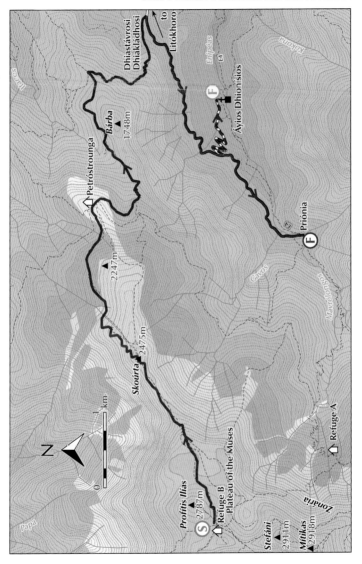

This is a beautiful but long and tiring descent, which brings you out on the forest road to Priónia at Dhiakládhosi (Dhiastávrosi on the Anávasi map).

Leaving the refuge, turn L/NE and continue to the edge of the Plateau of the Muses, where the path bends R round the head of a precipitous drop. Thereafter it follows the Lemós ridge dividing the Enipéas ravine R from the Pápa Réma ravine to the N as far as a rounded bump with a survey point on top: **Skoúrta** (2475m). Here, the coarse turf slopes down to a flat-topped ridge just clear of the highest trees. The path winds down

The monastery of Áyios Dhionísios

to this ridge, then traverses R into a broad shallow gully leading down into the trees. At around **2hr 15min** you come out on a rock-strewn shoulder among scattered Balkan pines, with an abandoned sheepfold among the boulders L. This is **Petróstrounga**; there is now another manned refuge here (May–end October), where you can stop for refreshment or overnight.

From this shoulder, drop down into an open grassy bowl and enter the trees again, where there is a signposted fork in the path. The R branch leads to a spring in 15min. You are heading S at this point. Keep straight on past the fork. There is another junction a little further on, where again you keep straight. The R branch leads in 10min to a rock overhang where an eccentric Greek landscape painter, Vassílis Ithakísios, once lived and painted.

The path now begins to descend steeply through mixed woods of beech and pine to a little patch of meadow known as **Bárba**, and thence first S, then E, to the road at **Dhiakládhosi** (**4hr 30min**).

Turn R and follow the tarmac for about an hour to return to the car park at **Priónia** (**5hr 30min**), where there is a good chance of a lift or you can ask the café to call a taxi to take you back down to Litókhoro.

> If you are planning to walk the E4 down to Litókhoro and are equipped to camp, instead of going all the way back to Priónia it makes more sense to turn left (after 2.5km) down to the ruins of **Áyios Dhionísios monastery** (a further 1.7km). There is water and a shady flat place to camp just before the monastery; or, better still, make your way down to the riverbank just upstream from the monastery – the E4 is on this bank at this point – where there is room to pitch a tent or spread a bivvy bag. By doing this, you save yourself the first 45min of the walk from Priónia in Stage 4.
>
> The heavily fortified monastery of Áyios Dhionísios is worth a visit. Founded by the saint in 1542, it was destroyed by the Germans in 1943 on suspicion of harbouring Resistance fighters.

STAGE 4

Priónia (1040m) to
Litókhoro (300m) by E4

Start point	Priónia
Distance	12km
Difficulty	2
Walking time	3hr 15min
Height gain	520m
Height loss	1520m
Waymarks	E4

The path, clearly marked E4, starts from the downhill corner of the car park by the café, crosses to the R bank of the Enipéas stream and shortly after returns to the L bank, which it follows all the way down to the **monastery of Áyios Dhionísios** (**45min**). There, it crosses back to the R bank, climbing up through cool beech woods to a tiny chapel (Áyio Spílio) built into a big rock overhang, with a resurgent stream (**1hr**). A few minutes later there is a fourth bridge by a spring, this time crossing a tributary stream descending from R. A 20min climb is followed by a steep descent. The gradient soon

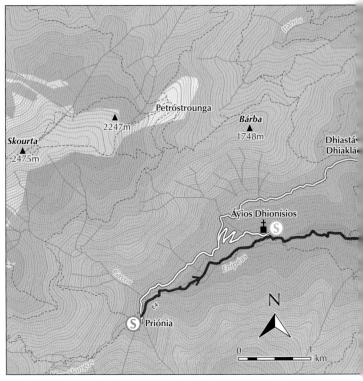

levels off, climbs steeply again to gain about 100m, levels off, then starts to climb again to reach the top of a jutting rocky pinnacle (**2hr 45min**), from which for the first time you can see Litókhoro and the coastal plain.

Áyio Spílio chapel built in a rock overhang

288

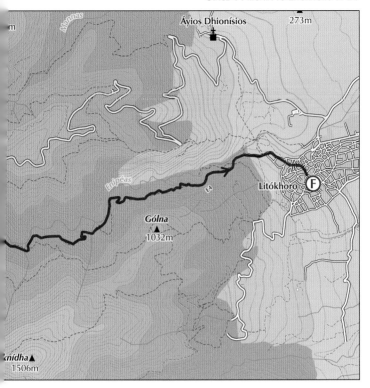

Some 10min later, you pass a bench beside the path; in another 10min you are taken over a rocky spur and down – ignore a turn down to the L. Pass a last rocky shoulder where there is a bench and caves above the path and a view ahead to the sea. There follows a short stretch on a concrete-covered water channel beside a green railing until, at **3hr 15min**, you turn L on a path that leads down to the first buildings and into the top of **Litókhoro**.

APPENDIX A
Route summary tables

Stage no	Title	Distance	Time	Height gain	Height loss	Page
The Peloponnese Way						
1	Dhiakoftó to Méga Spílio monastery	15km	4hr 30min	1000m	0m	33
2	Méga Spílio monastery to Áno Lousí	17km	6hr	750m	700m	37
3	Áno Lousí to Tourládha	17km	6hr	450m	750m	41
4	Near Tourládha to Dhára	18km	6hr	560m	600m	46
5	Nimfasía to Vitína	7km	2hr 50min	350m	240m	50
6	Vitína to Kardharás (or Kápsia)	17km (or 22km)	5hr 45min (or 6hr 45min)	930m	940m	55
7	Kardharás (or Kápsia) to Trípoli	19.5km (or 14.5km)	5hr 30min (or 4hr 20min)	350m	700m (or 380m)	60
8	Psilí Vrísi to Áyios Pétros	20km	6hr 15min	840m	630m	65
9	Malevís convent to Vamvakoú	17km	7hr	1120m	1090m	70
10	Vamvakoú to Paleogoulás	18km	4hr 10min	0m	480m	75
11	Mistrás to Anavrití	7.2km	2hr 45min	610m	100m	80
12	Anavrití to Taïgetos mountain refuge	12km	5hr	1050m	310m	84
13	Taïgetos mountain refuge to Árna	16km	6hr	570m	1340m	88
14	Árna to Pantazí beach	19km	6hr 40min	770m	1550m	92

Stage no	Title	Distance	Time	Height gain	Height loss	Page
The Píndos Way						
1	Ámfissa to Viniáni and Reká ravine	15km	4hr 30min	650m	200m	102
2	Mt Ghióna: Viniáni to Láka Karvoúni refuge	11km	5hr 15min	1250m	0m	106
3	Láka Karvoúni refuge to Sikiá	9km	4hr 40min	450m	1500m	109
4	Sikiá to Athanásios Dhiákos/Áno Mousounítsa	11km	4hr 5min	350m	70m	112
5	Mt Vardhoúsia: Athanásios Dhiákos/Áno Mousounítsa to Yiourtáki sheepfold	9.5km	3hr 25min	670m	120m	116
6	Yiourtáki sheepfold to Mt Oxiá/Sarádena refuge	15.5km	6hr 25min	830m	780m	119
7	Mt Oxiá/Sarádena refuge to Kokália obelisk/Rákhes Timfristoú	17km	5hr 30min	220m	370m	124
8	Kokália obelisk/Rákhes Timfristoú to Karpenísi	14km	3hr 30min	30m	500m	127
9	Karpenísi to Kerasokhóri	31.3km	9hr 15min	1040m	1000m	133
10	Kerasokhóri to Varvariádha	19km	6hr	200m	1000m	137
11	Varvariádha to Epinianá	12.5km	6hr 25min	1150m	230m	140
12	Epinianá to Spiliá monastery	25km	8hr 30min	1450m	1600m	144
13	Spiliá monastery to Petrotó	12km	5hr 45min	250m	300m	150
14	Petrotó to Kalí Kómi	10km	3hr	100m	200m	155
15	Kalí Kómi to Moskhófito	19km	4hr 30min	650m	450m	158

Stage no	Title	Distance	Time	Height gain	Height loss	Page
15A	Kalí Kómi to Mirófilo	9km	4hr	300m	120m	161
16	Moskhófito to Mesokhóra	9km	3hr 15min	400m	400m	164
16A	Mirófilo to Mesokhóra	17km	6hr 30min	1000m	1050m	166
17	Mesokhóra to Gardhíki (or Athamanía)	16.2km (or 15.1km)	4hr 50min (or 4hr 10min)	350m (or 250m)	100m	173
18	Gardhíki (or Athamanía) to Matsoúki	20.5km (or 21.1km)	7hr 30min (or 8hr)	1150m (or 1250m)	1150m	176
19	Matsoúki to Kalarítes	8km	2hr 45min	450m	300m	180
20	Kalarítes to Khalíki	23km	7hr 30min–8hr	850m	800m	183
20A	Kalarítes to Khalíki ridge route	24km	8hr 20min	1260m	1230m	188
21	Khalíki to Métsovo	17km	5hr 20min	940m	840m	193
22	Métsovo to Vália Kálda	28km (incl. tarmac); 15km (from Aóös lake)	5hr 30min (from Aóös lake)	1157m	907m	200
23	Vália Kálda to Vovoúsa	10km	3hr 20min–3hr 45min	100m	400m	204
24	Vovoúsa to Dhístrato	16km	5hr 30min	550m	700m	207
24A	Link: Vovoúsa to Skamnéli	30km	8hr +	1142m	1048m	211
25	Dhístrato to Samarína	15km	5hr 40min	850m	400m	215
25A	Dhístrato to Palioséli	24km	5–6hr	480m	420m	219
26	Samarína to Dhrakólimni	12.5km	6hr 30min	1547m	830m	221
26A	Palioséli to Dhrakólimni	8km	3hr 15min	1000m	0m	224
27	Dhrakólimni to Ayía Paraskeví/Kerásovo	7.5km	3hr	0m	1200m	227
28	Ayía Paraskeví/Kerásovo to Kefalokhóri	20.5km	6hr 45min	740m	990m	229

Stage no	Title	Distance	Time	Height gain	Height loss	Page
29	Kefalókhóri to Aetomilítsa/Dénsko	12km	4hr 55min	700m	0m	234
30	Aetomilítsa/Dénsko to Mt Grámos summit	11km	5hr (summit); 8–9hr (return)	1000m	130m	238

Zagóri and Mt Gamíla

Stage no	Title	Distance	Time	Height gain	Height loss	Page
1	Tsepélovo to Kípi via Kapésovo and Koukoúli	11km	3hr 10min	240m	520m	245
1A	Tsepélovo to Kípi via Khadzíou bridge	7.5km	2hr 40min	250m	550m	248
2	Kípi to Monodhéndhri	8km	3hr	300m	50m	250
3	Monodhéndhri to Pápingo	14.5km	6hr 10min	500m	600m	252
4	Pápingo to Astráka refuge	5km	3hr 30min	950m	0m	257
5	Astráka refuge to Tsepélovo (or Kapésovo)	13km (or 15.5km)	5hr 30min (or 6hr 15min)	350m (or 400m)	1150m (or 1200m)	260
5A	Astráka refuge to Kónitsa	12km	6hr 30min	0m	1250m	264
6	Skamnéli to Kónitsa	27km	11hr 30min	600m	1950m	266

Mt Olympus

Stage no	Title	Distance	Time	Height gain	Height loss	Page
1	Priónia to Spílios Agapitós/Refuge A	6km	2hr 30min	1050m	0m	279
2	Spílios Agapitós/Refuge A to Mítikas and Yíósos Apostolídhis/Refuge B	5km (via Kakí Skála and Loúki)	3hr 30min (via Kakí Skála); 3hr 15min (via Loúki)	968m (via Kakí Skála); 1010m (via Loúki)	338m (via Kakí Skála ; 278m (via Loúki)	281
3	Yíósos Apostolídhis/Refuge B to Priónia	21km	5hr 30min	200m	1630m	284
4	Priónia to Litókhoro	12km	3hr 15min	520m	1520m	287

293

APPENDIX B
Glossary

Language is going to be a bit of a problem for most users of this book, and obviously we cannot teach you Greek here. (The alphabet, incidentally, will probably be less of a problem than you might fear.)

Listed below are a number of Greek words and phrases that you may find useful, including terms relevant to a walk in the mountains. You are most likely to hear people using these to address you, so we have arranged them in simple categories with the Greek word first. If the spelling looks strange it is because we have tried to find combinations of English letters which, if pronounced in the normal 'English' way, will produce sounds as near as possible to the Greek. The accents show which syllables should be stressed. Stress is vital in Greek; if you get everything else in a word right, but put the stress on the wrong syllable, people will not understand you.

Pronunciation tips

- *a* is pronounced as in 'hat', *e* as in 'get', *o* as in 'hot', *ee* as in 'feet', *oo* as in 'food'
- the hard *g* (*g* before *a* or *o*) is slightly breathy – *gh*
- *kh* sounds like the *ch* in Scottish 'loch'
- *dh* sounds like *th* in 'then'
- *r* is rolled in the front of the mouth
- *s* is always as in 'soft'

Terrain and landmarks

aneefóra	ascent
apótomos	steep, precipitous
dhásos	wood, forest
dheemósyo	public road or track
dheeyakládhosee	fork, junction in road or path
dheeyáselo	saddle, col
dheeyastávrosee	crossroads
dhéndro	tree
dhrómos	road (some times means 'the way')
eedhragoyeéo	water channel, pipeline
eépsoma	height, knoll, bump
eésyoma	level ground
ekleeseéya	church, chapel
élata	fir trees
faránghee	ravine, gorge
gremós	cliff, precipice
kaldereémee	cobbled mule path
kaleéva	hut
katafeéyo	mountain refuge
kateefóra	descent
keeládha	valley
kharádhra	ravine, gorge
khomatódhromos	dirt road
khoráfee	field, cultivated patch

khoryó	village
kolónes	telegraph or electricity poles
kordhéles	zigzags, in path or road
koreefogrameé	summit ridge, peak line
korfeé	summit, peak
láka	grassy clearing or hollow, cwm
langádhee	gully, especially wooded
leémnee	lake, tarn
leevádhee	meadow, pasture
lófos	hill
loókee	couloir
loótsa	pond, tarn
magazeé	village shop, café
magazeés	keeper of a magazeé
mandreé	sheepfold
meélos	mill
monasteéree	monastery
monopátee	footpath
oksyá	beech tree
orthoplayá	vertical cliff
paraleéya	seashore
peeghádhee	well
peenakeédha	signpost
peeyeé	spring (of water)
péfka	pine trees
pétra	stone
platánee	plane tree
plateéya	(town/village) square
playá	slope, hillside
poornárya	prickly oak scrub
potámee	river

potamyá	riverbed
rákhee	ridge
reéza	foot of slope or cliff
réma	stream
rematyá	streambed, gully
sára	scree
skoleéyo	school
smeéksee	confluence of streams
speelyá	cave
speétee	house
stánee	sheepfold
stroónga	sheepfold
tabéla	signpost
teékhos	wall
thálasa	sea
tsombános	shepherd
velaneedyá	oak tree
vlákhos	Vlach (also, generically, 'shepherd')
voonó	mountain
voskós	shepherd
vrákhos/vrákhya	rock(s)
vreésee	spring (of water)
yeemnós	bare, treeless
yéfeera	bridge

Directions

ap'afteé tee meryá	on this side
apénandee	opposite
apó teen álee meryá	on the other side
aristerá	on the left
dheépla	next to, alongside
dheksyá	on the right
edhó	here
eésya	straight ahead
eésya káto	straight down

eésya páno	straight up
ekeé	there
kat'eftheéya	straight ahead
káto	down
khameelá	low down
kondá	near
makreeyá	far
mékhree	up to, as far as, until
páno	up
péra	over there, beyond
pros	towards
pseelá	high up
anevénees…	you go up…
katevénees…	you go down…
pas…	you go…
pernás…	you cross/pass…
mólees perásees…	as soon as you have crossed/passed
parakaló, o dhrómos ya…?	can you tell me, where is the way to…?
parakaló, to monopátee ya…?	can you tell me, where is the path to…?
póses óres eéne?	how many hours is it?

Weather

aéras	wind
andára	mist, cloud
astrapeé	lightning
booboonitá	thunder claps
eélyos	sun
feesáyee	it's windy
kateyeédha	storm
khyónee	snow
kreéyo	cold
omeékhlee	mist

seénefa	clouds
vrokheé	rain
zéstee	hot

Transport

aftokéeneeto	car, vehicle
forteeghó	lorry
leoforeéyo	bus
tee óra févyee	what time does it leave?
tee óra ftánee	what time does it arrive?
boreétee na me párete?	can you take me?

Eating and shopping

avghá	eggs
batereéya	battery
brizóla	large chop, usually pork or beef
elyés	olives
fayeé	food
ghála	milk
gházee	gas
kebábya	spit-roasted chunks of lamb
kheelópeeta	local pasta
kokorétsi	spit-roasted offal
konsérves	tinned food
kréas	meat
neró	water
omeléta	omelette
psomeé	bread
saláta	salad
speérta	matches
teereé	cheese
venzeénee	petrol

Sleeping and camping

dheékleeno	double room
dhomátyo	room

kameenéto	camping stove
krevátee	bed
ksenodhokheéyo	hotel
ksenónas	guesthouse
skeeneé	tent
boró na steéso lee skeeneé?	can I put my tent up?

Numbers

éna/meéya (masc/fem)	1
dheéyo	2
treés/treéya (masc/fem)	3
téseres/tésera (masc/fem)	4
pénde	5
éksee	6
eftá	7
októ	8
enyá	9
dhéka	10
éndheka	11
dhódheka	12
dhekatreés	13
dhekatéseres	14
dhekapénde	15
eékosee	20
treeyánda	30
saránda	40
peneénda	50
ekseénda	60
evdhomeénda	70
oghdhónda	80
eneneénda	90
ekató	100
dheeyakósya	200
pendakósya	500
kheélya	1000
dheéyo kheelyádhes	2000

Time

pénde leftá	five minutes
éna tétarto	quarter of an hour
meeseé óra	half an hour
méeya óra	an hour
meeyámeesee óres	one and a half hours
dheéyo óres	two hours
stees méeya	at one o'clock
stees trées ke tétarto	at quarter past three
stees tóseres pará pénde	at five to four
apóyevma	afternoon (generally means 5–6pm in Greece); early afternoon is meseeméree (noon)
ávreeyo	tomorrow
khthés	yesterday
méra	day, daytime
meseeméree	noon, early afternoon
neékhta	night, night-time
proeé	morning
seémera	today
vrádhee	evening (after 7–8pm)

Animals

agrioghoóroono	wild boar
agriokátsiko	wild goat
alepoódha	fox
álogho	horse
arkoódha	bear
asvós	badger
ayeládha	cow
ayetós	eagle
feédhee	snake
gháta	cat
ghayeedhoóree	donkey
katseékya	goats
khelóna	tortoise
koonávee	marten
laghós	hare
leékos	wolf

órnyo	vulture	*yeédhya*	goats
pondeékee	mouse, rat	*yerákee*	hawk
pooleé	bird	*zarkádhee*	deer
próvata	sheep	*zóa*	mules
skeeleé/skeelyá	dog/s		

Miscellaneous

ne	yes
ókhee	no
leégho	a little
poleé	a lot, very
parakaló	please
efkhareestó	thank you
meekró	small
meghálo	big
kaleé andámosee	till we meet again
kaló	good
kakó	bad
kaleeméra	good day
na pas sto kaló	'may you go to the good' (a common way of saying goodbye to the person leaving)
óra kaleé	an old-fashioned salutation on parting, meaning literally 'good hour'
yásoo/yásas	'good health to you' (singular/plural): the commonest way of saying hello
tee kánees	how are you?
póso kánee	how much is it?

APPENDIX C
Further reading

Books

Andrews, Kevin, *The Flight of Ikaros* (Penguin, 1984). A well-written and readable account of the author's experiences wandering about southern Greece during the Civil War in the late 1940s.

Boulay, Juliet du, *Portrait of a Greek Mountain Village* (Oxford, 1974). A detailed study based on the author's personal experience. Again, very interesting, although indigestibly academic in parts.

Campbell, JK, *Honour, Family and Patronage* (Oxford, 1964). A very interesting anthropological study of the Sarakatsani shepherds in the Mt Gamíla region in north-west Greece.

Cullen, Michael, *Landscapes of the Southern Peloponnese* (Sunflower Books, 2003) for more details of walks in this area.

Fermor, Patrick Leigh, *Mani* (John Murray, 1958) and *Roumeli* (John Murray, 1966). The two best travel books about remote rural and mountain Greece.

Foss, Arthur, *Epirus* (Faber, 1978). A readable, if unexciting, account of the history, traditions and people of Épiros.

Hunt, Sir John, and DE Sugden, 'A journey through the Pindus Mountains in 1963', *Journal of the Royal Geographical Society*, vol 130, no 3 (Sept 1964), pp 355–64.

Huxley, Anthony, and William Taylor, *Flowers of Greece and the Aegean* (Chatto and Windus, 1977). The best field guide by far.

Salmon, Tim, *The Unwritten Places* (Lycabettus Press, 1995, and Blackbird Digital Books, available on Amazon). An account of travels in the Píndos mountains and especially of life among the Vlachs. Obtainable in the UK from: Edward Stanford, 12–14 Long Acre, London WC2E 9LP (www.stanfords.co.uk) and Daunt Books, 83 Marylebone High St, London W1U 4QW (www.dauntbooks.co.uk).

Polunin, Oleg, *Flowers of Greece and the Balkans* (Oxford, 1980). Expensive and bulky. Its big attraction is that it describes in detail particularly good flower-hunting areas of the mountains.

Wace, AJB, and MS Thompson, *The Nomads of the Balkans* (Methuen, 1914). A fascinating account of living among the Vlachs, when Vlachs were truly Vlachs.

Woodhouse, CM, *The Struggle for Greece 1941–49* (Hart-Davis, MacGibbon, 1976). The best and most balanced account of the Resistance, with whom the author fought, and the ensuing Civil War.

Of the numerous general guidebooks, *The Rough Guide to Greece* remains the most readable and useful.

Online

The Great Greek Hike (www.greekhiking.com) is an evocative and charming blog by Jane and Alan Laurie telling the story of their epic 2014 walk through the mountains from the Albanian border to the southern Peloponnese. They followed a route always close and sometimes identical to ours. If you are contemplating a Greek hike, this is a really enticing taster.

Dhiava – The Autumn Journey (50min) (www.youtube.com/watch?v=RJfom155v_o) is a documentary made by Tim Salmon and David Hope about transhumant Vlach shepherds taking their flocks down from Samarína (Píndos Way, Stage 25) to the lowlands for the winter. It was first shown on Greek TV in 2001 and is available to view on YouTube. Our trial run, *Summer in Samarína, Píndos Mountains, Greece, 1995*, is also viewable on YouTube. Both give real insights into what life in the mountains has been like for many generations.

APPENDIX D
Useful contacts

Alpine Club branches
The two Athenian branches of EOS, the Hellenic Alpine Club, may be of interest:

- EOS Athinón, whose offices on the first floor of 23–25 Lekka St off the downhill right-hand corner of Síntagma Square (as you look out from the Parliament building) are open Tuesday–Friday, 5–8pm (tel 210-3212355, eosathinon@yahoo.gr, www.eosathinon.gr). You can always find someone who speaks good English.
- EOS Akharnón, 126 Filadelfias St in the rather out-of-the-way suburb of Akharnés (tel 210-2461528, eosa@otenet.gr, www.eosacharnon.gr). They publish a quarterly magazine called *Korfés* ('Peaks') with an English page.

Outdoor equipment in Athens
If you find yourself in need of any decent equipment (including camping gas cartridges), the place to go is Polo Center at 52 Leofóros Patisíon/corner with Metsóvou St, very near the National Archaeological Museum; open Monday–Thursday, Friday 9.30am–9pm, Saturday 9.30am–4pm (tel 210-8256840, patision@polocenter.gr, www.polo.gr/polo-center).

Maps
In the UK, maps are available from:

- Edward Stanford, 12–14 Long Acre, London WC2E 9LP (tel 020 7836 1321, www.stanfords.co.uk)
- The Map Shop, 15 High Street, Upton-upon-Severn, Worcestershire WR8 0HJ (freephone tel 0800 085 40 80, tel 01684 593146, themapshop@btinternet.com, www.themapshop.co.uk)

In Athens, both of the following addresses are five minutes' walk from the central Síntigma Square:

- Anávasi Bookshop, 32 Voulís St, 10557 Athens (tel 210-3218104, sales@anavasi.gr, www.anavasi.gr)
- Anávasi (Publisher), 34 Níkis St, 10557 Athens (tel 210-3210152, editions@anavasi.gr, www.anavasi.gr)

Route updates
Check out the authors' websites (www.thepindosway.com and www.thepeloponneseway.com) for news about the routes, including updates on accommodation.

NOTES

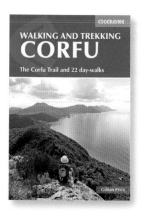
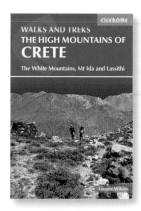
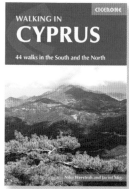
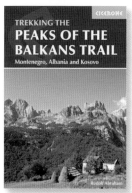

Walking – Trekking – Mountaineering – Climbing – Cycling

Over 40 years, Cicerone have built up an outstanding collection of over 300 guides, inspiring all sorts of amazing adventures.

Every guide comes from extensive exploration and research by our expert authors, all with a passion for their subjects. They are frequently praised, endorsed and used by clubs, instructors and outdoor organisations.

All our titles can now be bought as **e-books**, **ePubs** and **Kindle** files and we also have an online magazine – **Cicerone Extra** – with features to help cyclists, climbers, walkers and trekkers choose their next adventure, at home or abroad.

Our website shows any **new information** we've had in since a book was published. Please do let us know if you find anything has changed, so that we can publish the latest details. On our **website** you'll also find great ideas and lots of detailed information about what's inside every guide and you can buy **individual routes** from many of them online.

It's easy to keep in touch with what's going on at Cicerone by getting our monthly **free e-newsletter**, which is full of offers, competitions, up-to-date information and topical articles. You can subscribe on our home page and also follow us on **Facebook** and **Twitter** or dip into our **blog**.

Cicerone – the very best guides for exploring the world.

CICERONE

Juniper House, Murley Moss, Oxenholme Road, Kendal, Cumbria LA9 7RL
Tel: 015395 62069 info@cicerone.co.uk
www.cicerone.co.uk